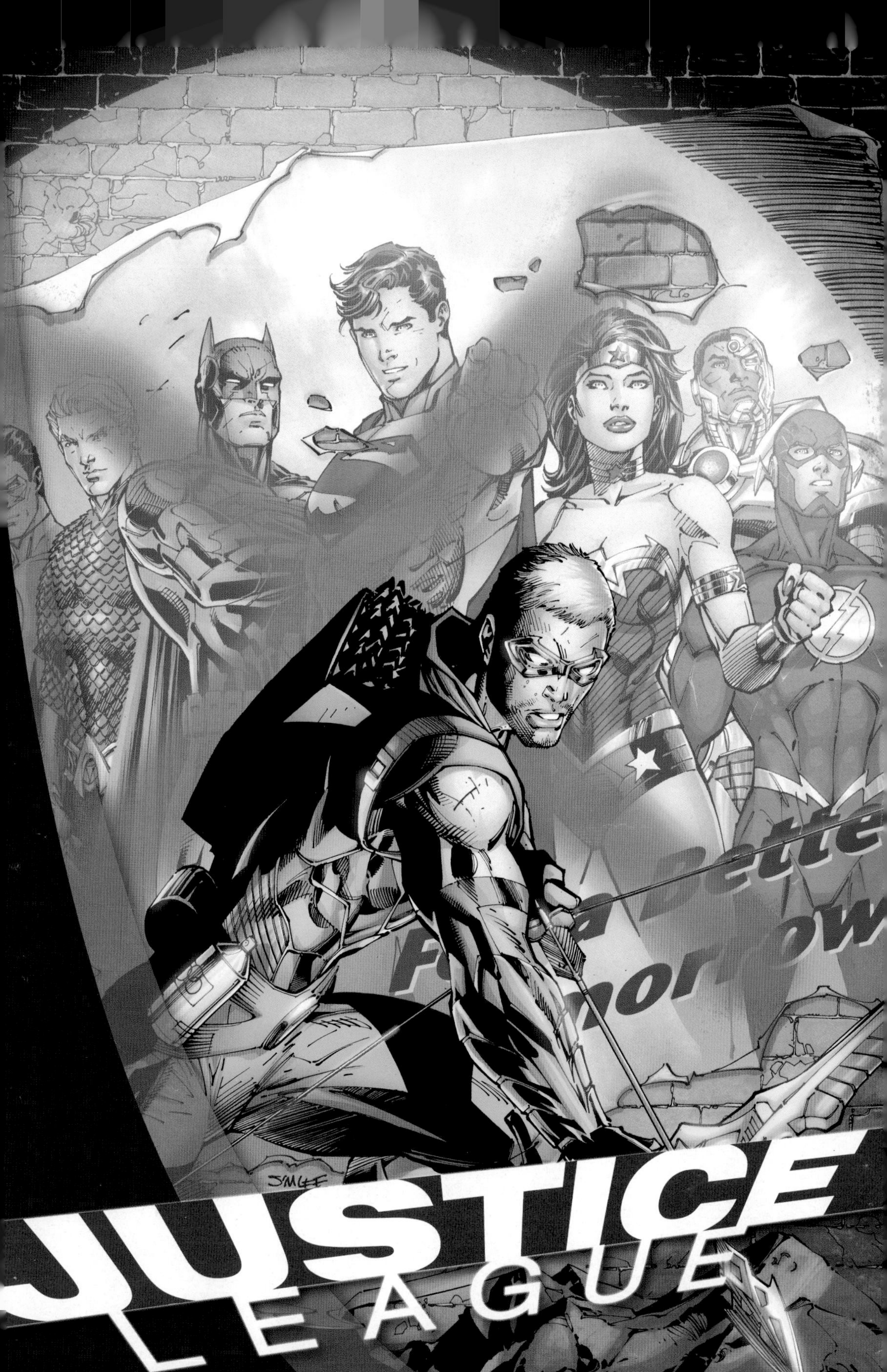

JUSTICE LEAGUE

VOLUME 2 THE VILLAIN'S JOURNEY

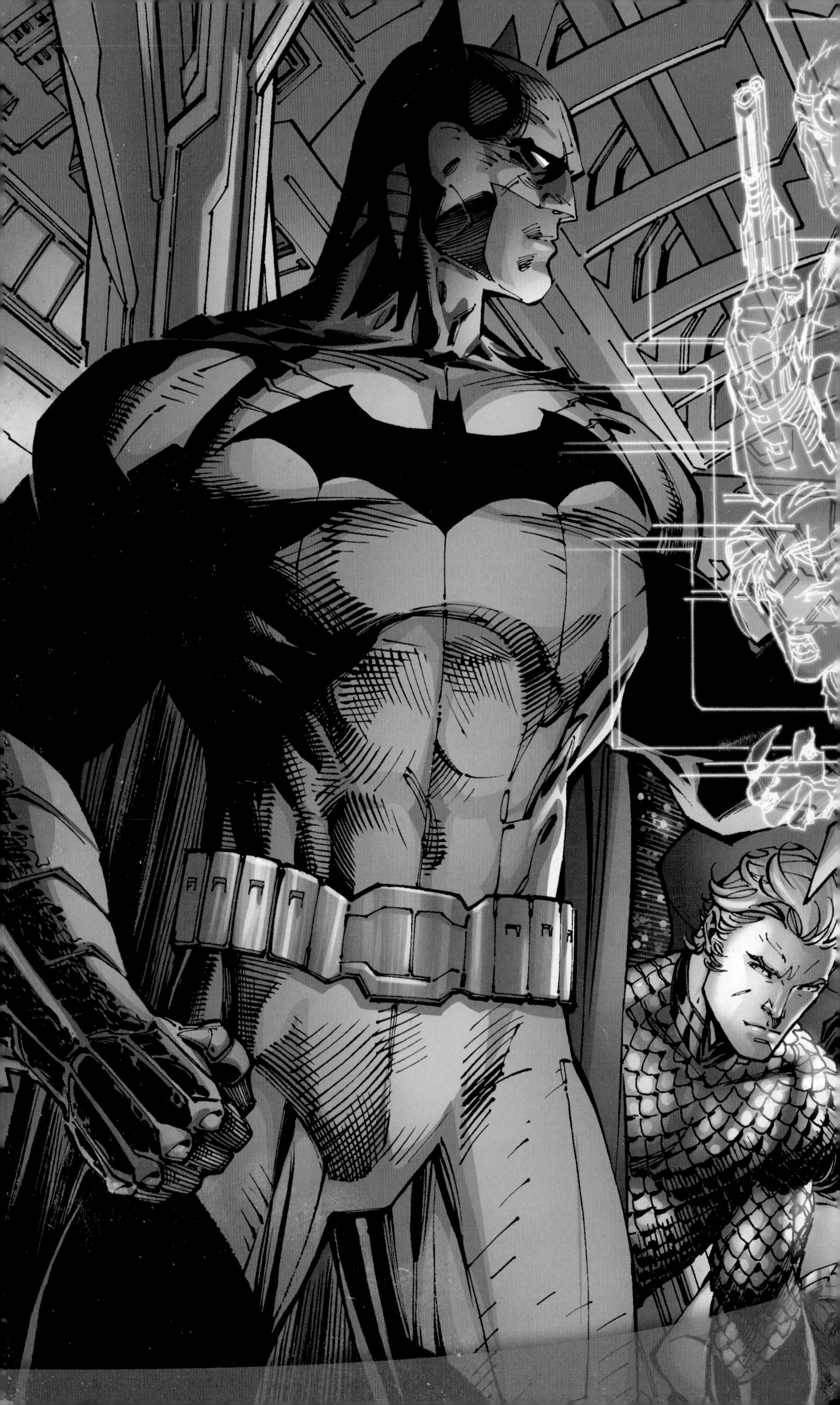

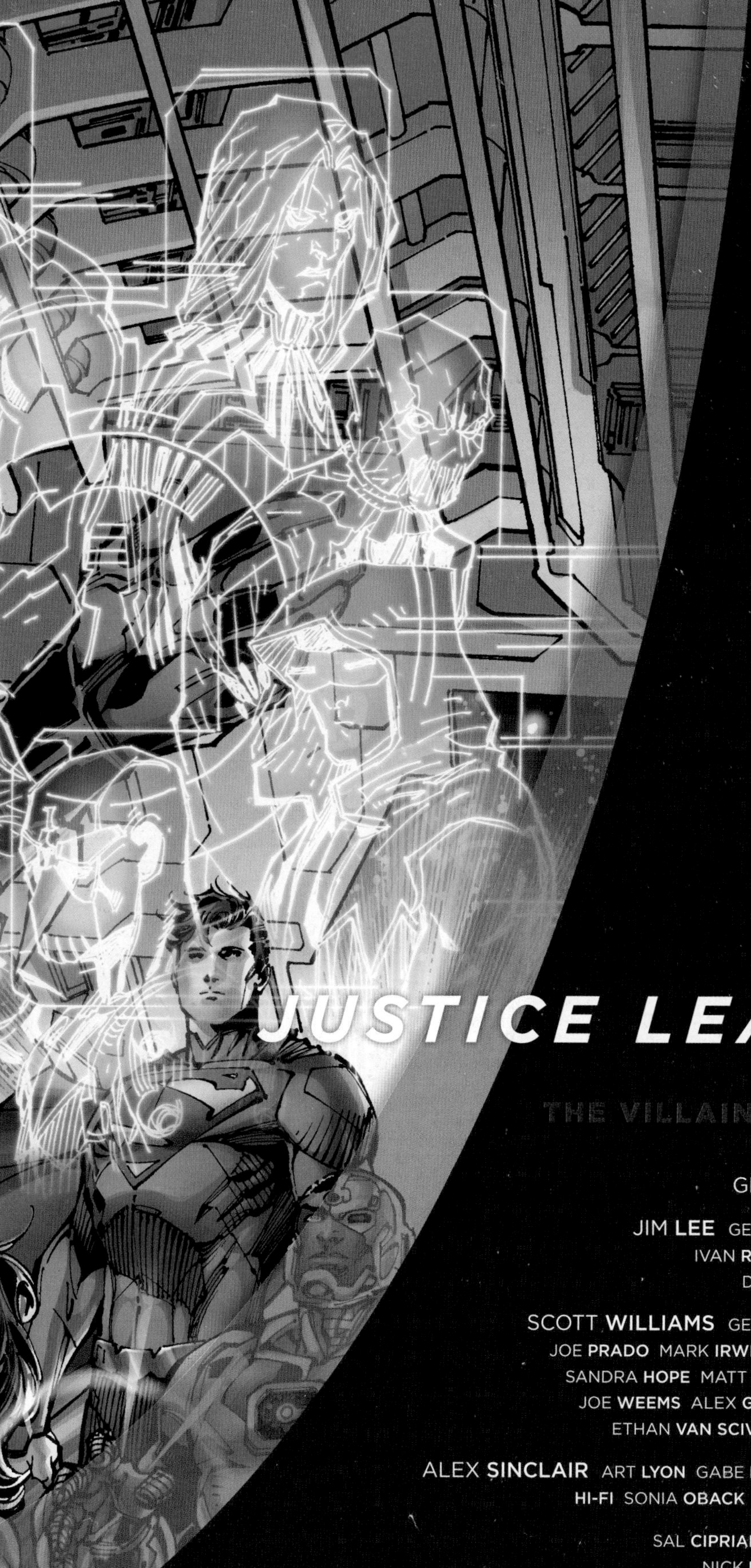

JUSTICE LEAGUE

VOLUME 2
THE VILLAIN'S JOURNEY

GEOFF **JOHNS** writer

JIM **LEE** GENE **HA** CARLOS **D'ANDA**
IVAN **REIS** ETHAN **VAN SCIVER**
DAVID **FINCH** pencillers

SCOTT **WILLIAMS** GENE **HA** CARLOS **D'ANDA**
JOE **PRADO** MARK **IRWIN** JONATHAN **GLAPION**
SANDRA **HOPE** MATT **BANNING** ROB **HUNTER**
JOE **WEEMS** ALEX **GARNER** TREVOR **SCOTT**
ETHAN **VAN SCIVER** DAVID **FINCH** inker

ALEX **SINCLAIR** ART **LYON** GABE **ELTAEB** PETE **PANTAZIS**
HI-FI SONIA **OBACK** TONY **AVINA** colorists

SAL **CIPRIANO** PATRICK **BROSSEAU**
NICK **NAPOLITANO** letterers

BRIAN CUNNINGHAM Editor – Original Series KATIE KUBERT DARREN SHAN Assistant Editors – Original Series
PETER HAMBOUSSI Editor ROBBIN BROSTERMAN Design Director – Books
ROBBIE BIEDERMAN Publication Design

BOB HARRAS VP – Editor-in-Chief

DIANE NELSON President DAN DIDIO and JIM LEE Co-Publishers
GEOFF JOHNS Chief Creative Officer
JOHN ROOD Executive VP – Sales, Marketing and Business Development
AMY GENKINS Senior VP – Business and Legal Affairs NAIRI GARDINER Senior VP – Finance
JEFF BOISON VP – Publishing Operations MARK CHIARELLO VP – Art Direction and Design
JOHN CUNNINGHAM VP – Marketing TERRI CUNNINGHAM VP – Talent Relations and Services
ALISON GILL Senior VP – Manufacturing and Operations HANK KANALZ Senior VP – Digital
JAY KOGAN VP – Business and Legal Affairs, Publishing JACK MAHAN VP – Business Affairs, Talent
NICK NAPOLITANO VP – Manufacturing Administration SUE POHJA VP – Book Sales
COURTNEY SIMMONS Senior VP – Publicity BOB WAYNE Senior VP – Sales

JUSTICE LEAGUE VOLUME 2: THE VILLAIN'S JOURNEY

DC Comics, 1700 Broadway, New York, NY 10019
A Warner Bros. Entertainment Company.
Printed by RR Donnelley, Salem, VA, USA. 12/28/12. First Printing.

HC ISBN: 978-1-4012-3764-6
SC ISBN: 978-1-4012-3765-3

Library of Congress Cataloging-in-Publication Data

Johns, Geoff, 1973-
Justice League. Volume 2, The villain's journey / Geoff Johns, Jim Lee.
p. cm.
"Originally published in single magazine form in Justice League 7-12."
ISBN 978-1-4012-3764-6
1. Graphic novels. I. Lee, Jim, 1964- II. Title. III. Title: Villain's journey.
PN6728.J87J653 2012
741.5'973—dc23
2012040572

SUSTAINABLE Certified Chain of Custody

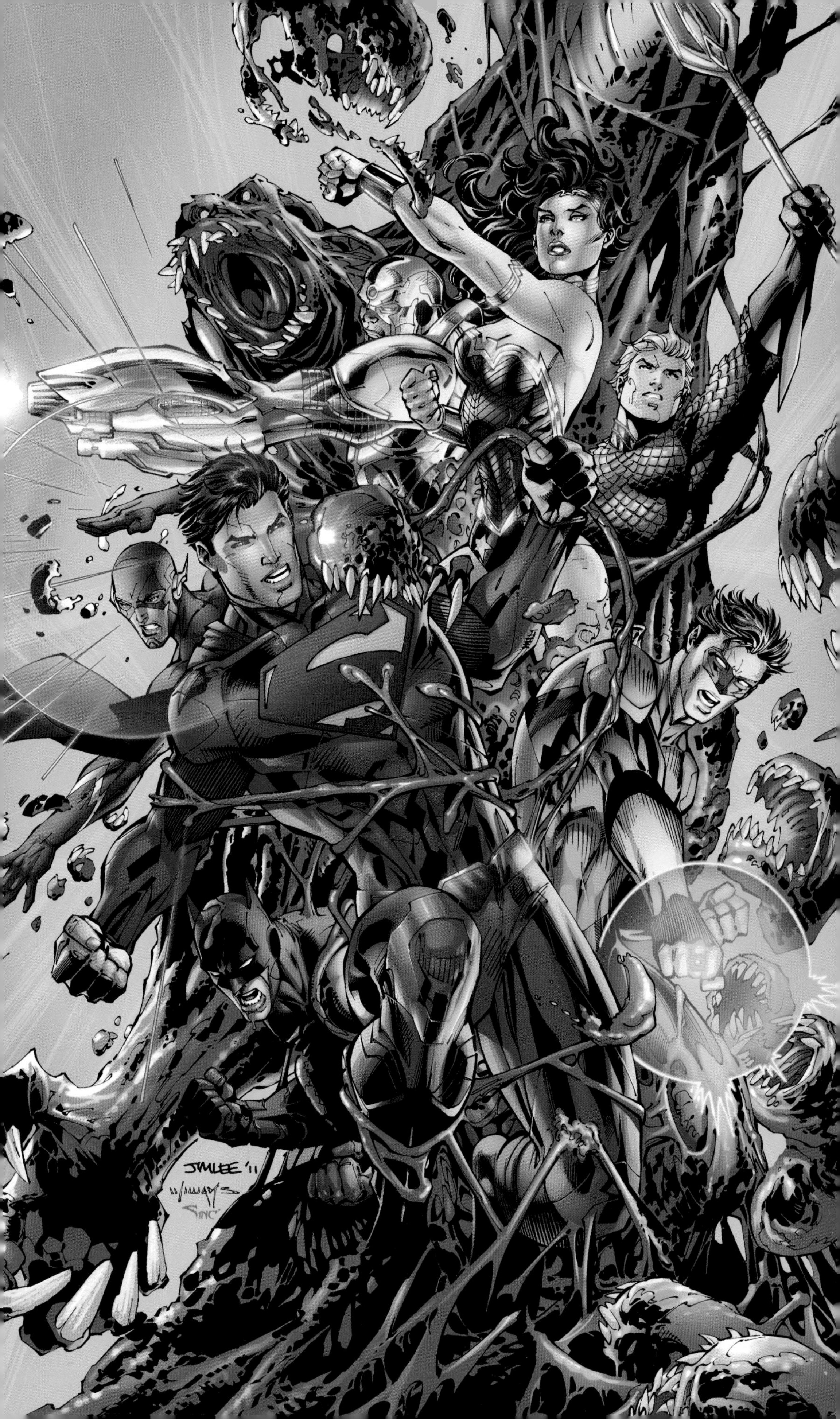
JIMLEE '11

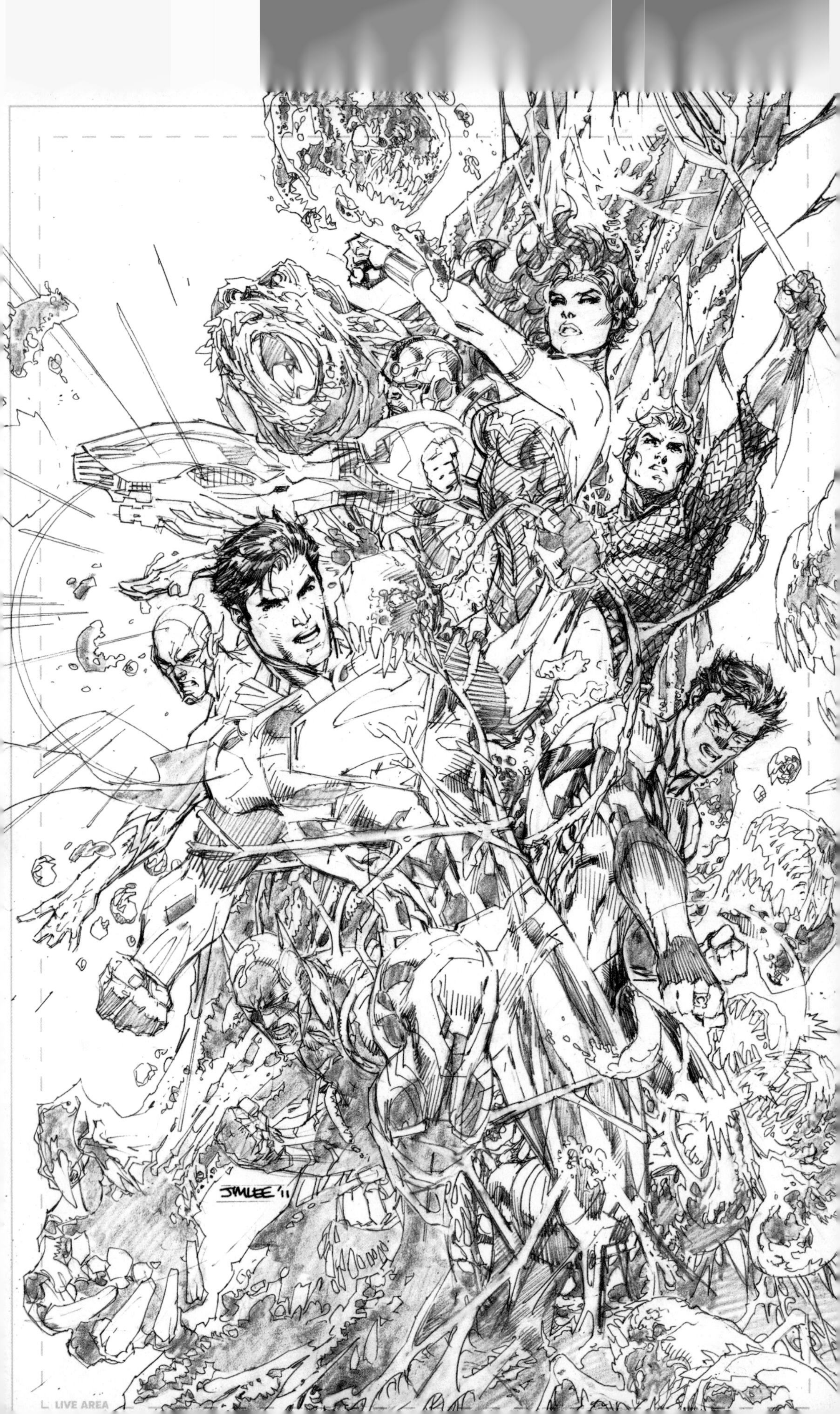
JIMLEE '11
LIVE AREA

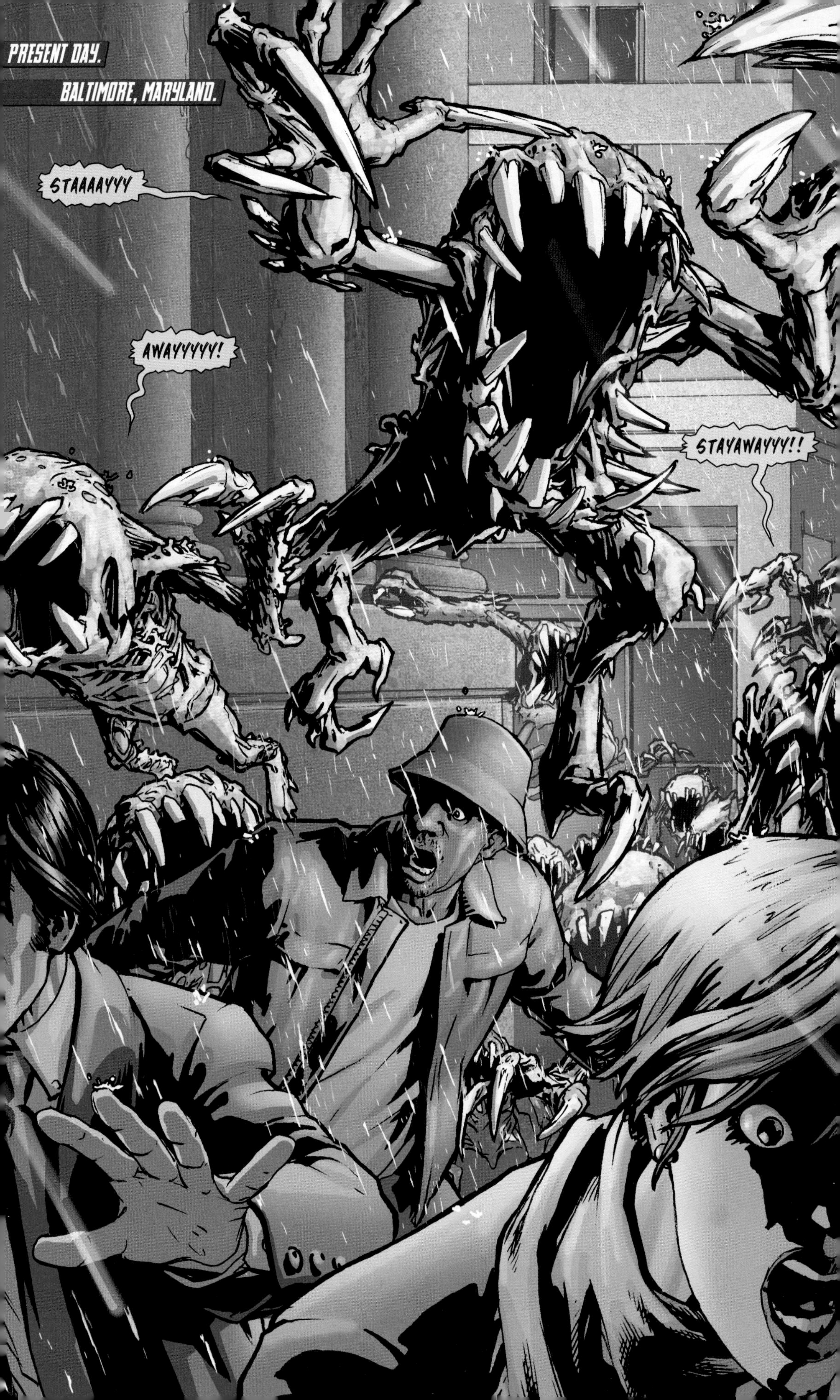
PRESENT DAY.
BALTIMORE, MARYLAND.
STAAAAYYY
AWAYYYYY!
STAYAWAYYY!!

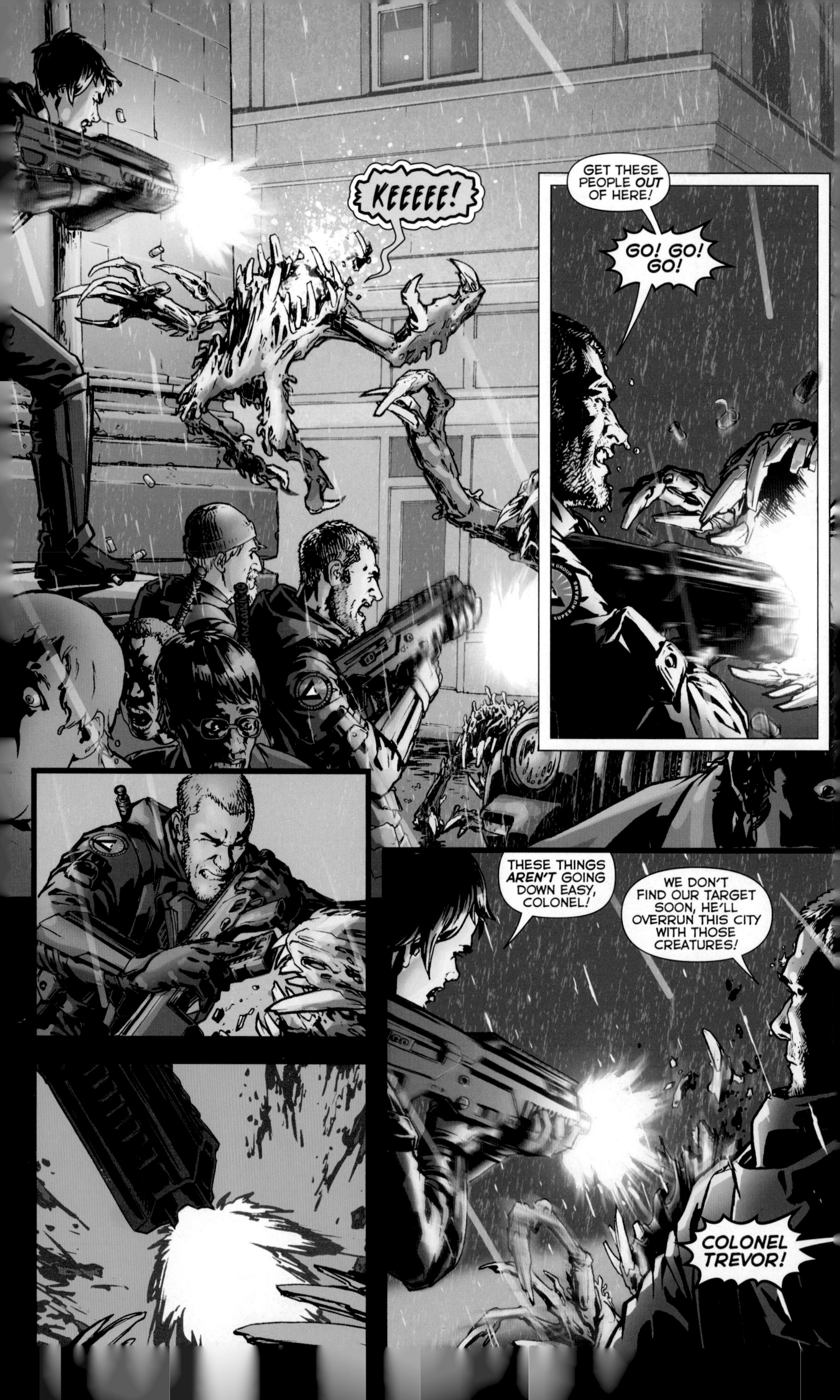
KEEEEE!
GET THESE PEOPLE OUT OF HERE!
GO! GO! GO!
THESE THINGS AREN'T GOING DOWN EASY, COLONEL!
WE DON'T FIND OUR TARGET SOON, HE'LL OVERRUN THIS CITY WITH THOSE CREATURES!
COLONEL TREVOR!

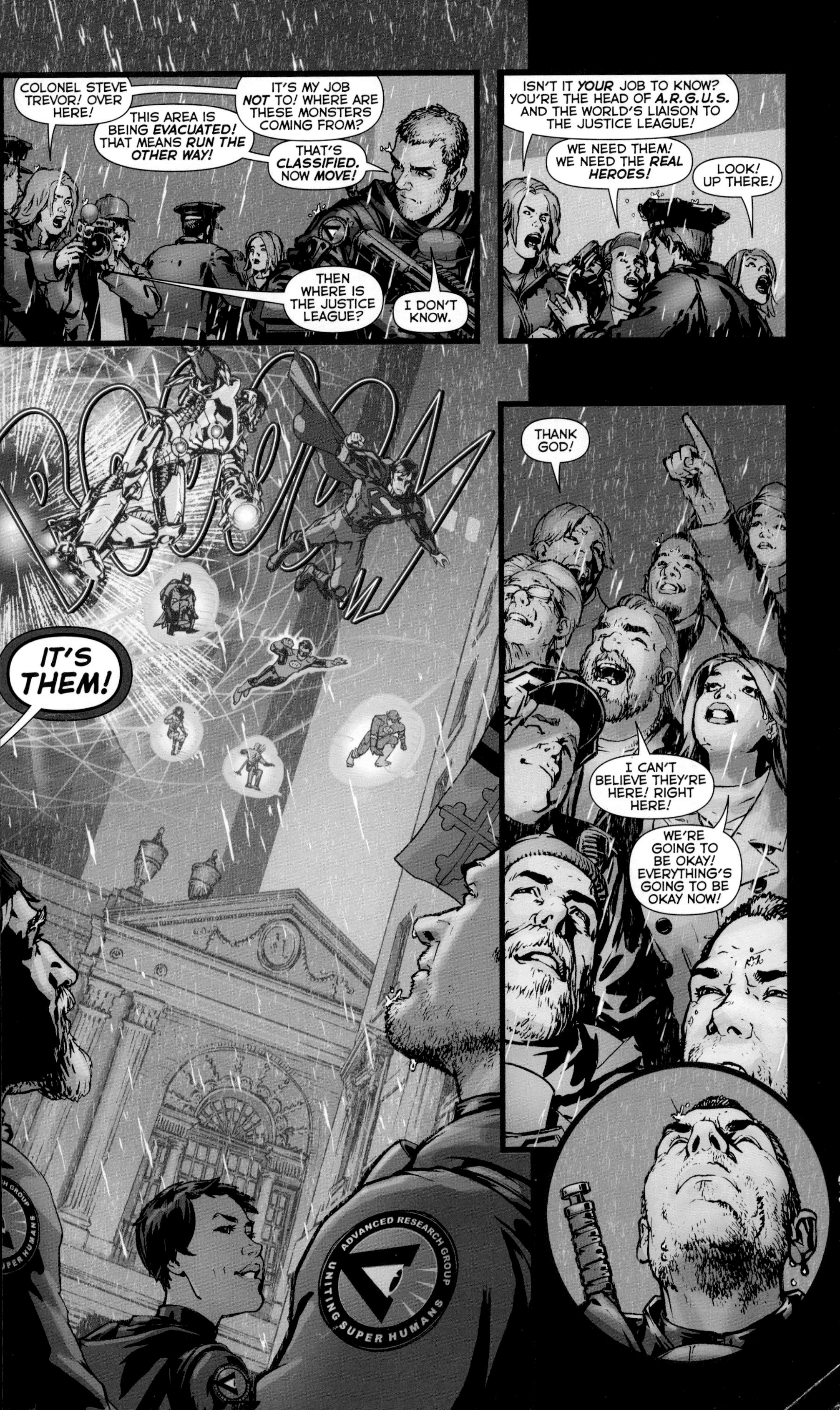

COLONEL STEVE TREVOR! OVER HERE!
IT'S MY JOB NOT TO! WHERE ARE THESE MONSTERS COMING FROM?
THIS AREA IS BEING EVACUATED! THAT MEANS RUN THE OTHER WAY!
THAT'S CLASSIFIED. NOW MOVE!
THEN WHERE IS THE JUSTICE LEAGUE?
I DON'T KNOW.
ISN'T IT YOUR JOB TO KNOW? YOU'RE THE HEAD OF A.R.G.U.S. AND THE WORLD'S LIAISON TO THE JUSTICE LEAGUE!
WE NEED THEM! WE NEED THE REAL HEROES!
LOOK! UP THERE!
THANK GOD!
IT'S THEM!
I CAN'T BELIEVE THEY'RE HERE! RIGHT HERE!
WE'RE GOING TO BE OKAY! EVERYTHING'S GOING TO BE OKAY NOW!
ADVANCED RESEARCH GROUP
UNITING SUPER HUMANS

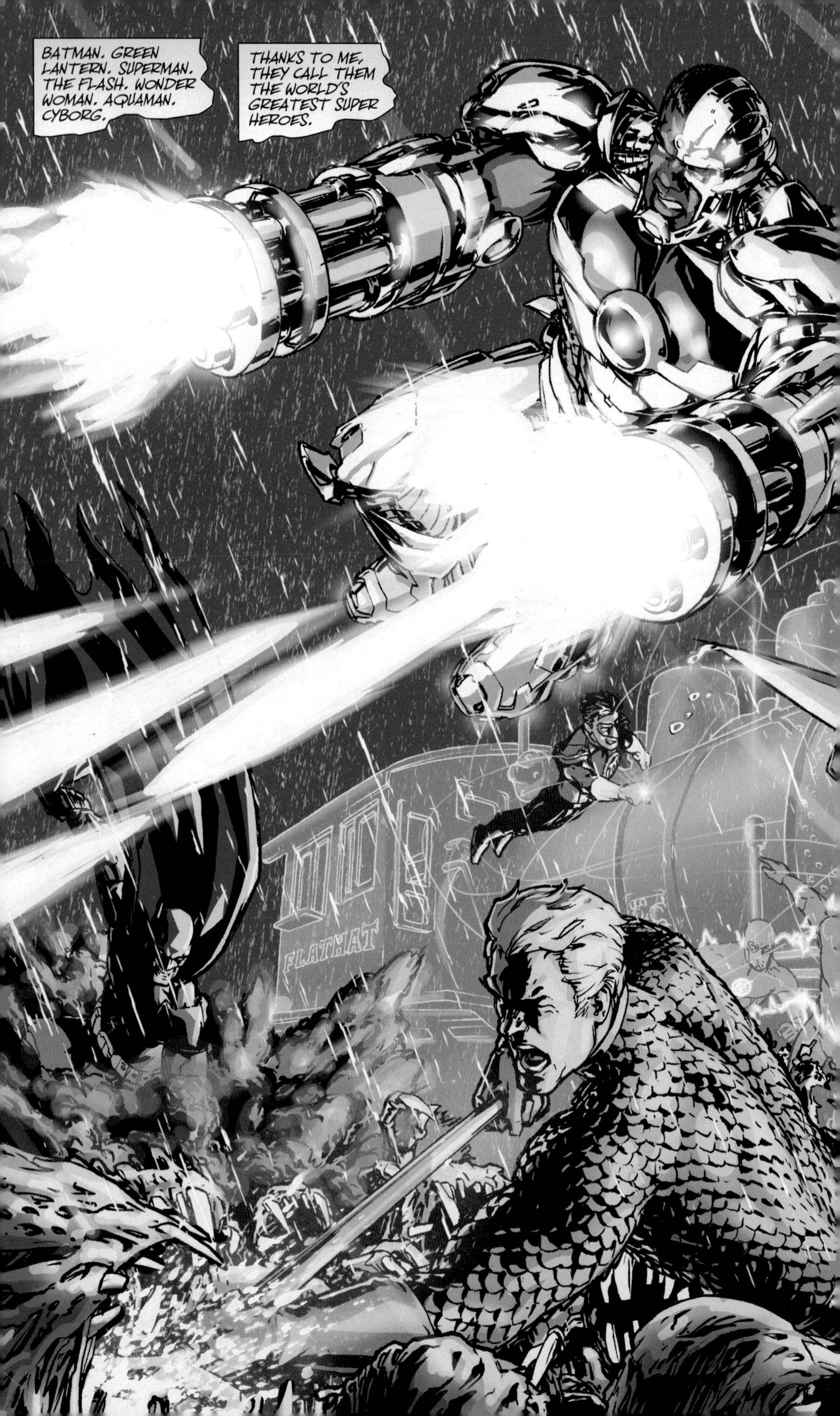

BATMAN. GREEN LANTERN. SUPERMAN. THE FLASH. WONDER WOMAN. AQUAMAN. CYBORG.
THANKS TO ME, THEY CALL THEM THE WORLD'S GREATEST SUPER HEROES.
FLATHAT

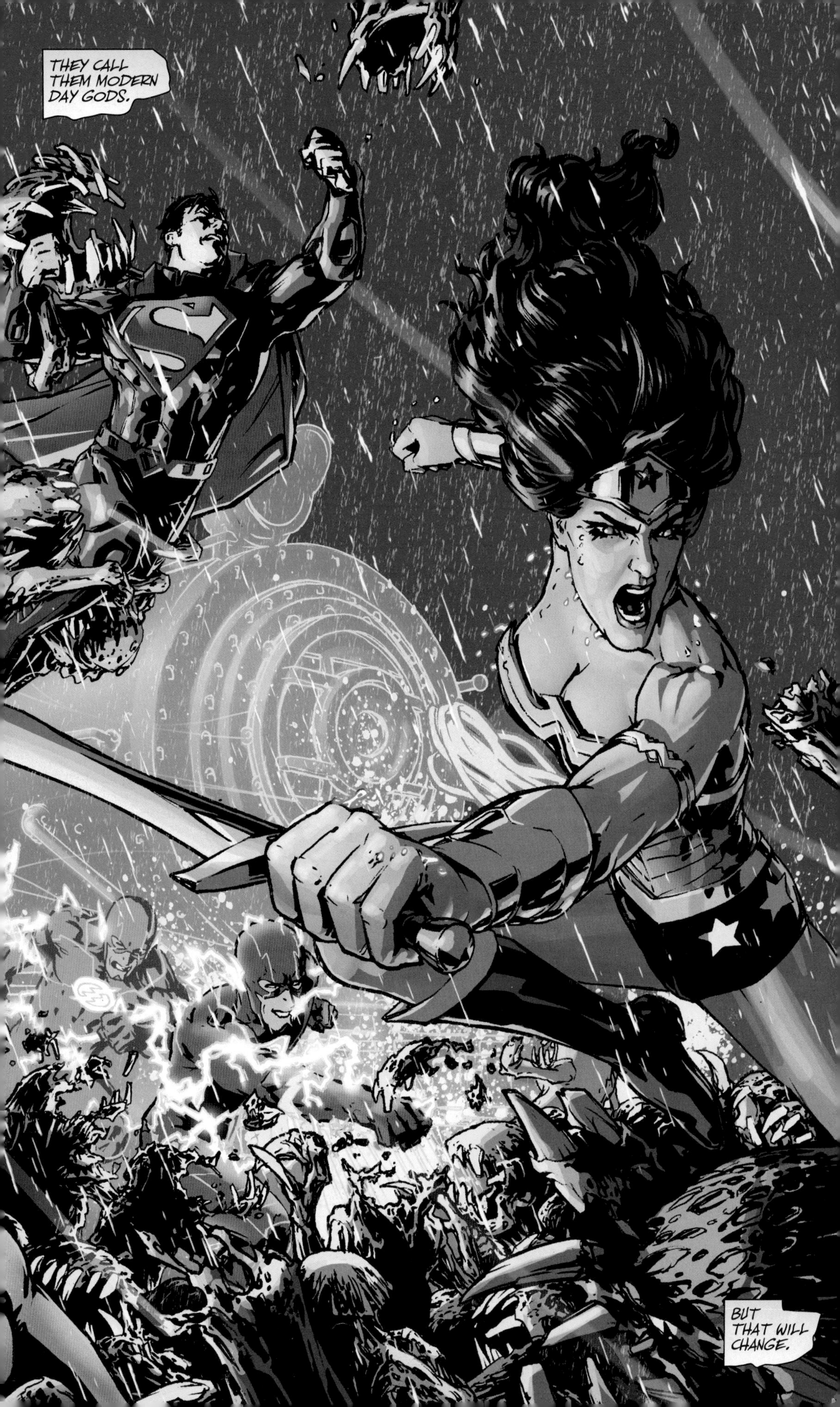
THEY CALL THEM MODERN DAY GODS.
BUT THAT WILL CHANGE.

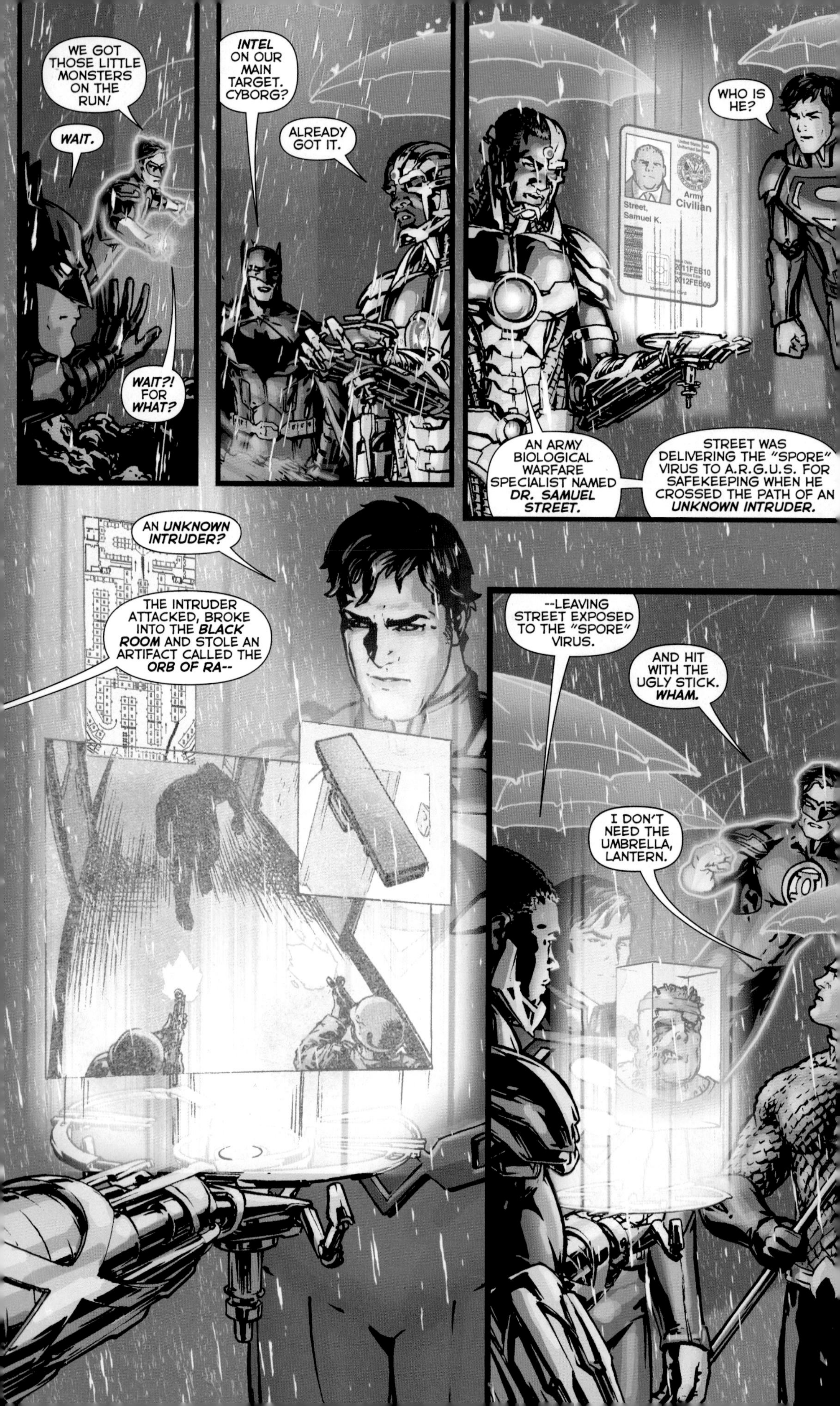

WE GOT THOSE LITTLE MONSTERS ON THE RUN!
WAIT.
WAIT?! FOR WHAT?
INTEL ON OUR MAIN TARGET. CYBORG?
ALREADY GOT IT.
Street, Samuel K.
Army Civilian
WHO IS HE?
AN ARMY BIOLOGICAL WARFARE SPECIALIST NAMED DR. SAMUEL STREET.
STREET WAS DELIVERING THE "SPORE" VIRUS TO A.R.G.U.S. FOR SAFEKEEPING WHEN HE CROSSED THE PATH OF AN UNKNOWN INTRUDER.
AN UNKNOWN INTRUDER?
THE INTRUDER ATTACKED, BROKE INTO THE BLACK ROOM AND STOLE AN ARTIFACT CALLED THE ORB OF RA--
--LEAVING STREET EXPOSED TO THE "SPORE" VIRUS.
AND HIT WITH THE UGLY STICK. WHAM.
I DON'T NEED THE UMBRELLA, LANTERN.

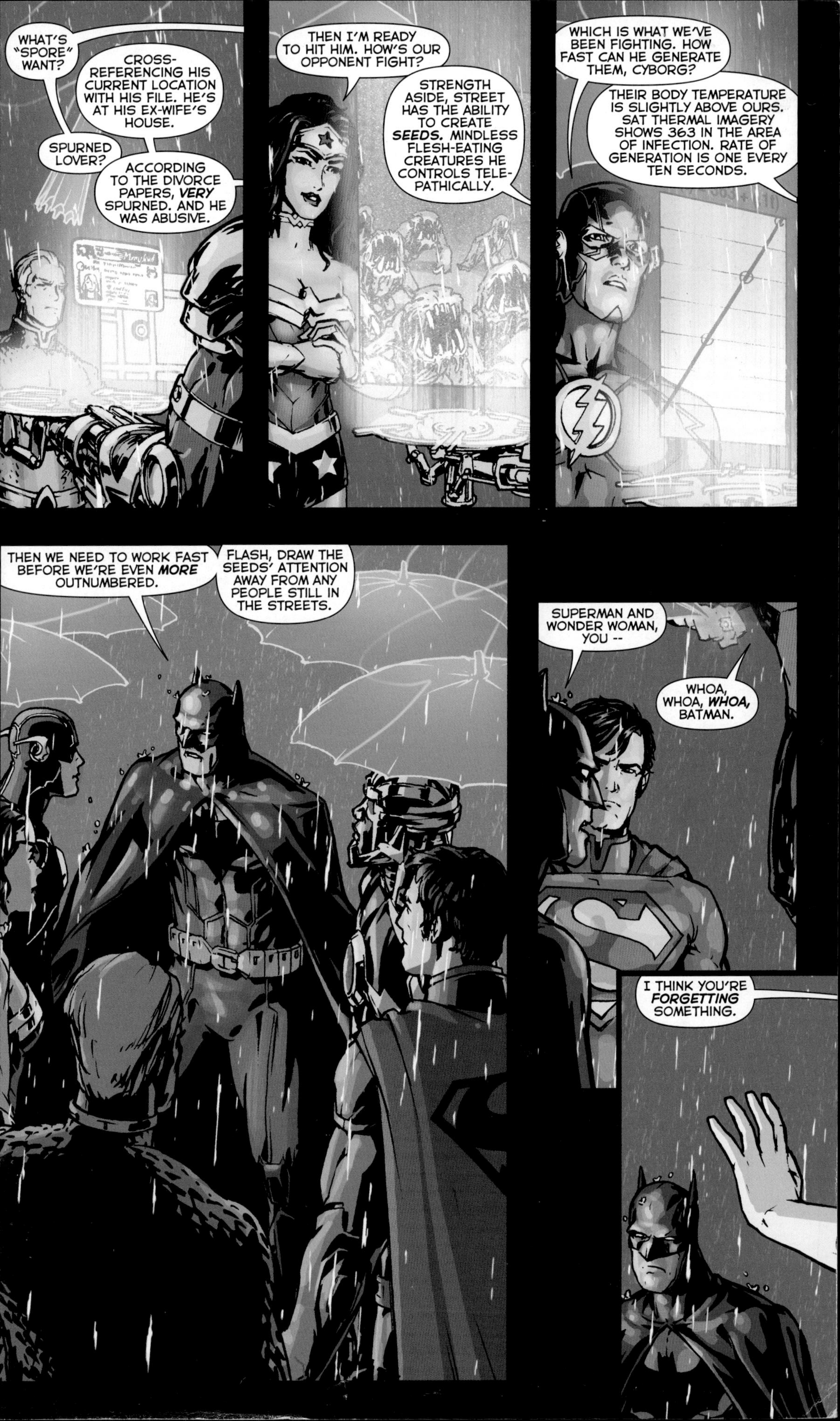
WHAT'S "SPORE" WANT?
CROSS-REFERENCING HIS CURRENT LOCATION WITH HIS FILE. HE'S AT HIS EX-WIFE'S HOUSE.
SPURNED LOVER?
ACCORDING TO THE DIVORCE PAPERS, *VERY* SPURNED. AND HE WAS ABUSIVE.
THEN I'M READY TO HIT HIM. HOW'S OUR OPPONENT FIGHT?
STRENGTH ASIDE, STREET HAS THE ABILITY TO CREATE *SEEDS.* MINDLESS FLESH-EATING CREATURES HE CONTROLS TELE-PATHICALLY.
WHICH IS WHAT WE'VE BEEN FIGHTING. HOW FAST CAN HE GENERATE THEM, CYBORG?
THEIR BODY TEMPERATURE IS SLIGHTLY ABOVE OURS. SAT THERMAL IMAGERY SHOWS 363 IN THE AREA OF INFECTION. RATE OF GENERATION IS ONE EVERY TEN SECONDS.
THEN WE NEED TO WORK FAST BEFORE WE'RE EVEN *MORE* OUTNUMBERED.
FLASH, DRAW THE SEEDS' ATTENTION AWAY FROM ANY PEOPLE STILL IN THE STREETS.
SUPERMAN AND WONDER WOMAN, YOU --
WHOA, WHOA, *WHOA,* BATMAN.
I THINK YOU'RE *FORGETTING* SOMETHING.

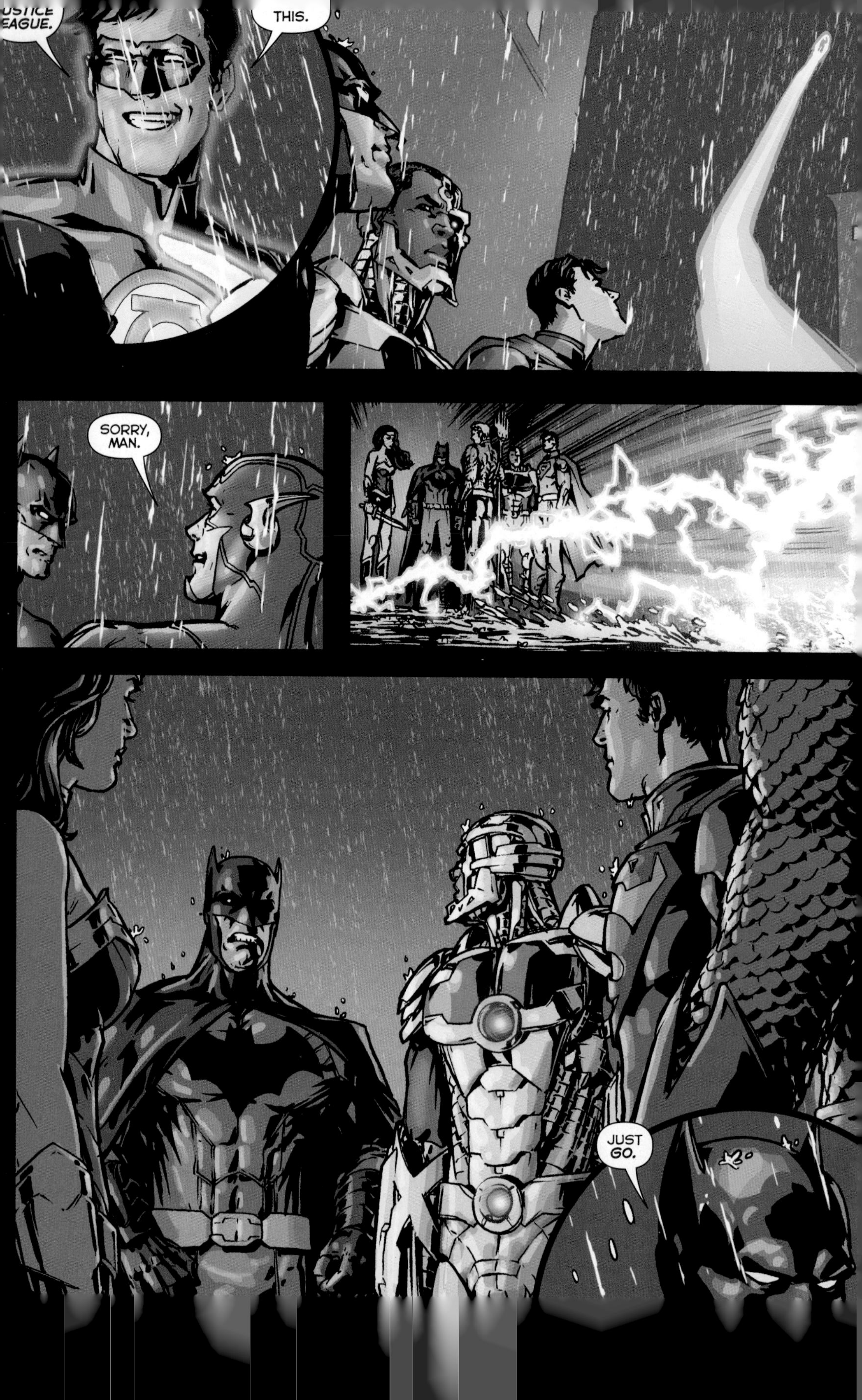
USTICE
EAGUE.
THIS.
SORRY, MAN.
JUST GO.

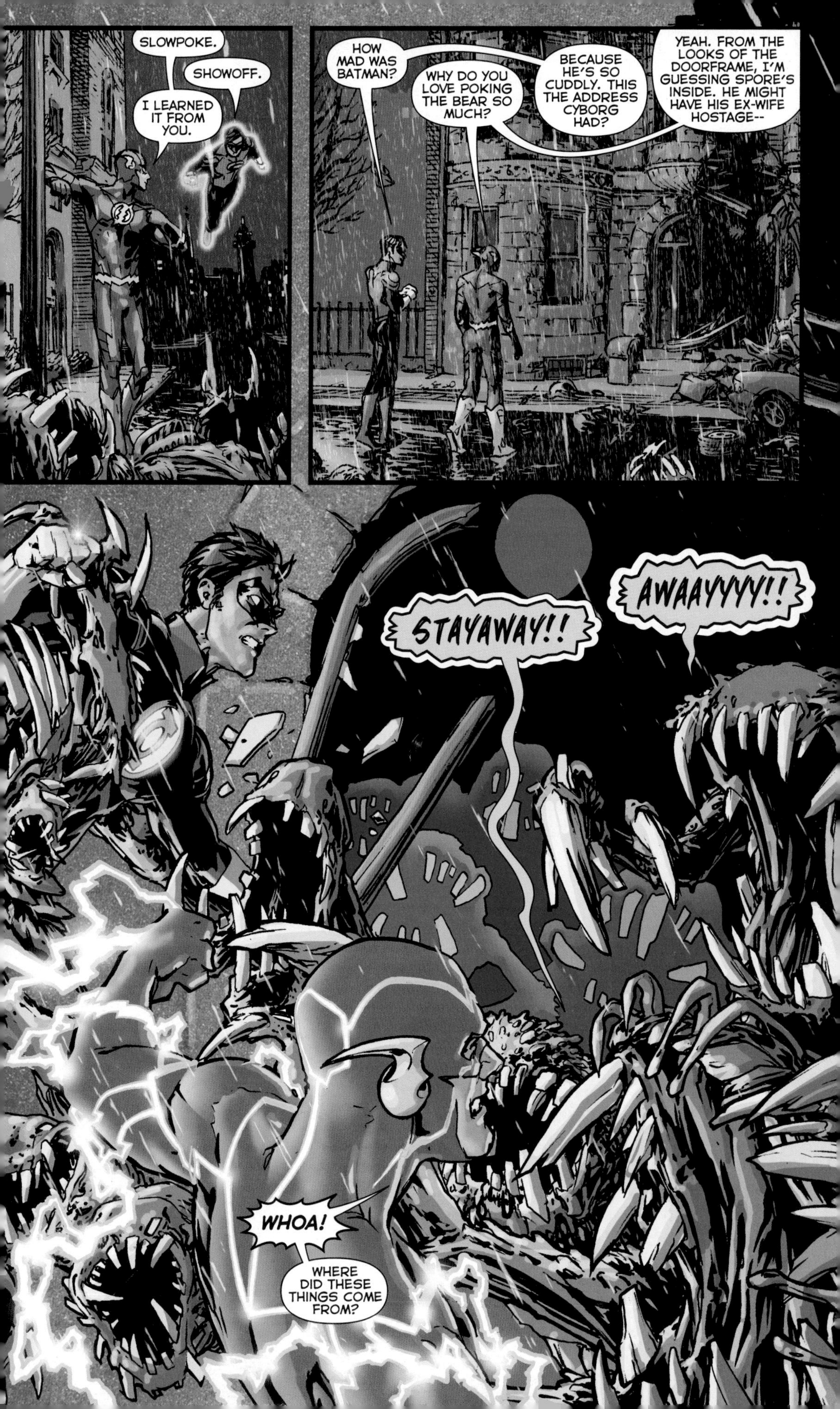
SLOWPOKE.
SHOWOFF.
I LEARNED IT FROM YOU.
HOW MAD WAS BATMAN?
WHY DO YOU LOVE POKING THE BEAR SO MUCH?
BECAUSE HE'S SO CUDDLY. THIS THE ADDRESS CYBORG HAD?
YEAH. FROM THE LOOKS OF THE DOORFRAME, I'M GUESSING SPORE'S INSIDE. HE MIGHT HAVE HIS EX-WIFE HOSTAGE--
STAYAWAY!!
AWAAYYYY!!
WHOA!
WHERE DID THESE THINGS COME FROM?

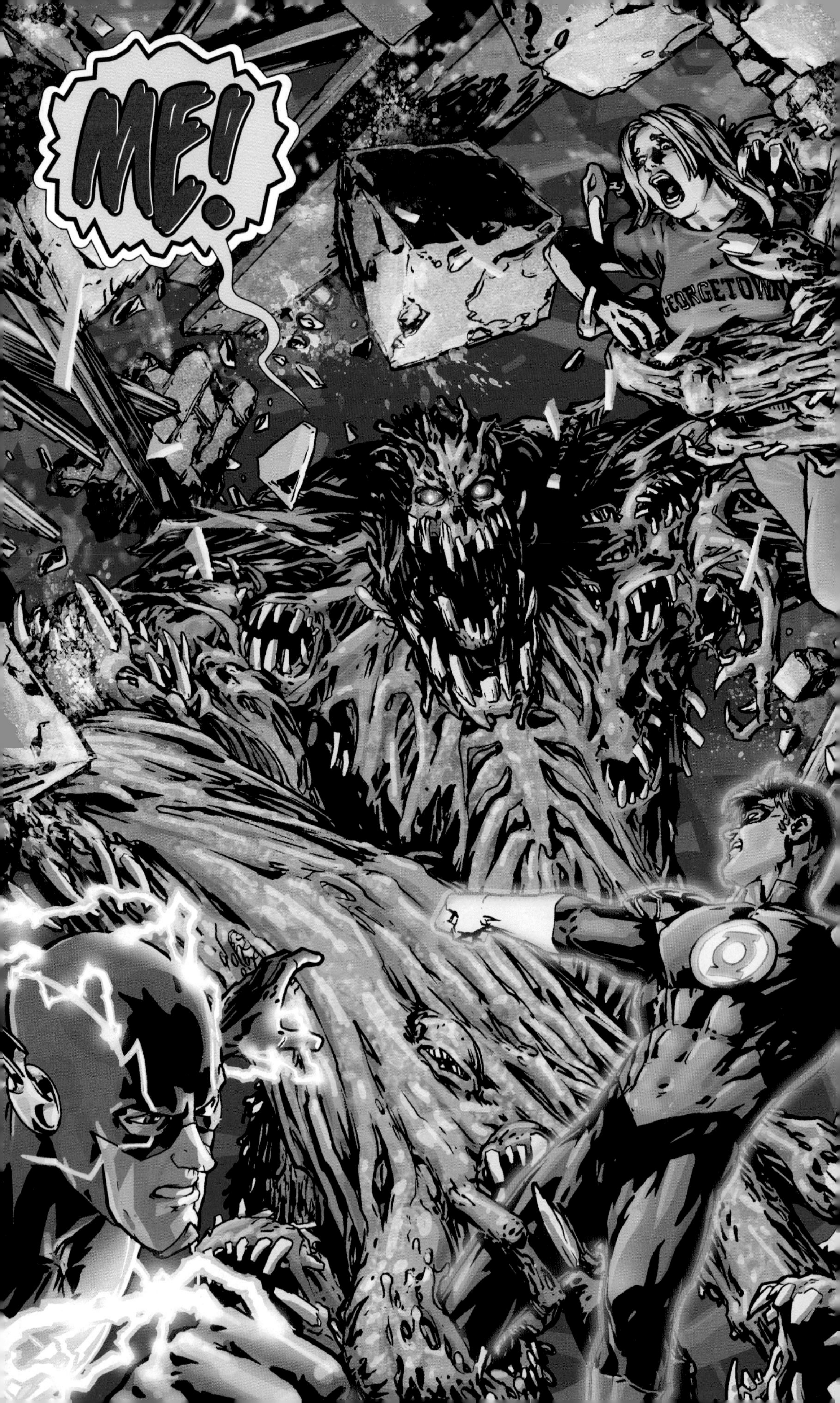
ME!
GEORGETOWN

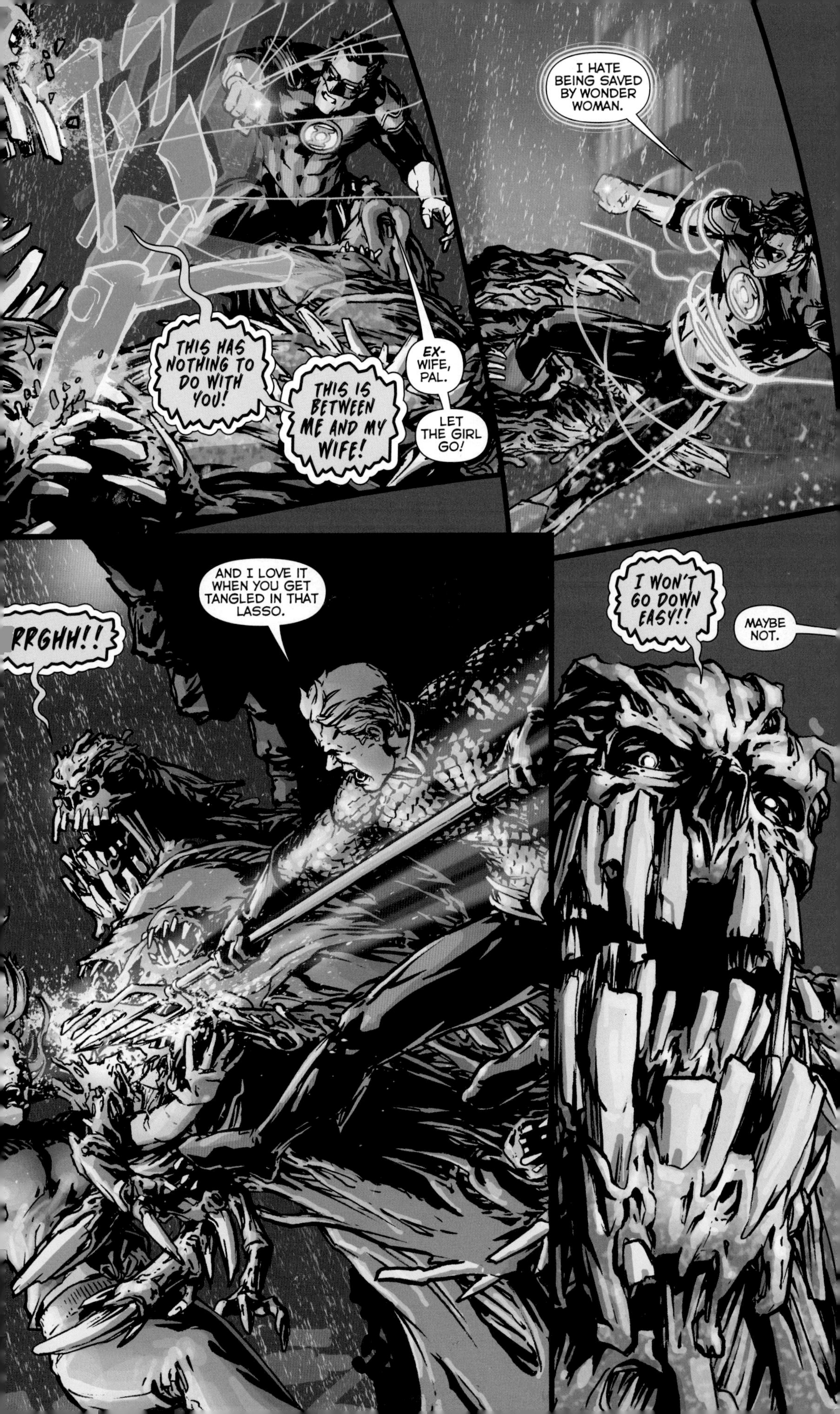
THIS HAS NOTHING TO DO WITH YOU!
THIS IS BETWEEN ME AND MY WIFE!
EX-WIFE, PAL.
LET THE GIRL GO!
I HATE BEING SAVED BY WONDER WOMAN.
RRGHH!!
AND I LOVE IT WHEN YOU GET TANGLED IN THAT LASSO.
I WON'T GO DOWN EASY!!
MAYBE NOT.

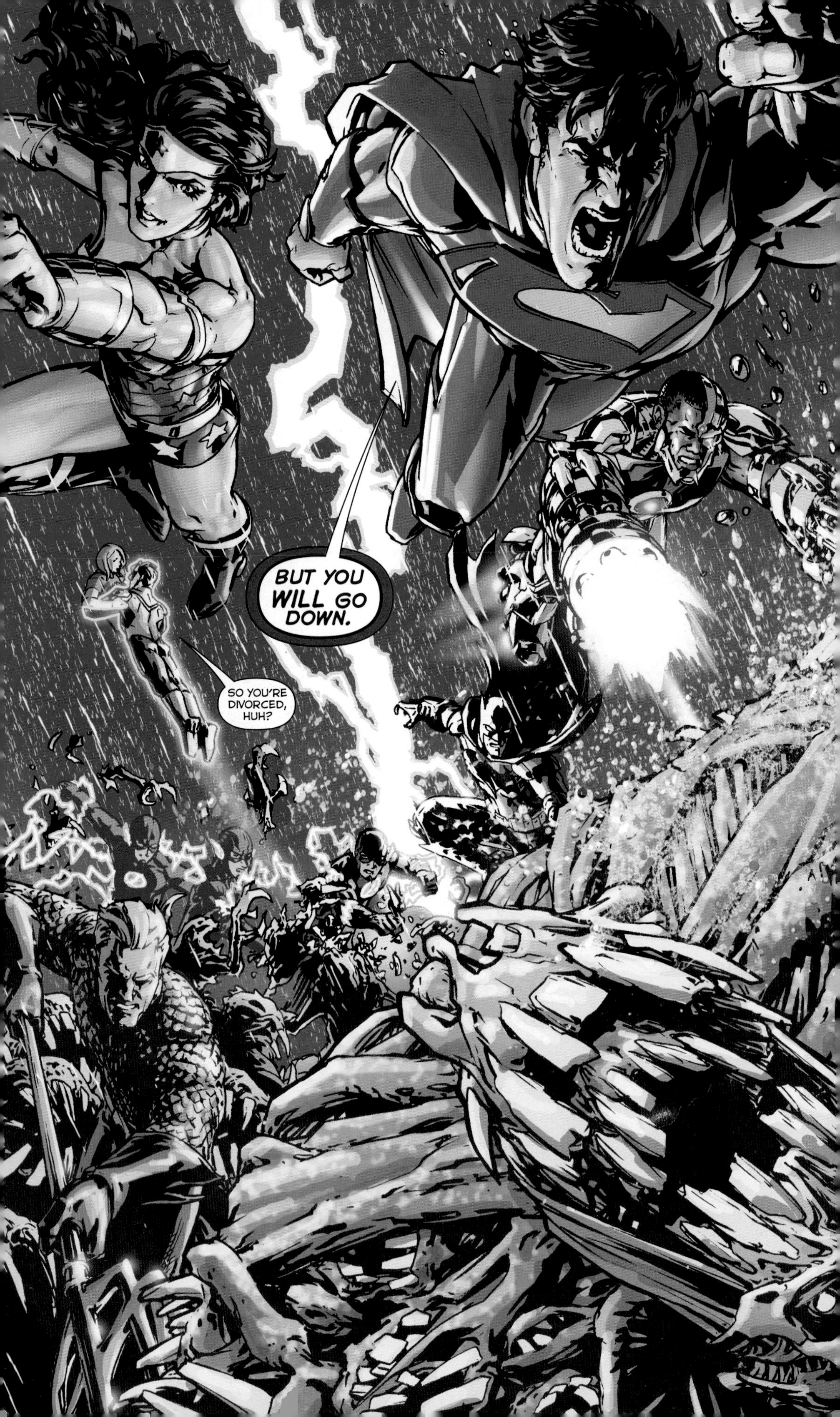
BUT YOU WILL GO DOWN.
SO YOU'RE DIVORCED, HUH?

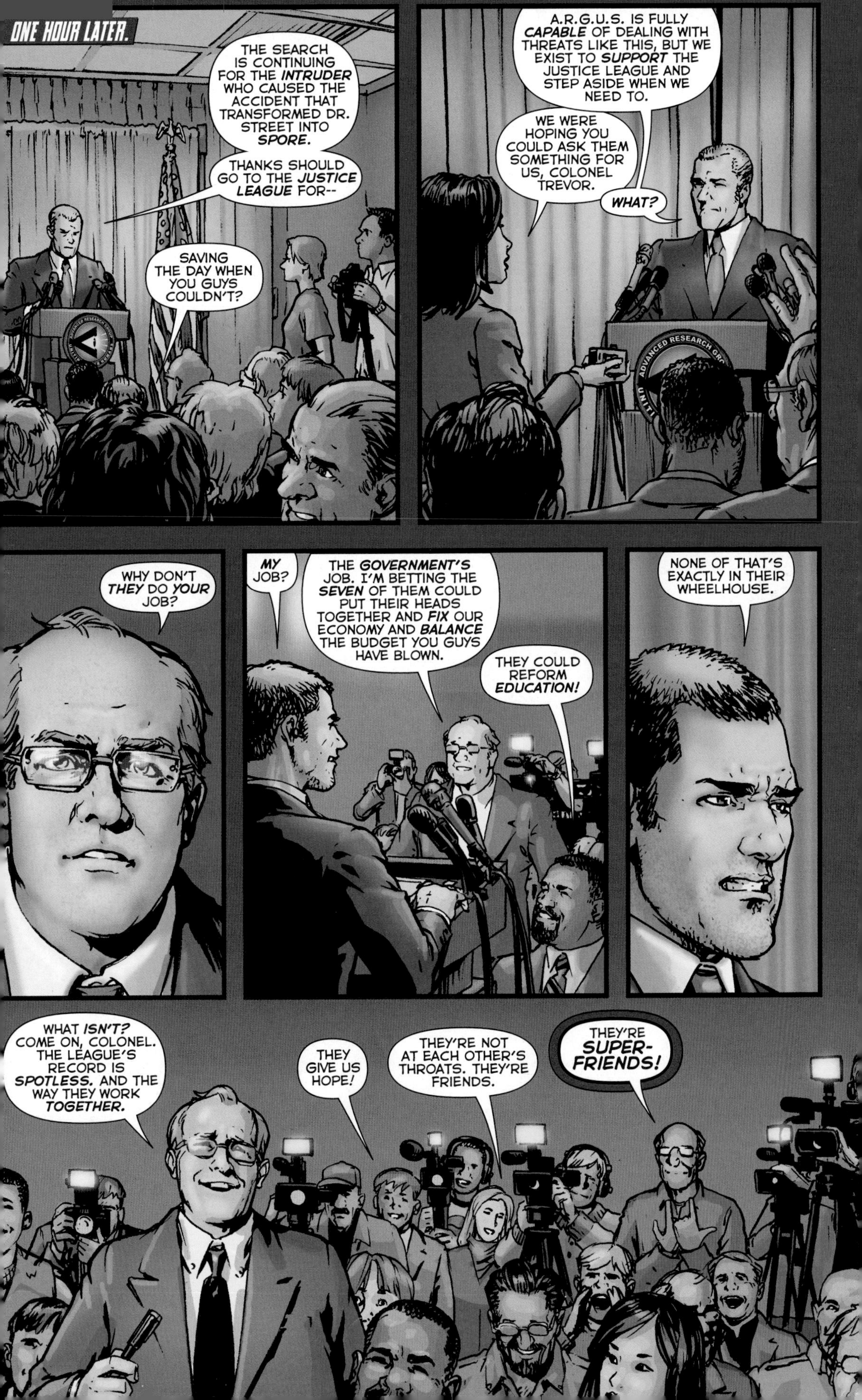
ONE HOUR LATER.
THE SEARCH IS CONTINUING FOR THE INTRUDER WHO CAUSED THE ACCIDENT THAT TRANSFORMED DR. STREET INTO SPORE.
THANKS SHOULD GO TO THE JUSTICE LEAGUE FOR--
SAVING THE DAY WHEN YOU GUYS COULDN'T?
A.R.G.U.S. IS FULLY CAPABLE OF DEALING WITH THREATS LIKE THIS, BUT WE EXIST TO SUPPORT THE JUSTICE LEAGUE AND STEP ASIDE WHEN WE NEED TO.
WE WERE HOPING YOU COULD ASK THEM SOMETHING FOR US, COLONEL TREVOR.
WHAT?
WHY DON'T THEY DO YOUR JOB?
MY JOB?
THE GOVERNMENT'S JOB. I'M BETTING THE SEVEN OF THEM COULD PUT THEIR HEADS TOGETHER AND FIX OUR ECONOMY AND BALANCE THE BUDGET YOU GUYS HAVE BLOWN.
THEY COULD REFORM EDUCATION!
NONE OF THAT'S EXACTLY IN THEIR WHEELHOUSE.
WHAT ISN'T? COME ON, COLONEL. THE LEAGUE'S RECORD IS SPOTLESS. AND THE WAY THEY WORK TOGETHER.
THEY GIVE US HOPE!
THEY'RE NOT AT EACH OTHER'S THROATS. THEY'RE FRIENDS.
THEY'RE SUPER-FRIENDS!

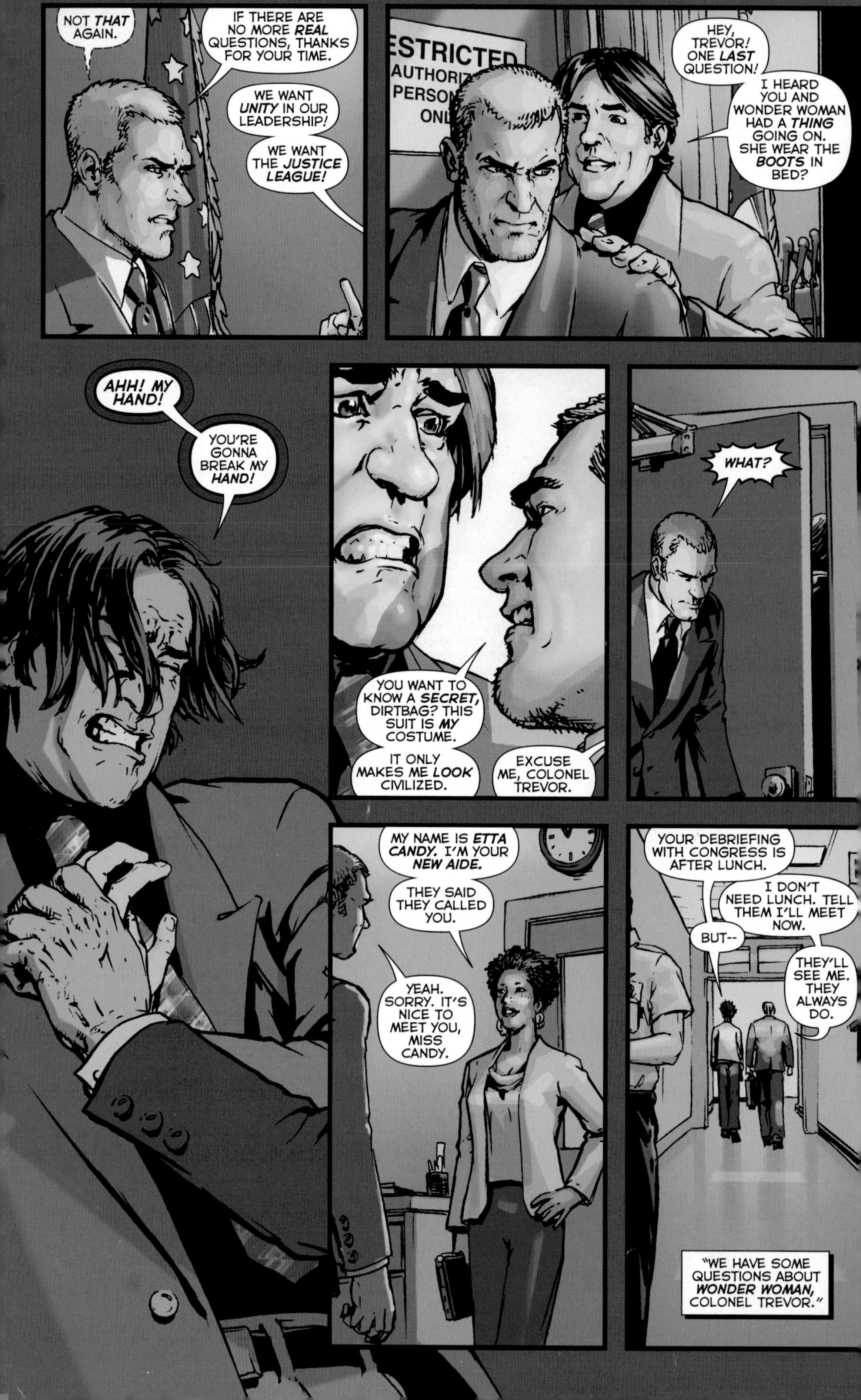
NOT THAT AGAIN.
IF THERE ARE NO MORE REAL QUESTIONS, THANKS FOR YOUR TIME.
WE WANT UNITY IN OUR LEADERSHIP!
WE WANT THE JUSTICE LEAGUE!
ESTRICTED AUTHORIZ PERSON ONL
HEY, TREVOR! ONE LAST QUESTION!
I HEARD YOU AND WONDER WOMAN HAD A THING GOING ON. SHE WEAR THE BOOTS IN BED?
AHH! MY HAND!
YOU'RE GONNA BREAK MY HAND!
YOU WANT TO KNOW A SECRET, DIRTBAG? THIS SUIT IS MY COSTUME.
IT ONLY MAKES ME LOOK CIVILIZED.
EXCUSE ME, COLONEL TREVOR.
WHAT?
MY NAME IS ETTA CANDY. I'M YOUR NEW AIDE.
THEY SAID THEY CALLED YOU.
YEAH. SORRY. IT'S NICE TO MEET YOU, MISS CANDY.
YOUR DEBRIEFING WITH CONGRESS IS AFTER LUNCH.
I DON'T NEED LUNCH. TELL THEM I'LL MEET NOW.
BUT--
THEY'LL SEE ME. THEY ALWAYS DO.
"WE HAVE SOME QUESTIONS ABOUT WONDER WOMAN, COLONEL TREVOR."

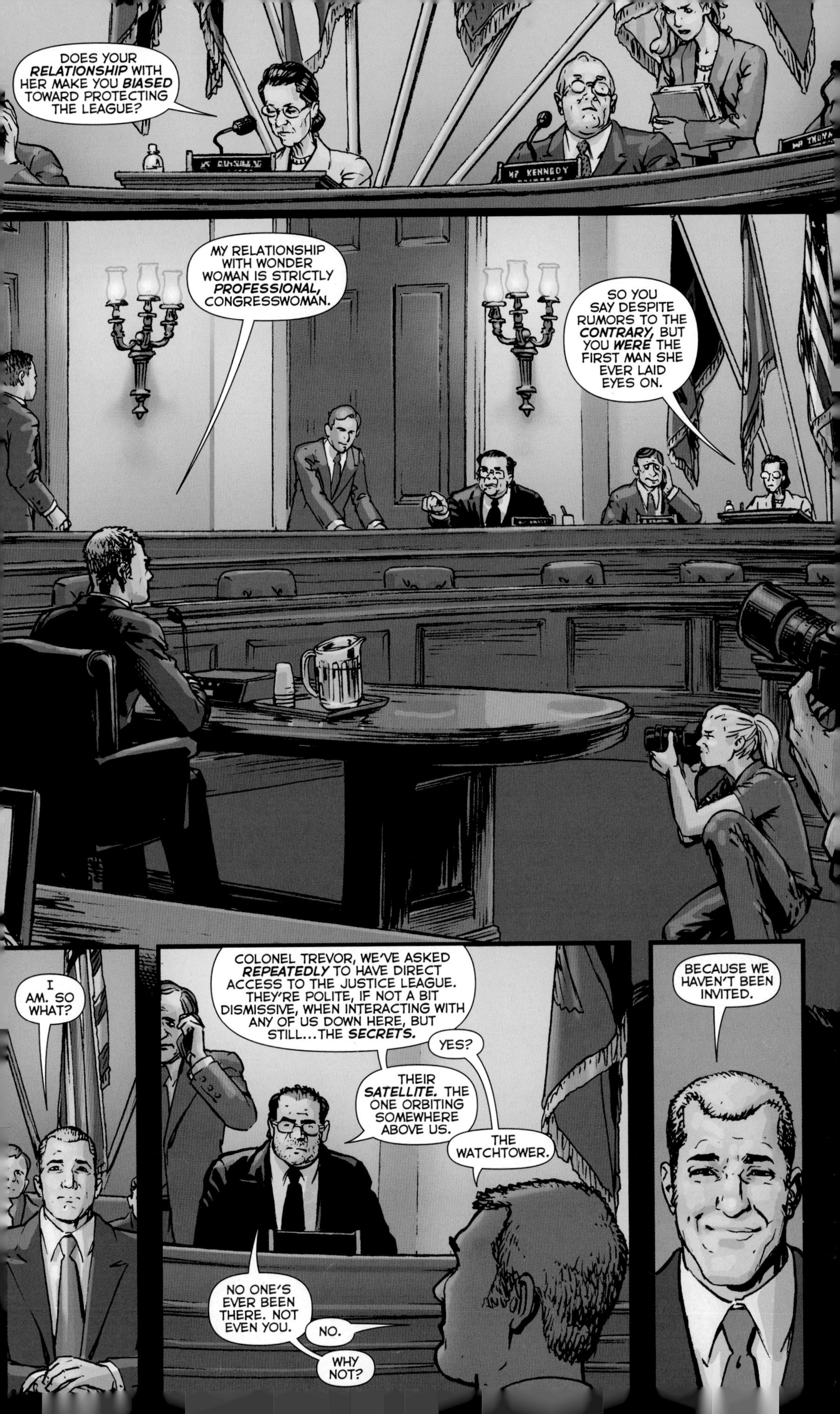
DOES YOUR *RELATIONSHIP* WITH HER MAKE YOU *BIASED* TOWARD PROTECTING THE LEAGUE?
MR KENNEDY
MY RELATIONSHIP WITH WONDER WOMAN IS STRICTLY *PROFESSIONAL,* CONGRESSWOMAN.
SO YOU SAY DESPITE RUMORS TO THE *CONTRARY,* BUT YOU *WERE* THE FIRST MAN SHE EVER LAID EYES ON.
I AM. SO WHAT?
COLONEL TREVOR, WE'VE ASKED *REPEATEDLY* TO HAVE DIRECT ACCESS TO THE JUSTICE LEAGUE. THEY'RE POLITE, IF NOT A BIT DISMISSIVE, WHEN INTERACTING WITH ANY OF US DOWN HERE, BUT STILL... THE *SECRETS.*
YES?
THEIR *SATELLITE.* THE ONE ORBITING SOMEWHERE ABOVE US.
THE WATCHTOWER.
NO ONE'S EVER BEEN THERE. NOT EVEN YOU.
NO.
WHY NOT?
BECAUSE WE HAVEN'T BEEN INVITED.

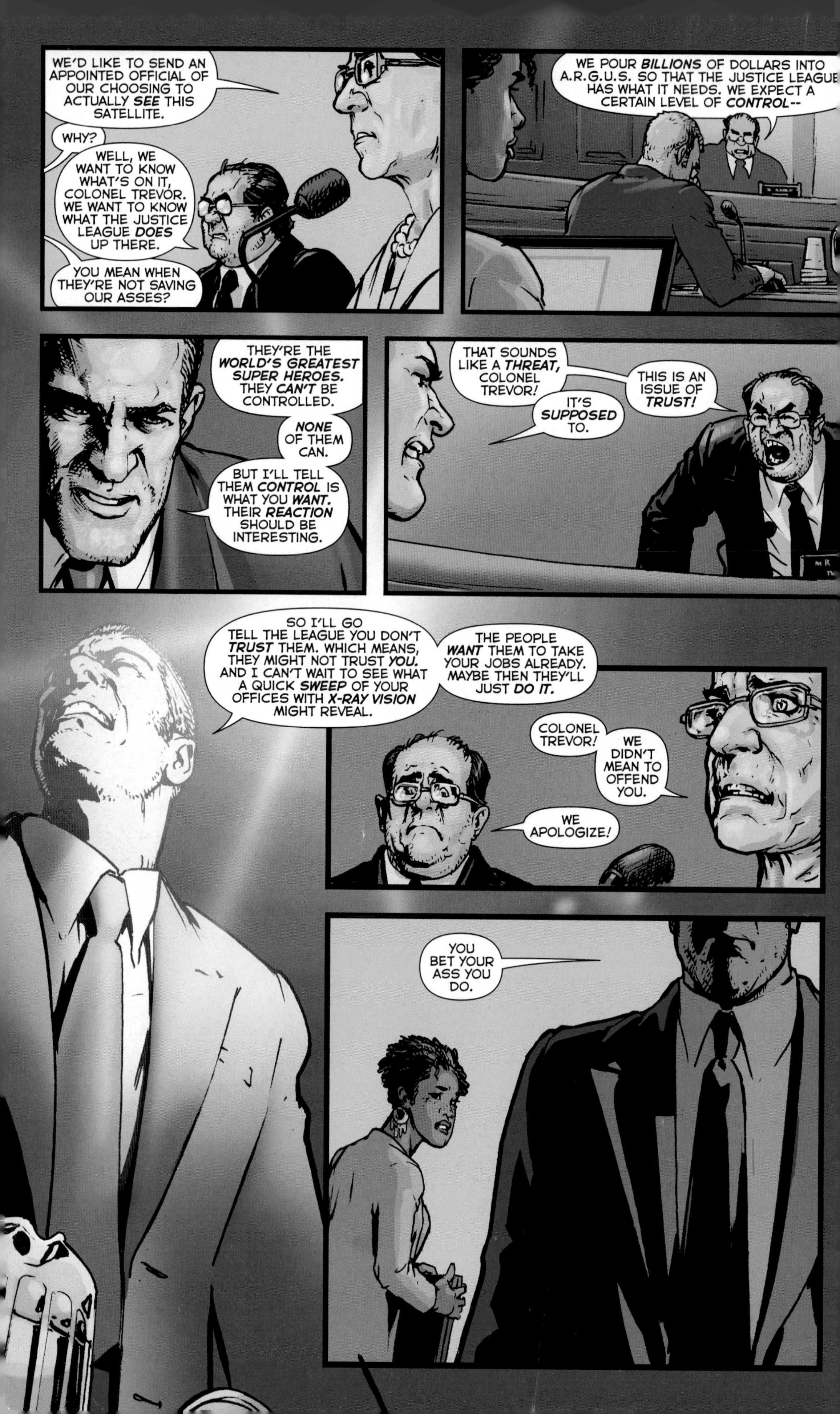
WE'D LIKE TO SEND AN APPOINTED OFFICIAL OF OUR CHOOSING TO ACTUALLY SEE THIS SATELLITE.
WHY?
WELL, WE WANT TO KNOW WHAT'S ON IT, COLONEL TREVOR. WE WANT TO KNOW WHAT THE JUSTICE LEAGUE DOES UP THERE.
YOU MEAN WHEN THEY'RE NOT SAVING OUR ASSES?
WE POUR BILLIONS OF DOLLARS INTO A.R.G.U.S. SO THAT THE JUSTICE LEAGUE HAS WHAT IT NEEDS. WE EXPECT A CERTAIN LEVEL OF CONTROL--
THEY'RE THE WORLD'S GREATEST SUPER HEROES. THEY CAN'T BE CONTROLLED.
NONE OF THEM CAN.
BUT I'LL TELL THEM CONTROL IS WHAT YOU WANT. THEIR REACTION SHOULD BE INTERESTING.
THAT SOUNDS LIKE A THREAT, COLONEL TREVOR!
IT'S SUPPOSED TO.
THIS IS AN ISSUE OF TRUST!
SO I'LL GO TELL THE LEAGUE YOU DON'T TRUST THEM. WHICH MEANS, THEY MIGHT NOT TRUST YOU. AND I CAN'T WAIT TO SEE WHAT A QUICK SWEEP OF YOUR OFFICES WITH X-RAY VISION MIGHT REVEAL.
THE PEOPLE WANT THEM TO TAKE YOUR JOBS ALREADY. MAYBE THEN THEY'LL JUST DO IT.
COLONEL TREVOR!
WE DIDN'T MEAN TO OFFEND YOU.
WE APOLOGIZE!
YOU BET YOUR ASS YOU DO.

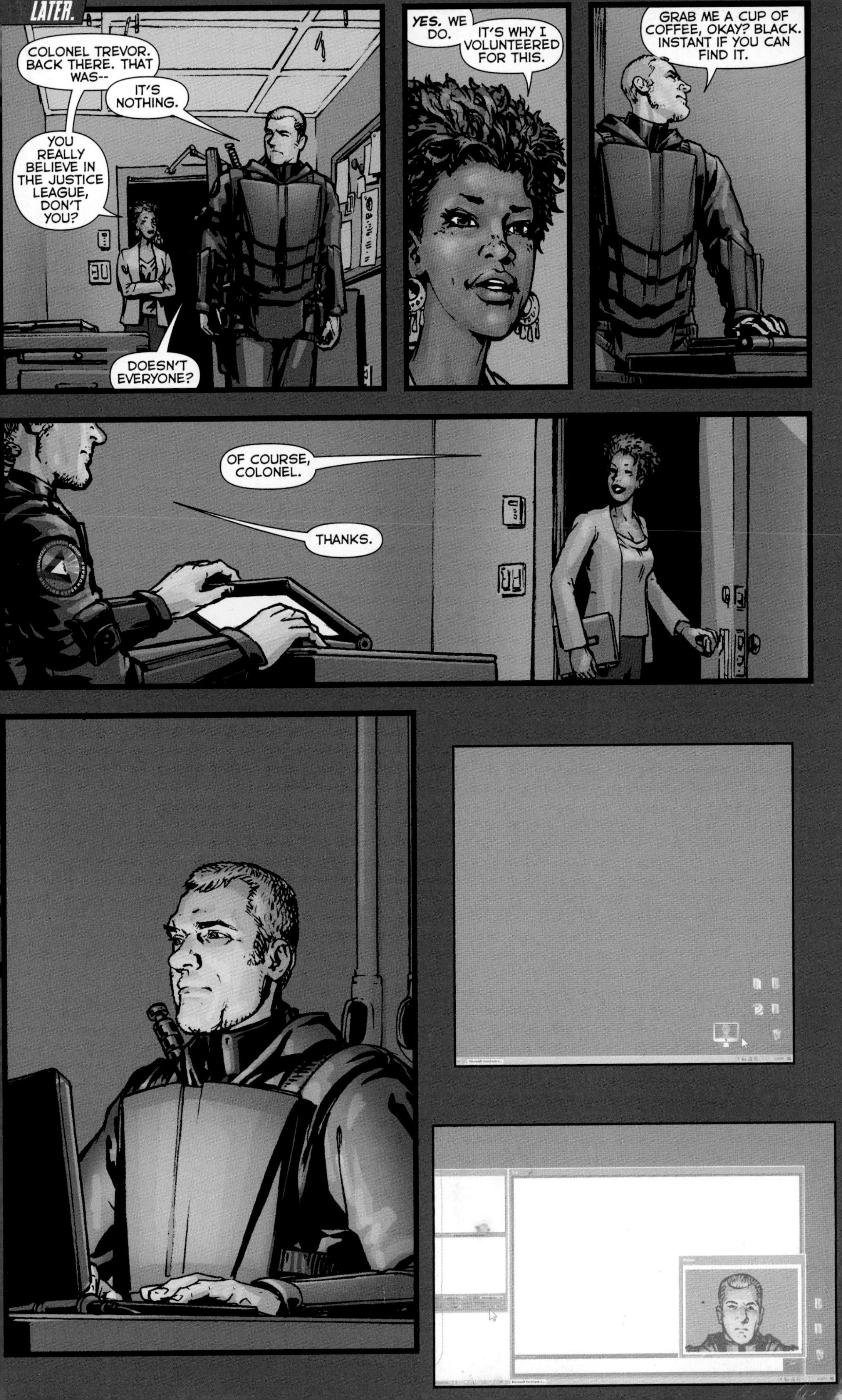
LATER.
COLONEL TREVOR. BACK THERE. THAT WAS--
IT'S NOTHING.
YOU REALLY BELIEVE IN THE JUSTICE LEAGUE, DON'T YOU?
DOESN'T EVERYONE?
YES. WE DO.
IT'S WHY I VOLUNTEERED FOR THIS.
GRAB ME A CUP OF COFFEE, OKAY? BLACK. INSTANT IF YOU CAN FIND IT.
OF COURSE, COLONEL.
THANKS.

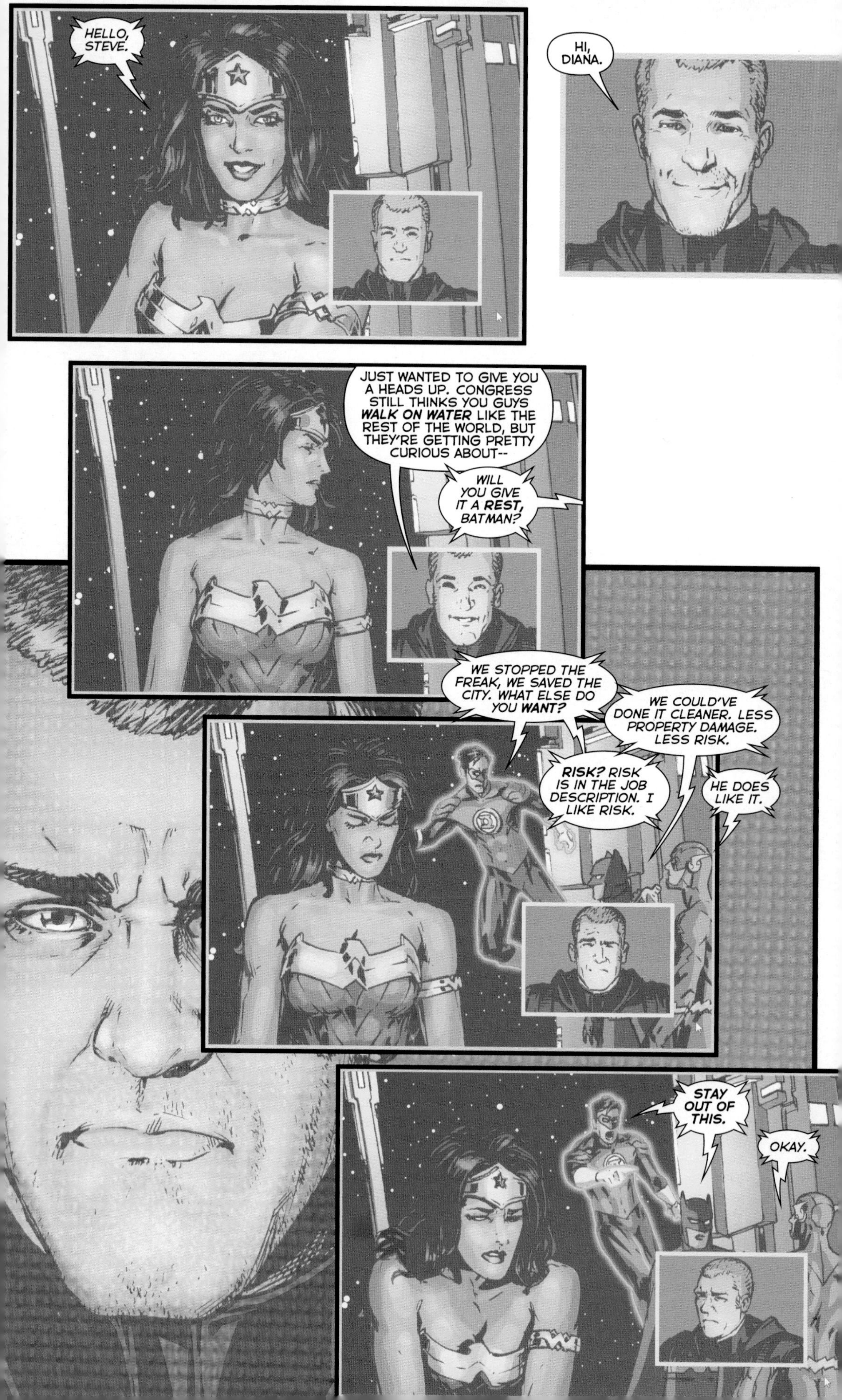
HELLO, STEVE.
HI, DIANA.
JUST WANTED TO GIVE YOU A HEADS UP. CONGRESS STILL THINKS YOU GUYS WALK ON WATER LIKE THE REST OF THE WORLD, BUT THEY'RE GETTING PRETTY CURIOUS ABOUT--
WILL YOU GIVE IT A REST, BATMAN?
WE STOPPED THE FREAK, WE SAVED THE CITY. WHAT ELSE DO YOU WANT?
WE COULD'VE DONE IT CLEANER. LESS PROPERTY DAMAGE. LESS RISK.
RISK? RISK IS IN THE JOB DESCRIPTION. I LIKE RISK.
HE DOES LIKE IT.
STAY OUT OF THIS.
OKAY.

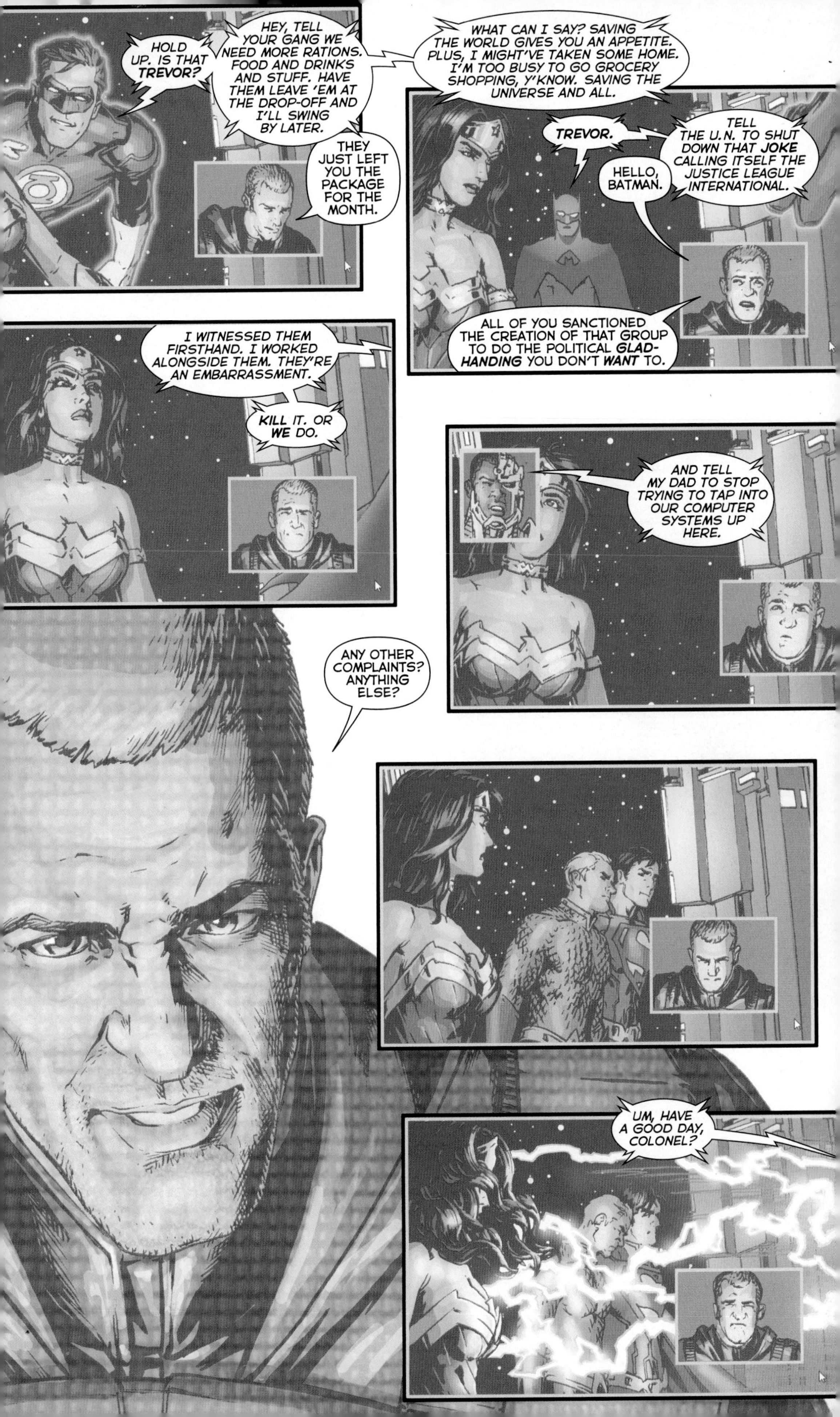
HOLD UP. IS THAT TREVOR?
HEY, TELL YOUR GANG WE NEED MORE RATIONS. FOOD AND DRINKS AND STUFF. HAVE THEM LEAVE 'EM AT THE DROP-OFF AND I'LL SWING BY LATER.
THEY JUST LEFT YOU THE PACKAGE FOR THE MONTH.
WHAT CAN I SAY? SAVING THE WORLD GIVES YOU AN APPETITE. PLUS, I MIGHT'VE TAKEN SOME HOME. I'M TOO BUSY TO GO GROCERY SHOPPING, Y'KNOW. SAVING THE UNIVERSE AND ALL.
TREVOR.
TELL THE U.N. TO SHUT DOWN THAT JOKE CALLING ITSELF THE JUSTICE LEAGUE INTERNATIONAL.
HELLO, BATMAN.
ALL OF YOU SANCTIONED THE CREATION OF THAT GROUP TO DO THE POLITICAL GLAD-HANDING YOU DON'T WANT TO.
I WITNESSED THEM FIRSTHAND. I WORKED ALONGSIDE THEM. THEY'RE AN EMBARRASSMENT.
KILL IT. OR WE DO.
AND TELL MY DAD TO STOP TRYING TO TAP INTO OUR COMPUTER SYSTEMS UP HERE.
ANY OTHER COMPLAINTS? ANYTHING ELSE?
UM, HAVE A GOOD DAY, COLONEL?

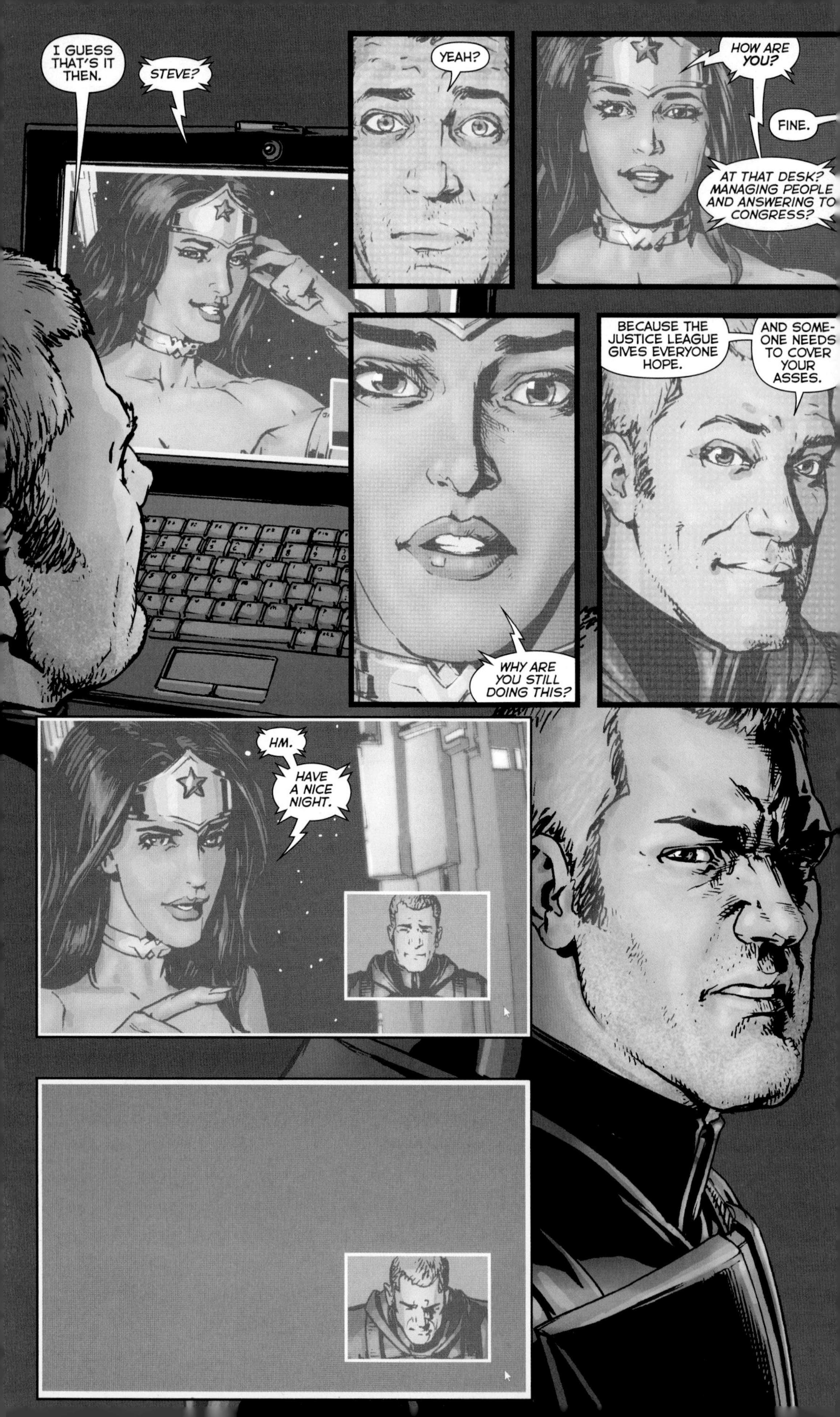
I GUESS THAT'S IT THEN.
STEVE?
YEAH?
HOW ARE YOU?
FINE.
AT THAT DESK? MANAGING PEOPLE AND ANSWERING TO CONGRESS?
WHY ARE YOU STILL DOING THIS?
BECAUSE THE JUSTICE LEAGUE GIVES EVERYONE HOPE.
AND SOME-ONE NEEDS TO COVER YOUR ASSES.
HM.
HAVE A NICE NIGHT.

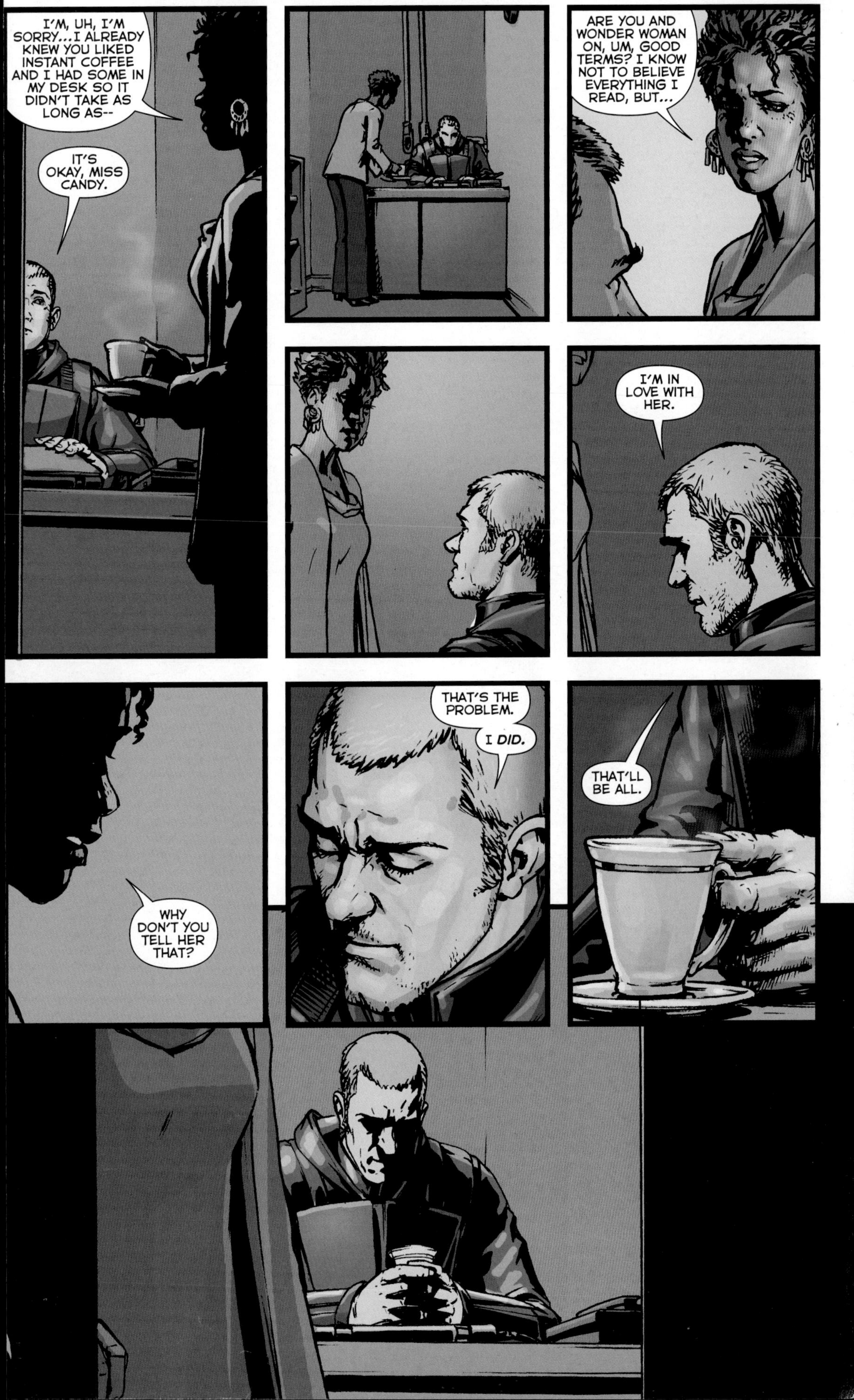
I'M, UH, I'M SORRY...I ALREADY KNEW YOU LIKED INSTANT COFFEE AND I HAD SOME IN MY DESK SO IT DIDN'T TAKE AS LONG AS--
IT'S OKAY, MISS CANDY.
ARE YOU AND WONDER WOMAN ON, UM, GOOD TERMS? I KNOW NOT TO BELIEVE EVERYTHING I READ, BUT...
I'M IN LOVE WITH HER.
WHY DON'T YOU TELL HER THAT?
THAT'S THE PROBLEM.
I DID.
THAT'LL BE ALL.

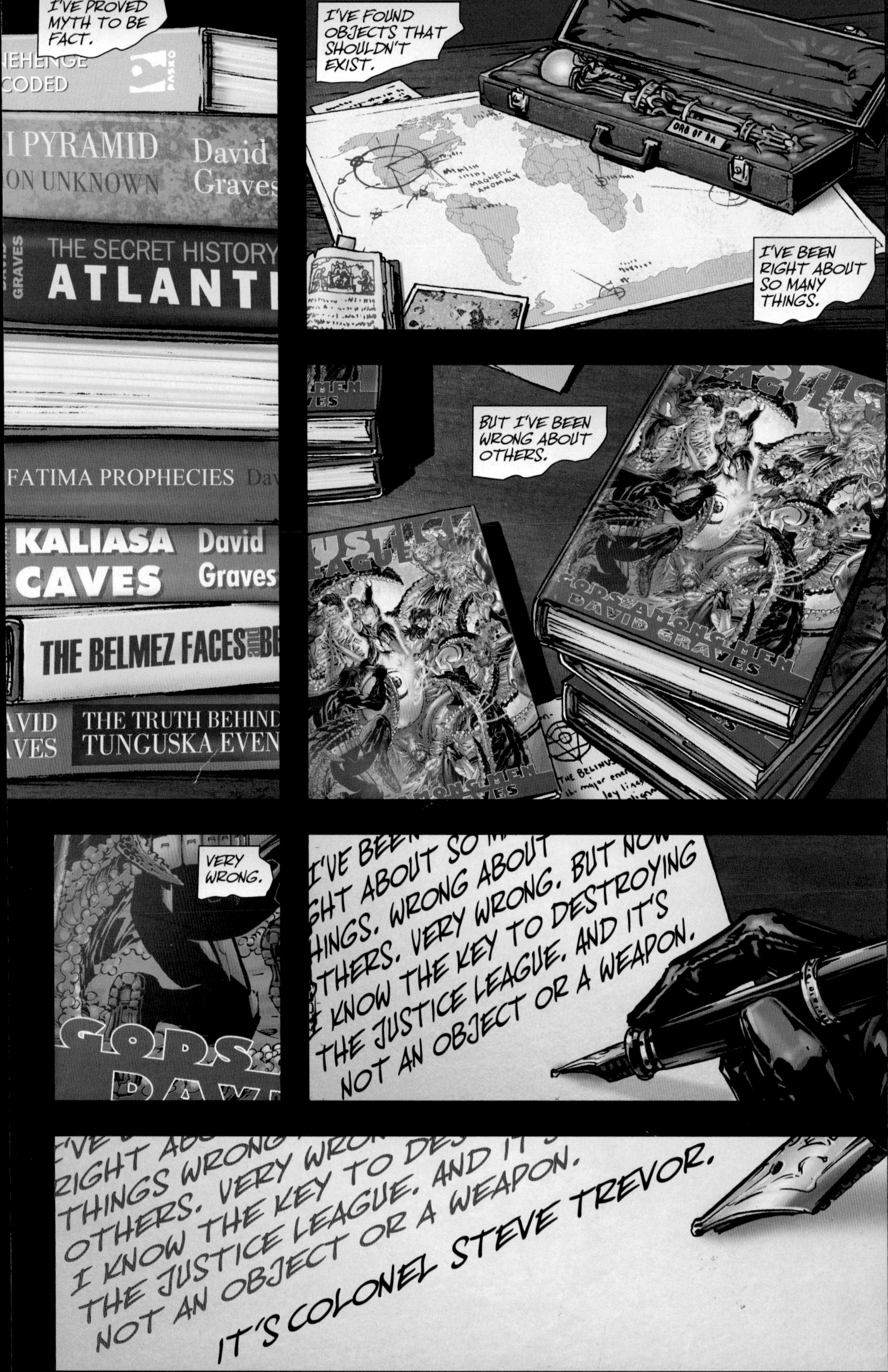
I'VE PROVED MYTH TO BE FACT.
NEHENGE
CODED
PASKO
I PYRAMID David
ON UNKNOWN Graves
THE SECRET HISTORY
ATLANTI
GRAVES
FATIMA PROPHECIES Dav
KALIASA CAVES David Graves
THE BELMEZ FACES
AVID
AVES
THE TRUTH BEHIND
TUNGUSKA EVEN
I'VE FOUND OBJECTS THAT SHOULDN'T EXIST.
ORB OF RA
MAGNETIC ANOMALY
I'VE BEEN RIGHT ABOUT SO MANY THINGS.
BUT I'VE BEEN WRONG ABOUT OTHERS.
DAVID GRAVES
VERY WRONG.
I KNOW THE KEY TO DESTROYING
THE JUSTICE LEAGUE. AND IT'S
NOT AN OBJECT OR A WEAPON.
IT'S COLONEL STEVE TREVOR.

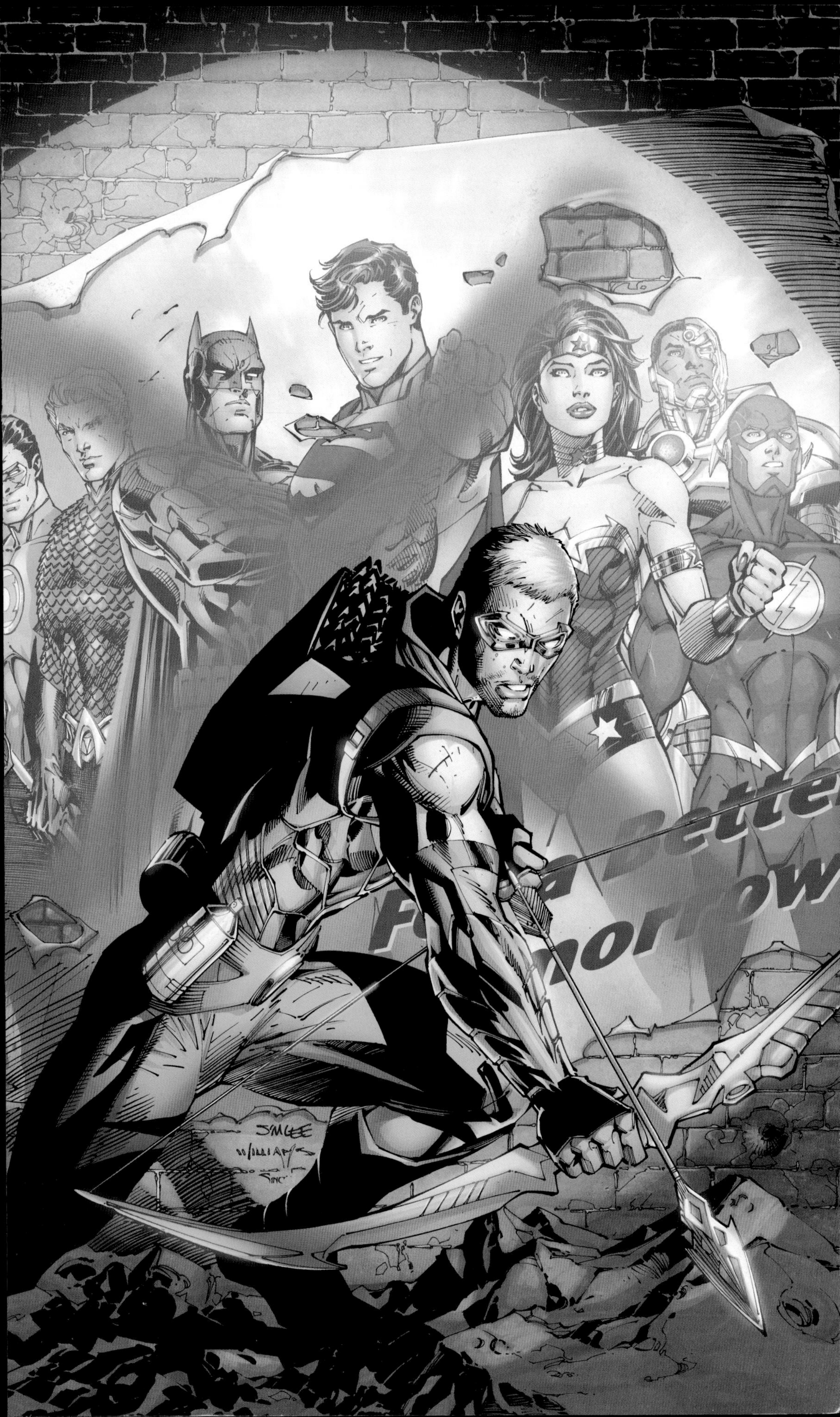

JUSTICE LEAGUE TEAM-UP: GREEN ARR

GEOFF JOHNS writer **CARLOS D'ANDA WITH IVAN REIS & JOE PRADO** artists cover by **JIM LEE, SCOTT WILLIAMS & ALEX SINCLAIR**

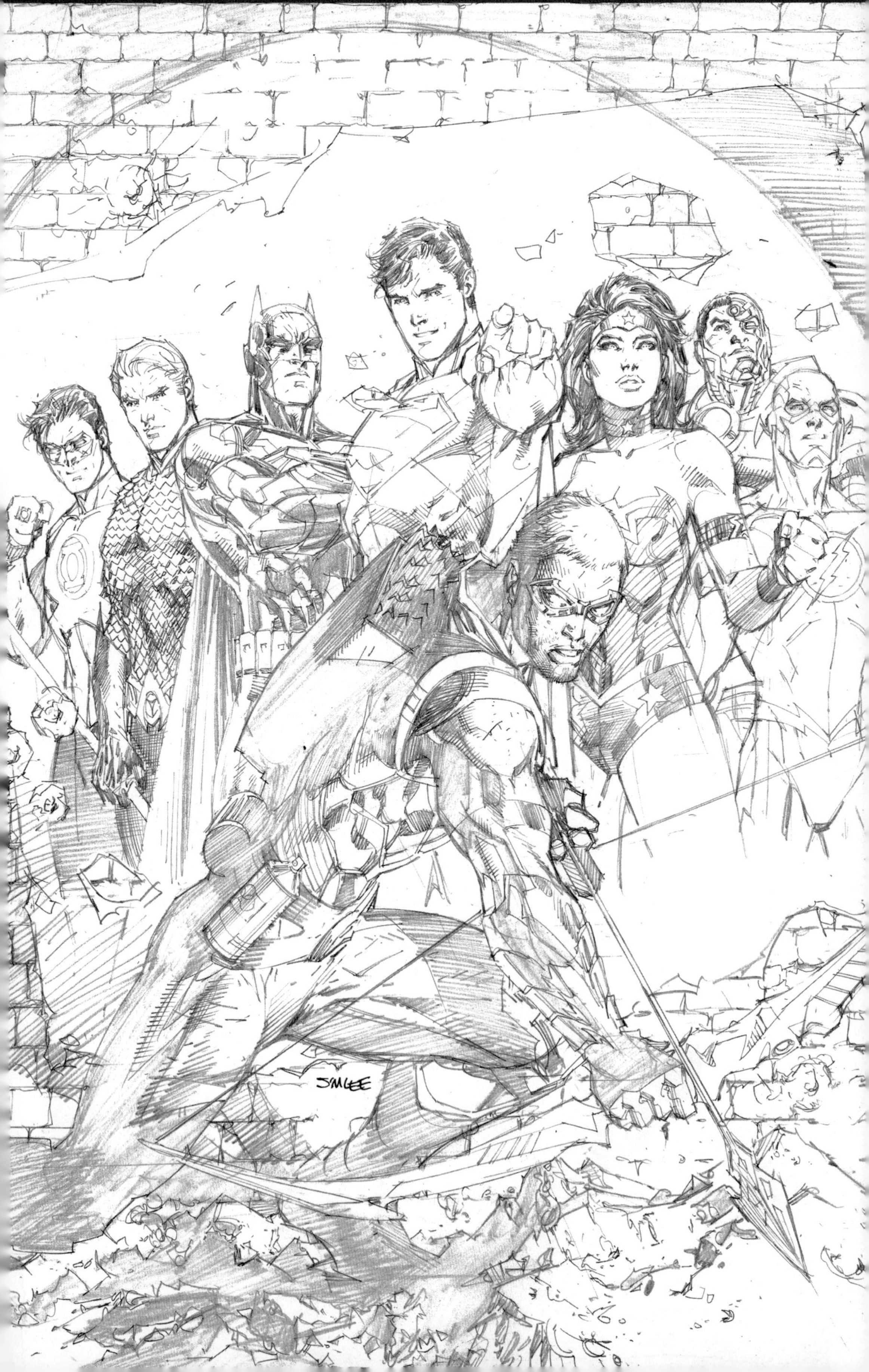

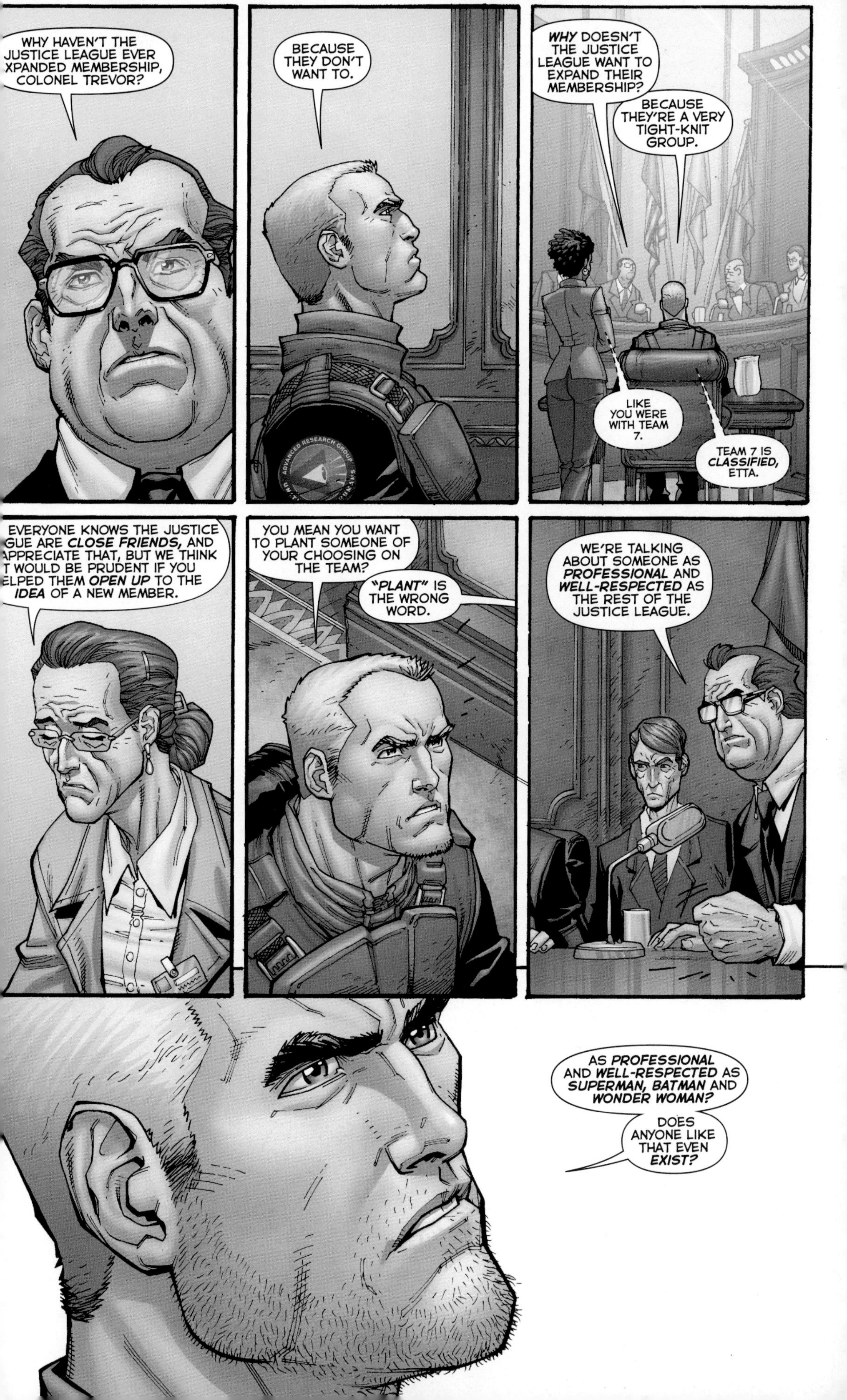

WHY HAVEN'T THE JUSTICE LEAGUE EVER XPANDED MEMBERSHIP, COLONEL TREVOR?
BECAUSE THEY DON'T WANT TO.
WHY DOESN'T THE JUSTICE LEAGUE WANT TO EXPAND THEIR MEMBERSHIP?
BECAUSE THEY'RE A VERY TIGHT-KNIT GROUP.
LIKE YOU WERE WITH TEAM 7.
TEAM 7 IS CLASSIFIED, ETTA.
EVERYONE KNOWS THE JUSTICE GUE ARE CLOSE FRIENDS, AND APPRECIATE THAT, BUT WE THINK T WOULD BE PRUDENT IF YOU ELPED THEM OPEN UP TO THE IDEA OF A NEW MEMBER.
YOU MEAN YOU WANT TO PLANT SOMEONE OF YOUR CHOOSING ON THE TEAM?
"PLANT" IS THE WRONG WORD.
WE'RE TALKING ABOUT SOMEONE AS PROFESSIONAL AND WELL-RESPECTED AS THE REST OF THE JUSTICE LEAGUE.
AS PROFESSIONAL AND WELL-RESPECTED AS SUPERMAN, BATMAN AND WONDER WOMAN?
DOES ANYONE LIKE THAT EVEN EXIST?

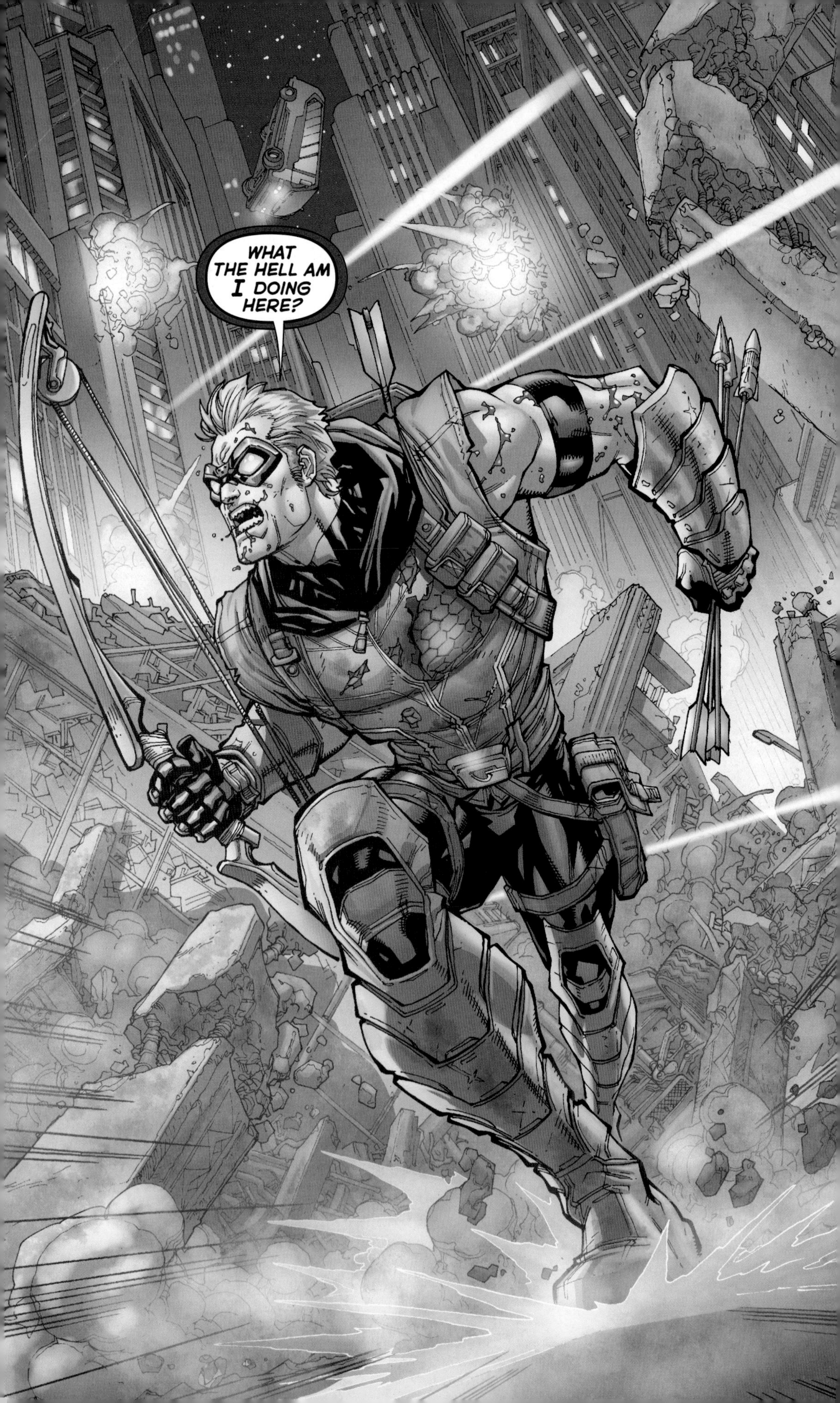
WHAT THE HELL AM I DOING HERE?

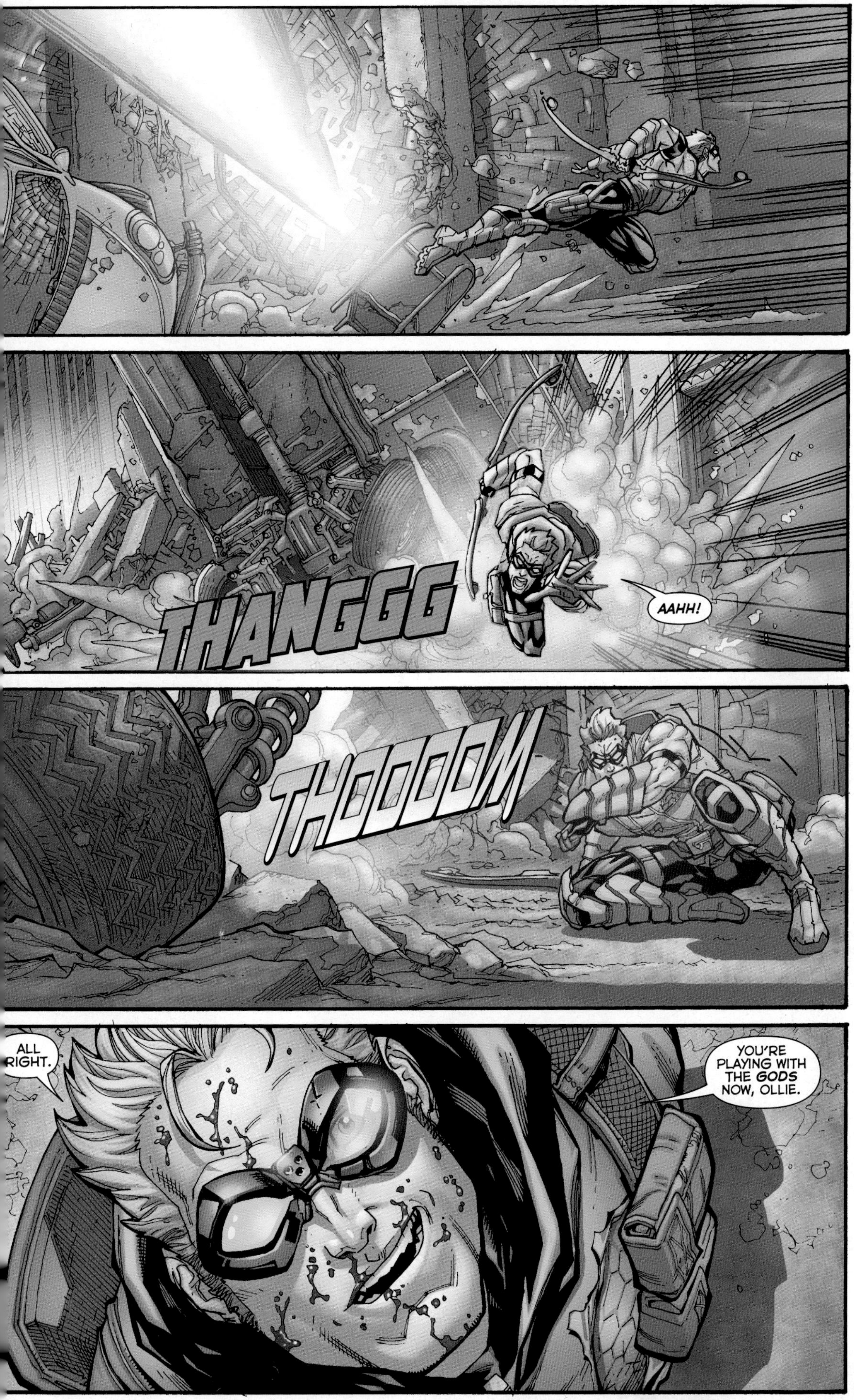
THANGGG
AAHH!
THOOOOM
ALL RIGHT.
YOU'RE PLAYING WITH THE GODS NOW, OLLIE.

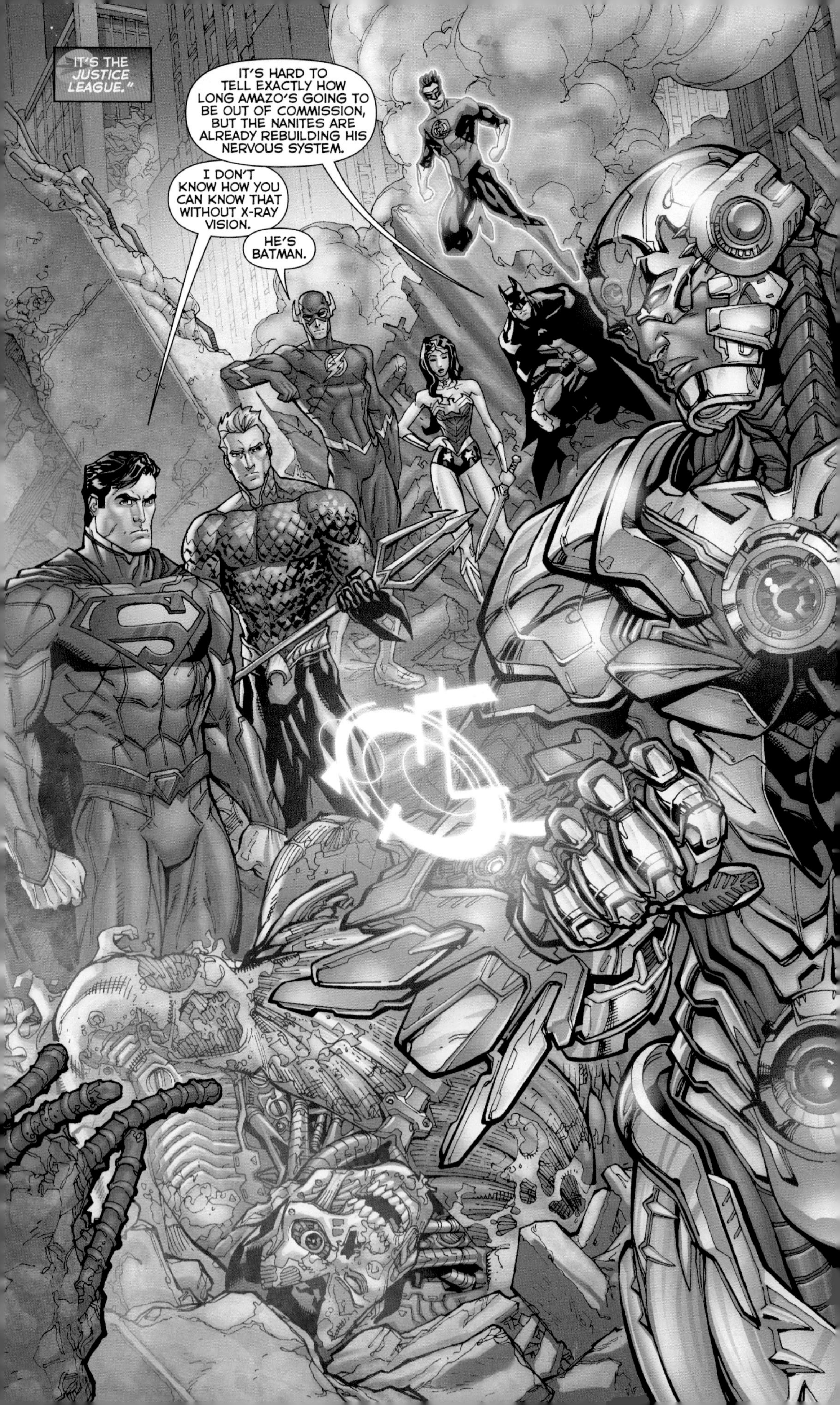
IT'S THE JUSTICE LEAGUE."
IT'S HARD TO TELL EXACTLY HOW LONG AMAZO'S GOING TO BE OUT OF COMMISSION, BUT THE NANITES ARE ALREADY REBUILDING HIS NERVOUS SYSTEM.
I DON'T KNOW HOW YOU CAN KNOW THAT WITHOUT X-RAY VISION.
HE'S BATMAN.

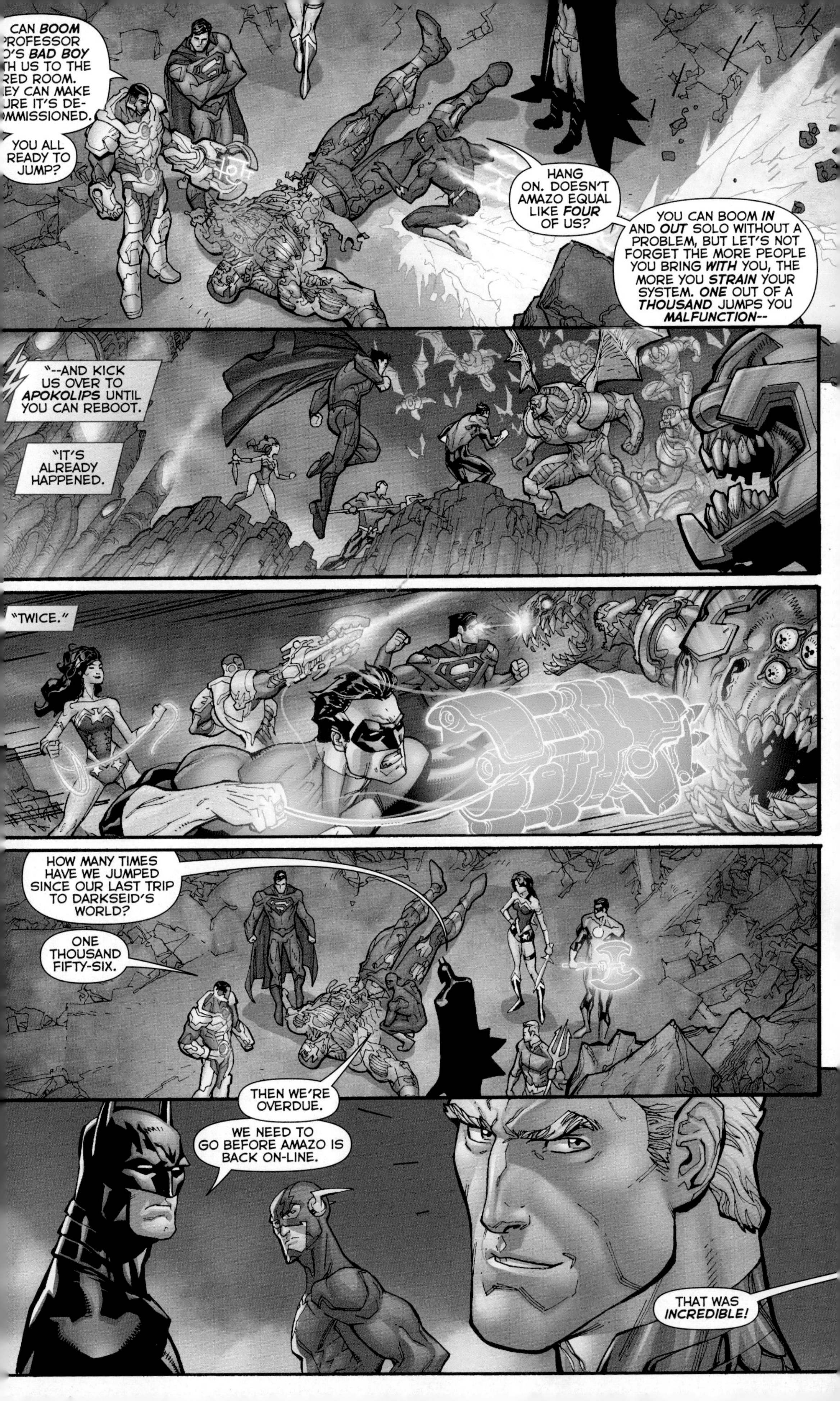

CAN BOOM PROFESSOR O'S BAD BOY TH US TO THE RED ROOM. EY CAN MAKE URE IT'S DE-MMISSIONED.
YOU ALL READY TO JUMP?
HANG ON. DOESN'T AMAZO EQUAL LIKE FOUR OF US?
YOU CAN BOOM IN AND OUT SOLO WITHOUT A PROBLEM, BUT LET'S NOT FORGET THE MORE PEOPLE YOU BRING WITH YOU, THE MORE YOU STRAIN YOUR SYSTEM. ONE OUT OF A THOUSAND JUMPS YOU MALFUNCTION--
"--AND KICK US OVER TO APOKOLIPS UNTIL YOU CAN REBOOT.
"IT'S ALREADY HAPPENED.
"TWICE."
HOW MANY TIMES HAVE WE JUMPED SINCE OUR LAST TRIP TO DARKSEID'S WORLD?
ONE THOUSAND FIFTY-SIX.
THEN WE'RE OVERDUE.
WE NEED TO GO BEFORE AMAZO IS BACK ON-LINE.
THAT WAS INCREDIBLE!

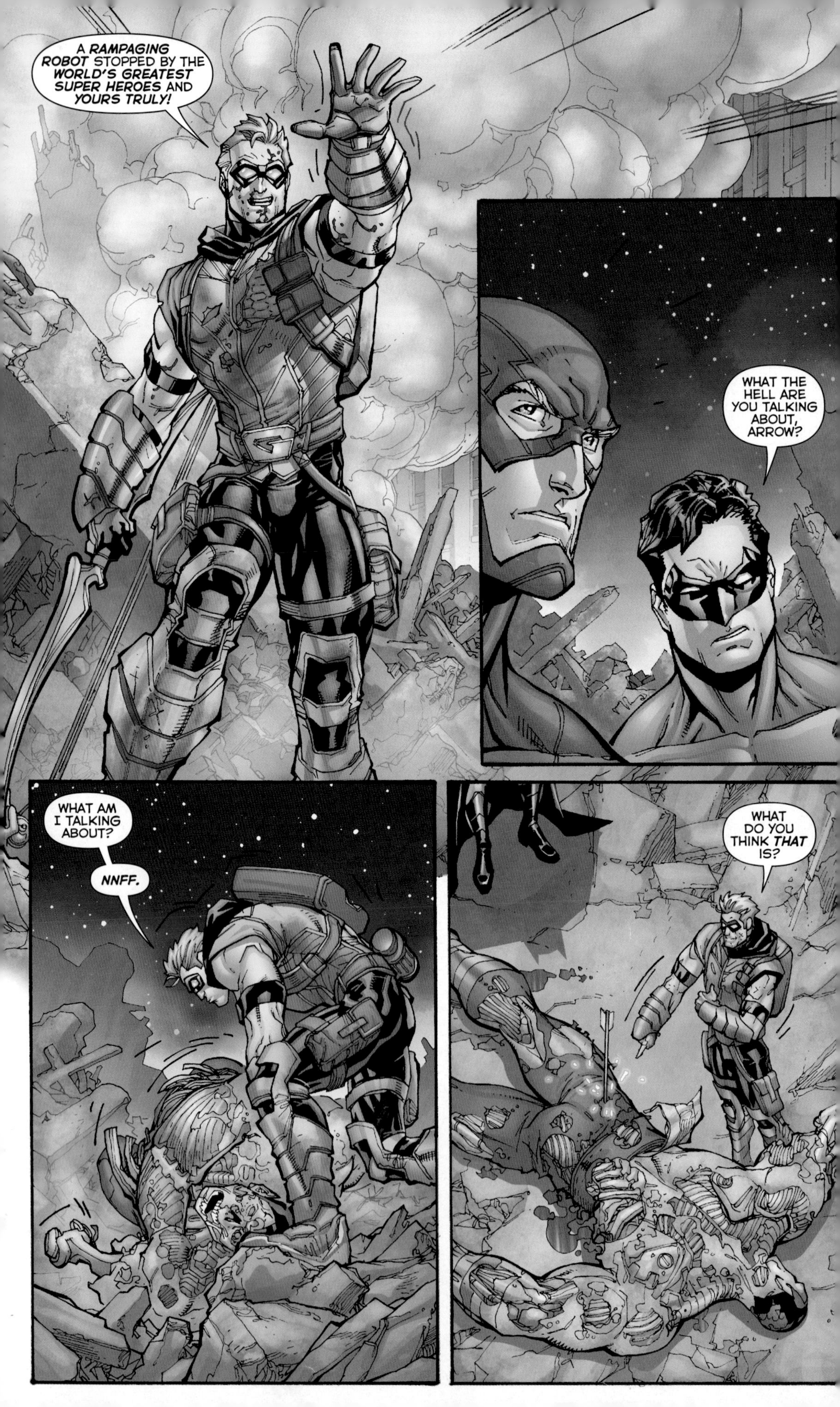
A RAMPAGING ROBOT STOPPED BY THE WORLD'S GREATEST SUPER HEROES AND YOURS TRULY!
WHAT THE HELL ARE YOU TALKING ABOUT, ARROW?
WHAT AM I TALKING ABOUT?
NNFF.
WHAT DO YOU THINK THAT IS?

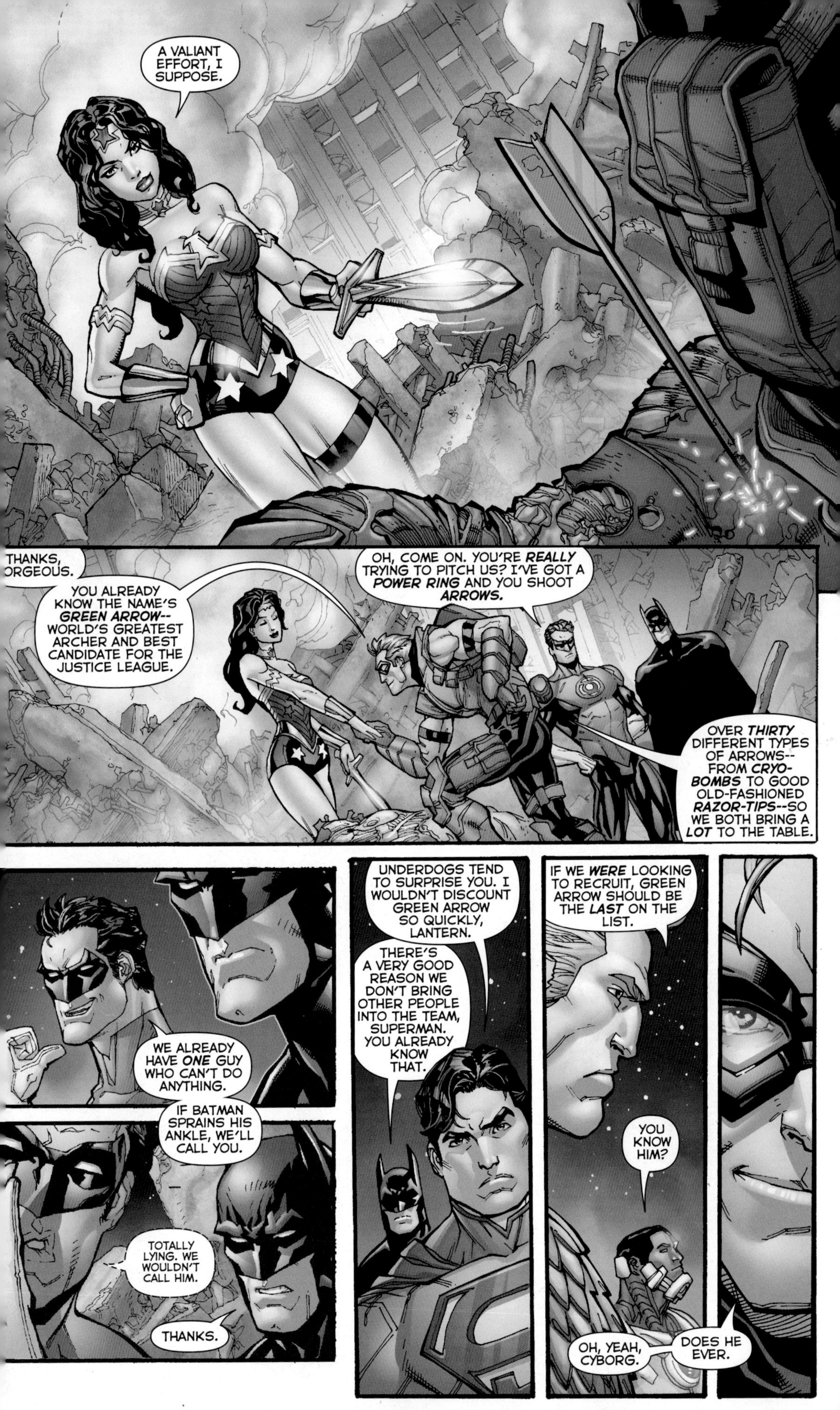
A VALIANT EFFORT, I SUPPOSE.
THANKS, GORGEOUS.
YOU ALREADY KNOW THE NAME'S GREEN ARROW-- WORLD'S GREATEST ARCHER AND BEST CANDIDATE FOR THE JUSTICE LEAGUE.
OH, COME ON. YOU'RE REALLY TRYING TO PITCH US? I'VE GOT A POWER RING AND YOU SHOOT ARROWS.
OVER THIRTY DIFFERENT TYPES OF ARROWS-- FROM CRYO-BOMBS TO GOOD OLD-FASHIONED RAZOR-TIPS--SO WE BOTH BRING A LOT TO THE TABLE.
WE ALREADY HAVE ONE GUY WHO CAN'T DO ANYTHING.
IF BATMAN SPRAINS HIS ANKLE, WE'LL CALL YOU.
TOTALLY LYING. WE WOULDN'T CALL HIM.
THANKS.
UNDERDOGS TEND TO SURPRISE YOU. I WOULDN'T DISCOUNT GREEN ARROW SO QUICKLY, LANTERN.
THERE'S A VERY GOOD REASON WE DON'T BRING OTHER PEOPLE INTO THE TEAM, SUPERMAN. YOU ALREADY KNOW THAT.
IF WE WERE LOOKING TO RECRUIT, GREEN ARROW SHOULD BE THE LAST ON THE LIST.
YOU KNOW HIM?
OH, YEAH, CYBORG.
DOES HE EVER.

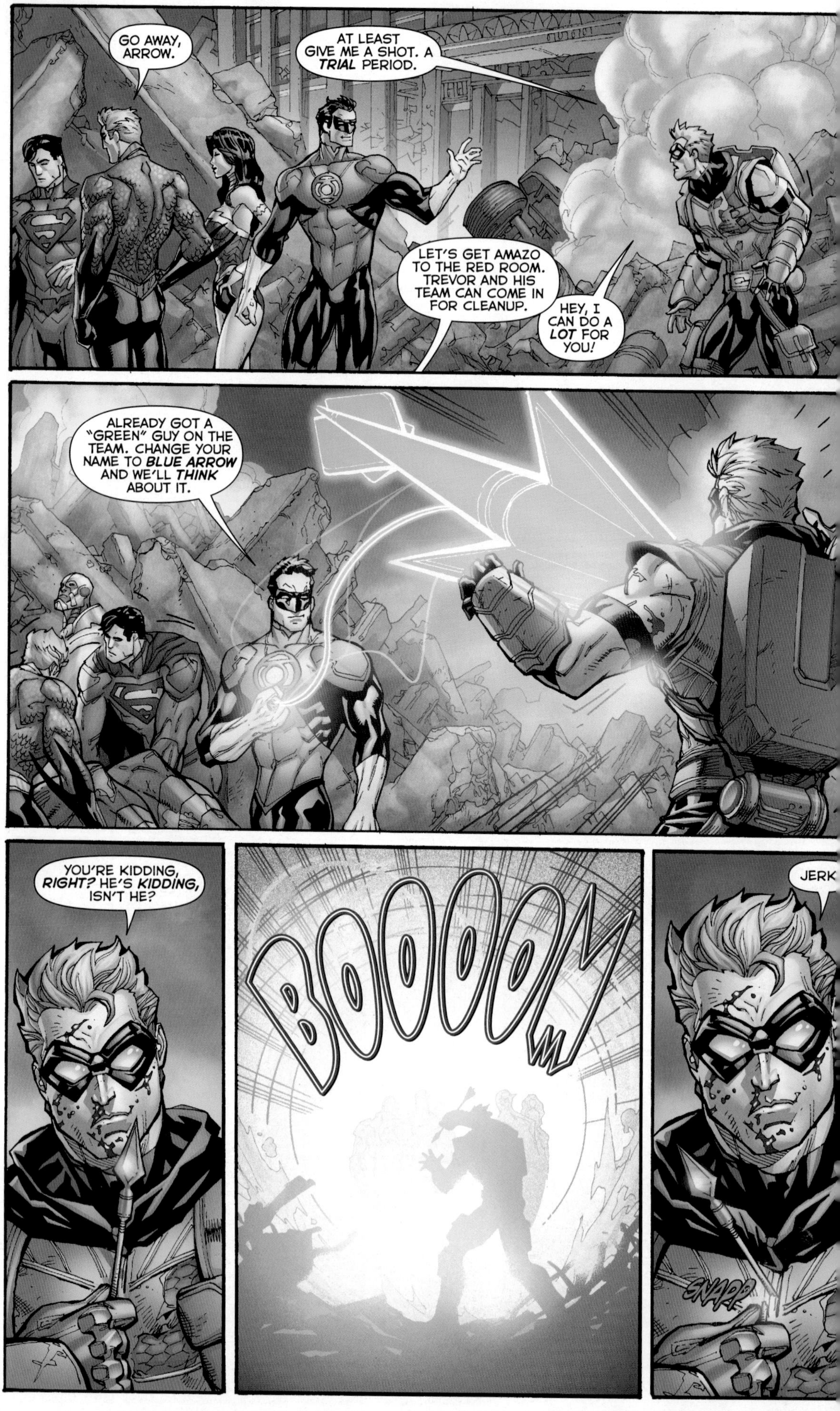
GO AWAY, ARROW.
AT LEAST GIVE ME A SHOT. A TRIAL PERIOD.
LET'S GET AMAZO TO THE RED ROOM. TREVOR AND HIS TEAM CAN COME IN FOR CLEANUP.
HEY, I CAN DO A LOT FOR YOU!
ALREADY GOT A "GREEN" GUY ON THE TEAM. CHANGE YOUR NAME TO BLUE ARROW AND WE'LL THINK ABOUT IT.
YOU'RE KIDDING, RIGHT? HE'S KIDDING, ISN'T HE?
BOOOOOM
JERK
SNAPP

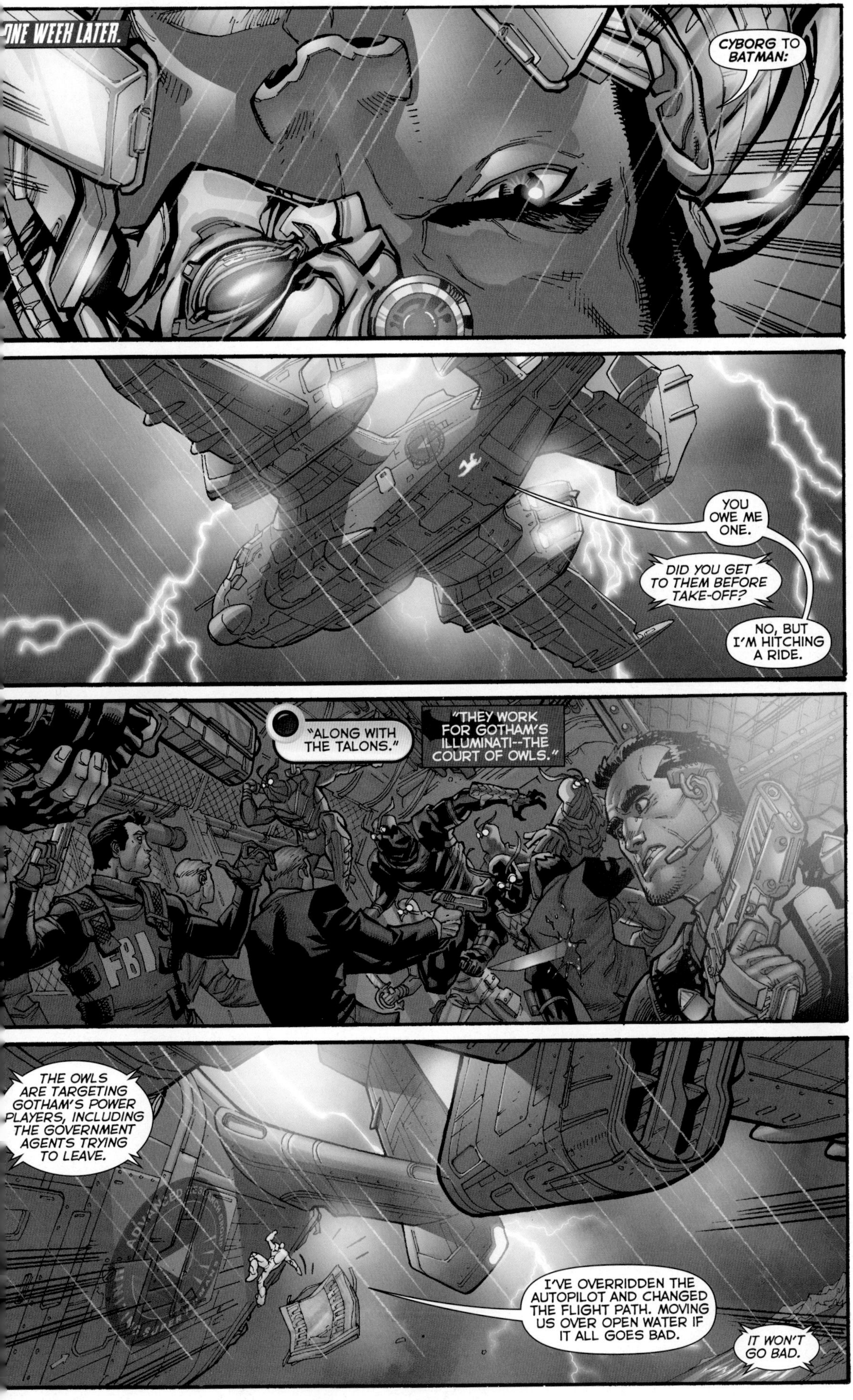
ONE WEEK LATER.
CYBORG TO BATMAN:
YOU OWE ME ONE.
DID YOU GET TO THEM BEFORE TAKE-OFF?
NO, BUT I'M HITCHING A RIDE.
"ALONG WITH THE TALONS."
"THEY WORK FOR GOTHAM'S ILLUMINATI--THE COURT OF OWLS."
FBI
THE OWLS ARE TARGETING GOTHAM'S POWER PLAYERS, INCLUDING THE GOVERNMENT AGENTS TRYING TO LEAVE.
I'VE OVERRIDDEN THE AUTOPILOT AND CHANGED THE FLIGHT PATH. MOVING US OVER OPEN WATER IF IT ALL GOES BAD.
IT WON'T GO BAD.

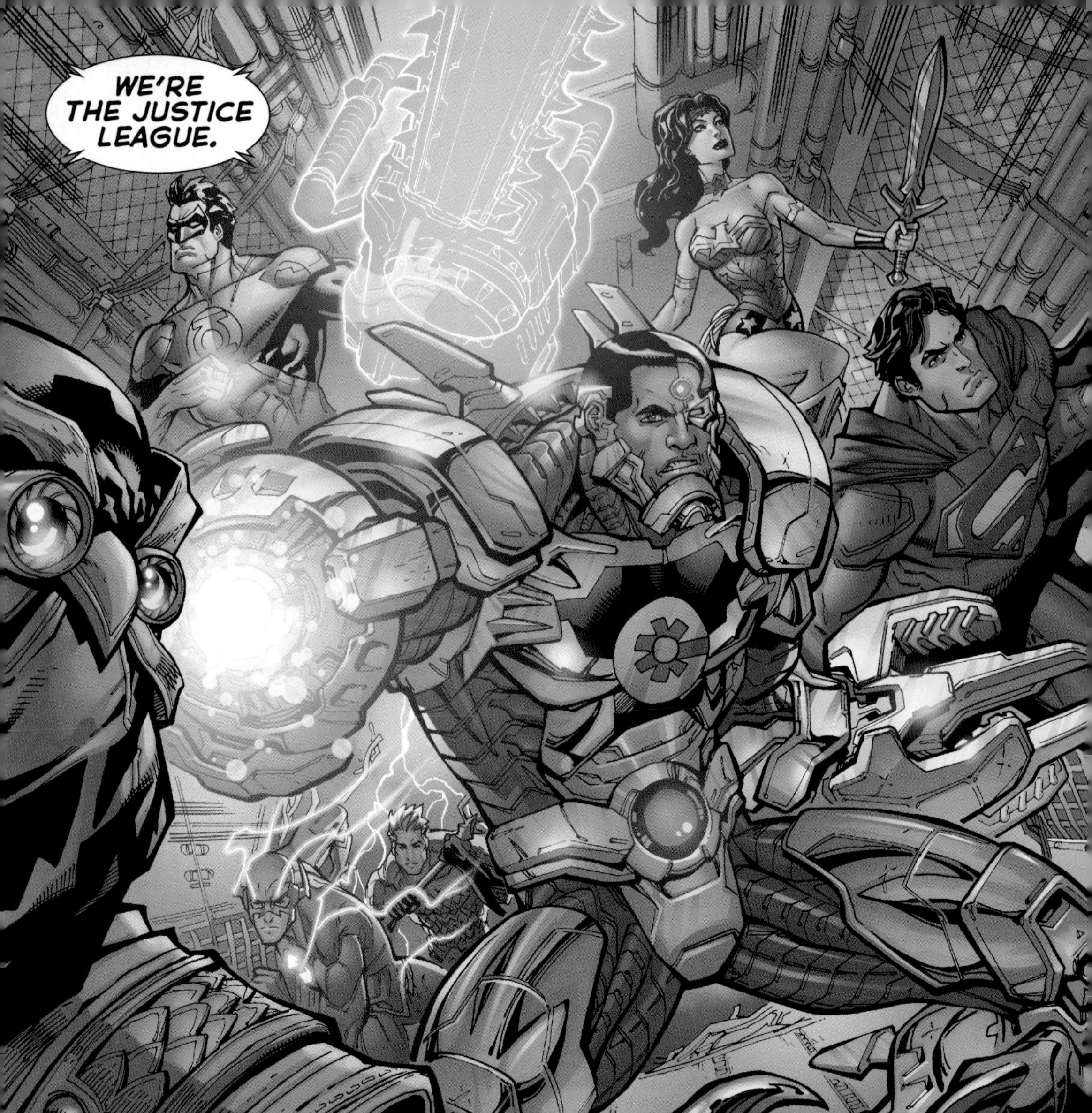
WE'RE THE JUSTICE LEAGUE.

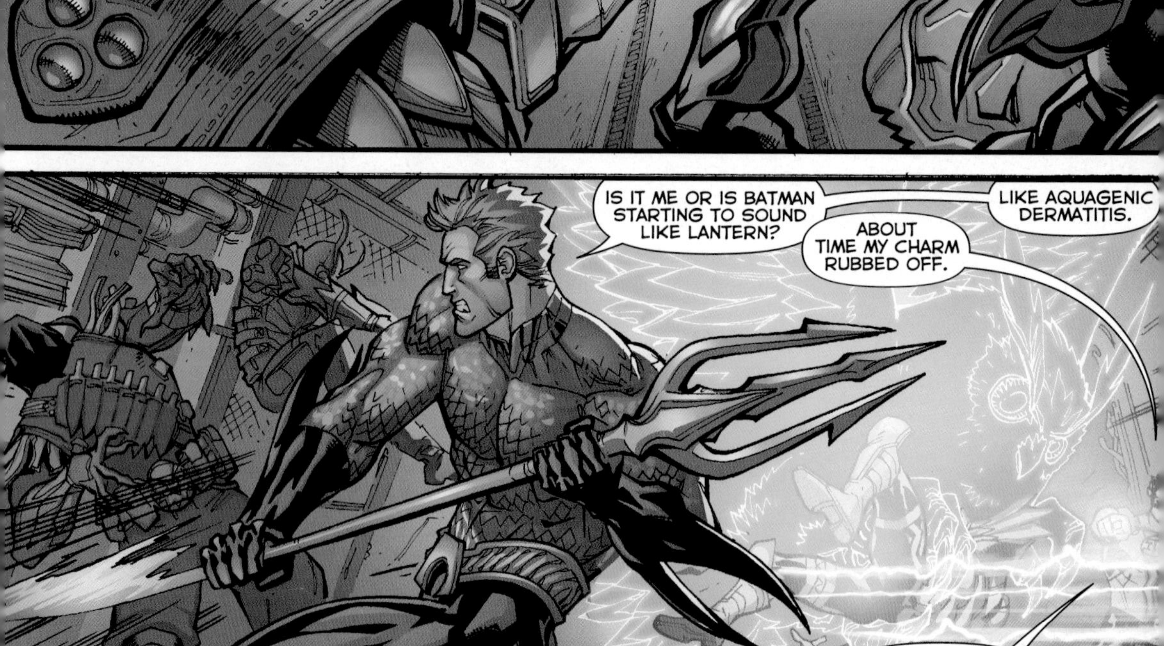
IS IT ME OR IS BATMAN STARTING TO SOUND LIKE LANTERN?
LIKE AQUAGENIC DERMATITIS.
ABOUT TIME MY CHARM RUBBED OFF.
LOOK WHO FOUND A SENSE OF HUMOR. I THINK.

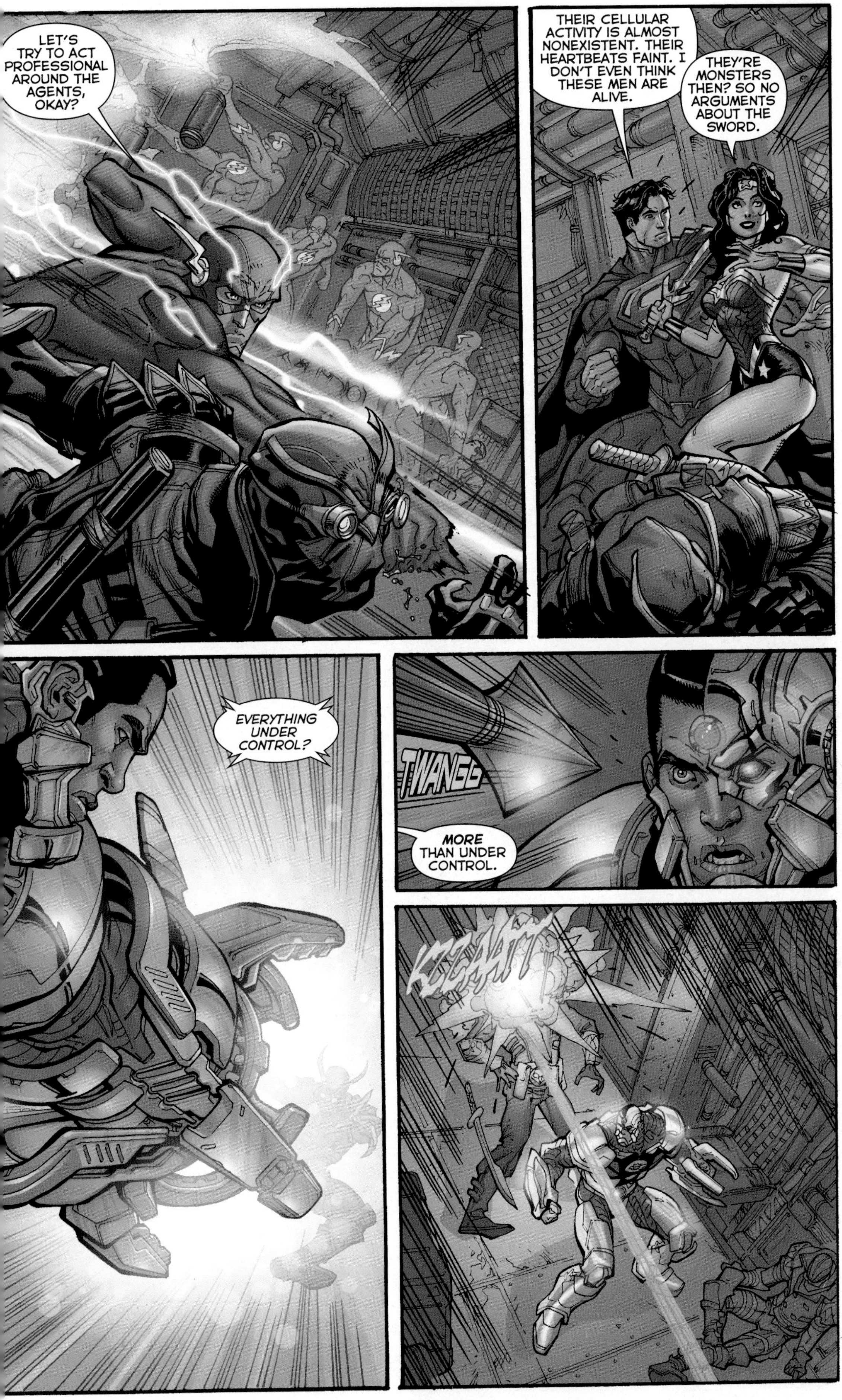
LET'S TRY TO ACT PROFESSIONAL AROUND THE AGENTS, OKAY?
THEIR CELLULAR ACTIVITY IS ALMOST NONEXISTENT. THEIR HEARTBEATS FAINT. I DON'T EVEN THINK THESE MEN ARE ALIVE.
THEY'RE MONSTERS THEN? SO NO ARGUMENTS ABOUT THE SWORD.
EVERYTHING UNDER CONTROL?
TWANGG
MORE THAN UNDER CONTROL.

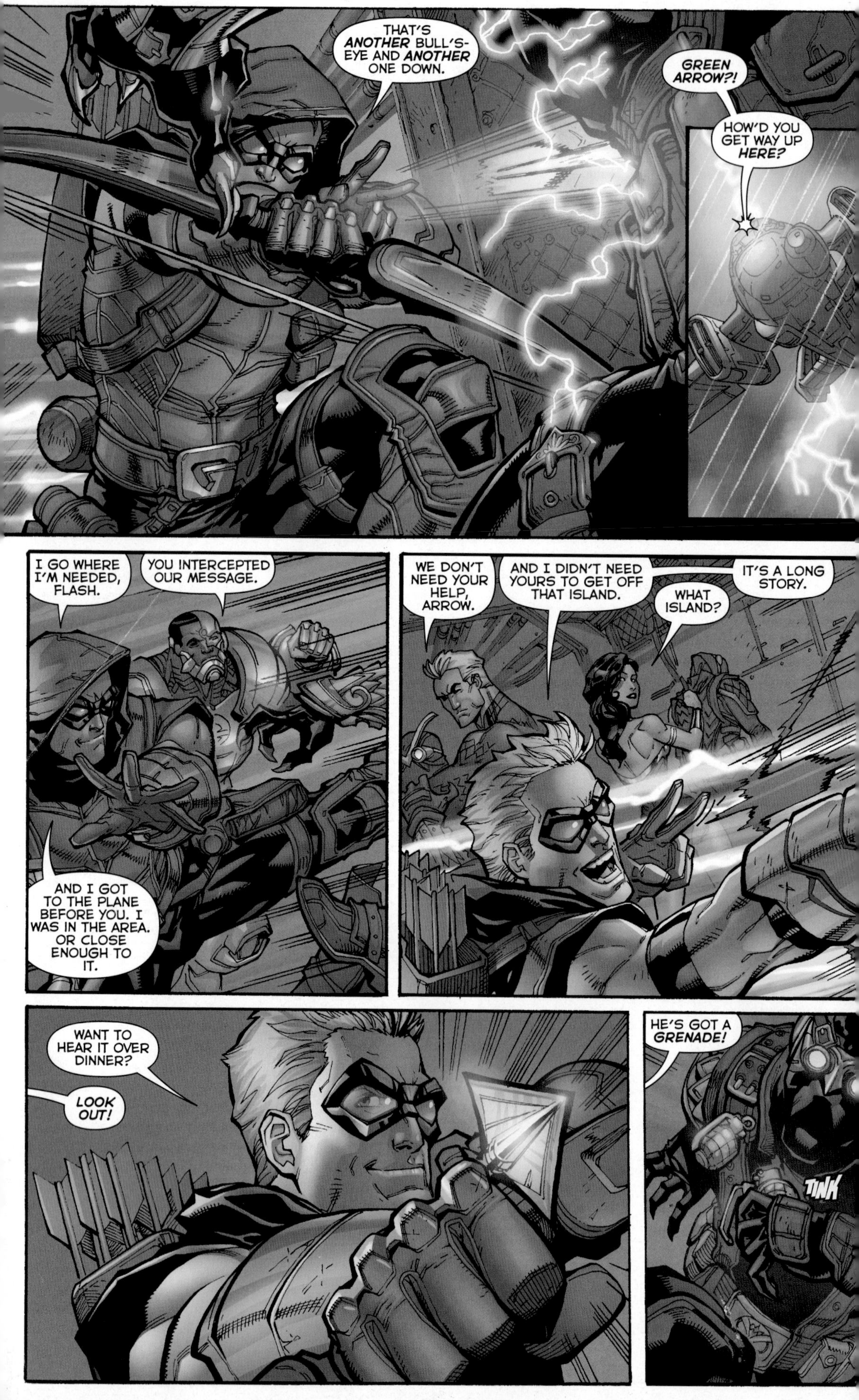

THAT'S ANOTHER BULL'S-EYE AND ANOTHER ONE DOWN.
GREEN ARROW?!
HOW'D YOU GET WAY UP HERE?
I GO WHERE I'M NEEDED, FLASH.
YOU INTERCEPTED OUR MESSAGE.
AND I GOT TO THE PLANE BEFORE YOU. I WAS IN THE AREA. OR CLOSE ENOUGH TO IT.
WE DON'T NEED YOUR HELP, ARROW.
AND I DIDN'T NEED YOURS TO GET OFF THAT ISLAND.
WHAT ISLAND?
IT'S A LONG STORY.
WANT TO HEAR IT OVER DINNER?
LOOK OUT!
HE'S GOT A GRENADE!
TINK

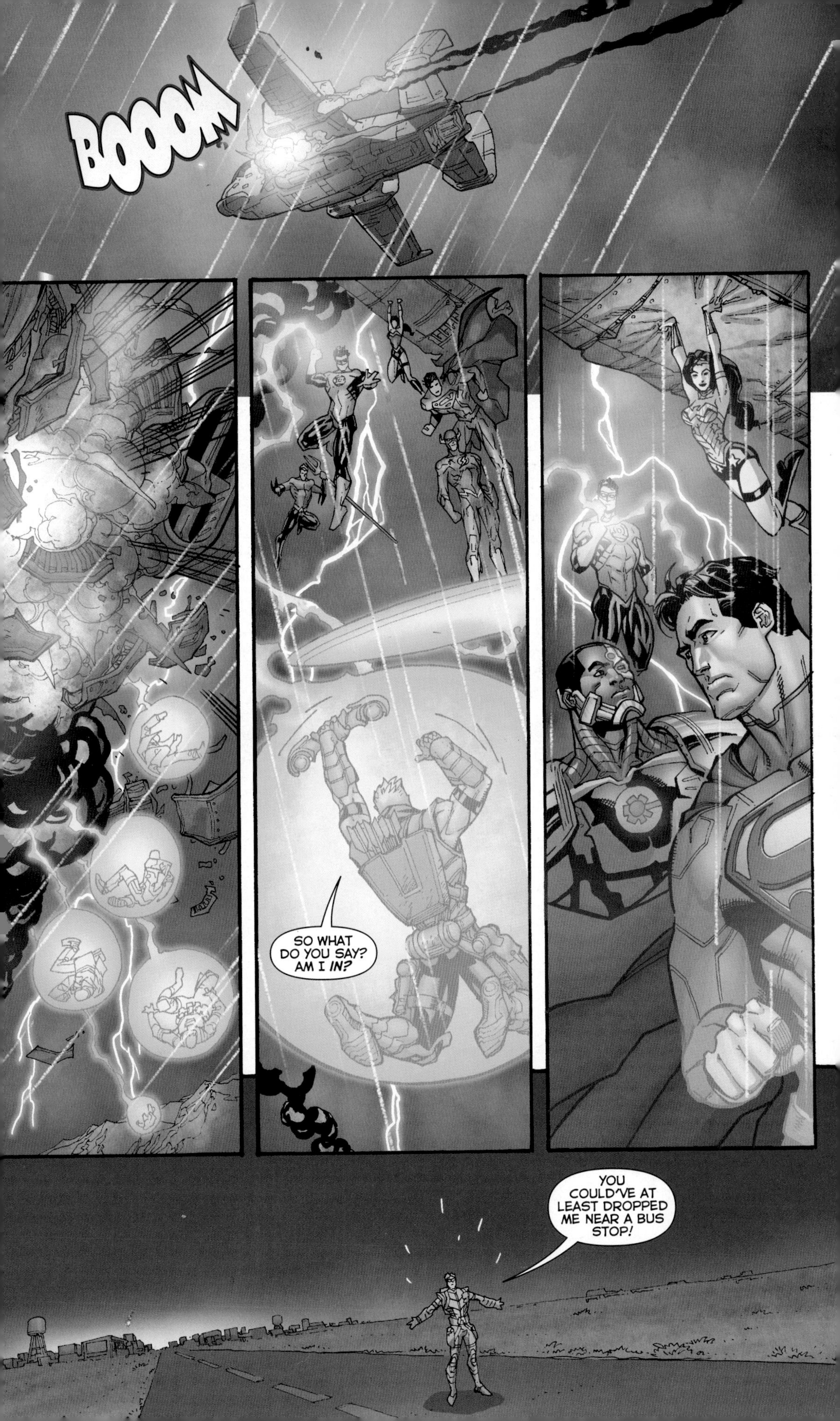
BOOOM
SO WHAT DO YOU SAY? AM I *IN?*
YOU COULD'VE AT LEAST DROPPED ME NEAR A BUS STOP!

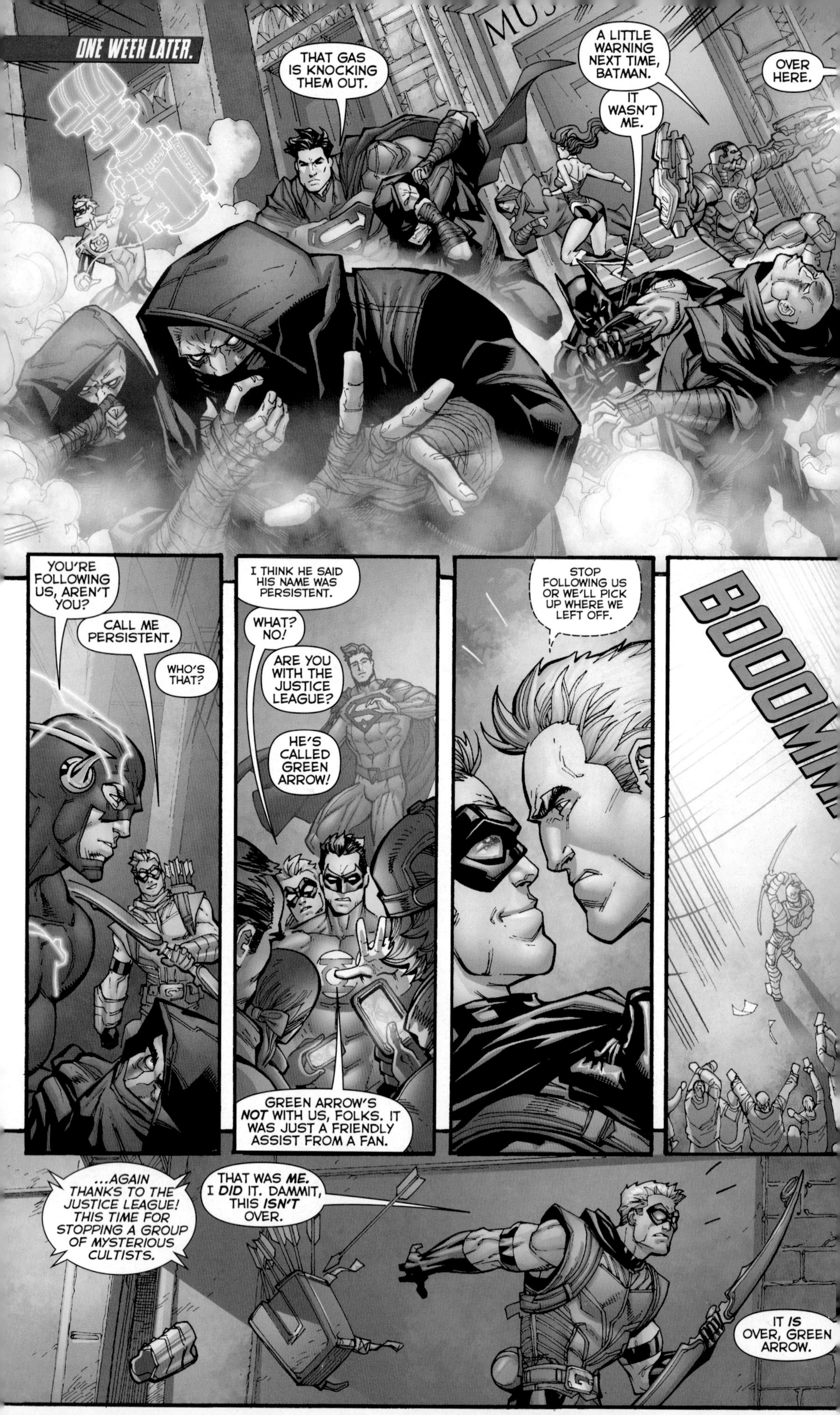
ONE WEEK LATER.
THAT GAS IS KNOCKING THEM OUT.
A LITTLE WARNING NEXT TIME, BATMAN.
IT WASN'T ME.
OVER HERE.
YOU'RE FOLLOWING US, AREN'T YOU?
CALL ME PERSISTENT.
WHO'S THAT?
I THINK HE SAID HIS NAME WAS PERSISTENT.
WHAT? NO!
ARE YOU WITH THE JUSTICE LEAGUE?
HE'S CALLED GREEN ARROW!
GREEN ARROW'S *NOT* WITH US, FOLKS. IT WAS JUST A FRIENDLY ASSIST FROM A FAN.
STOP FOLLOWING US OR WE'LL PICK UP WHERE WE LEFT OFF.
BOOOMM!
...AGAIN THANKS TO THE JUSTICE LEAGUE! THIS TIME FOR STOPPING A GROUP OF MYSTERIOUS CULTISTS.
THAT WAS *ME*. I *DID* IT. DAMMIT, THIS *ISN'T* OVER.
IT *IS* OVER, GREEN ARROW.

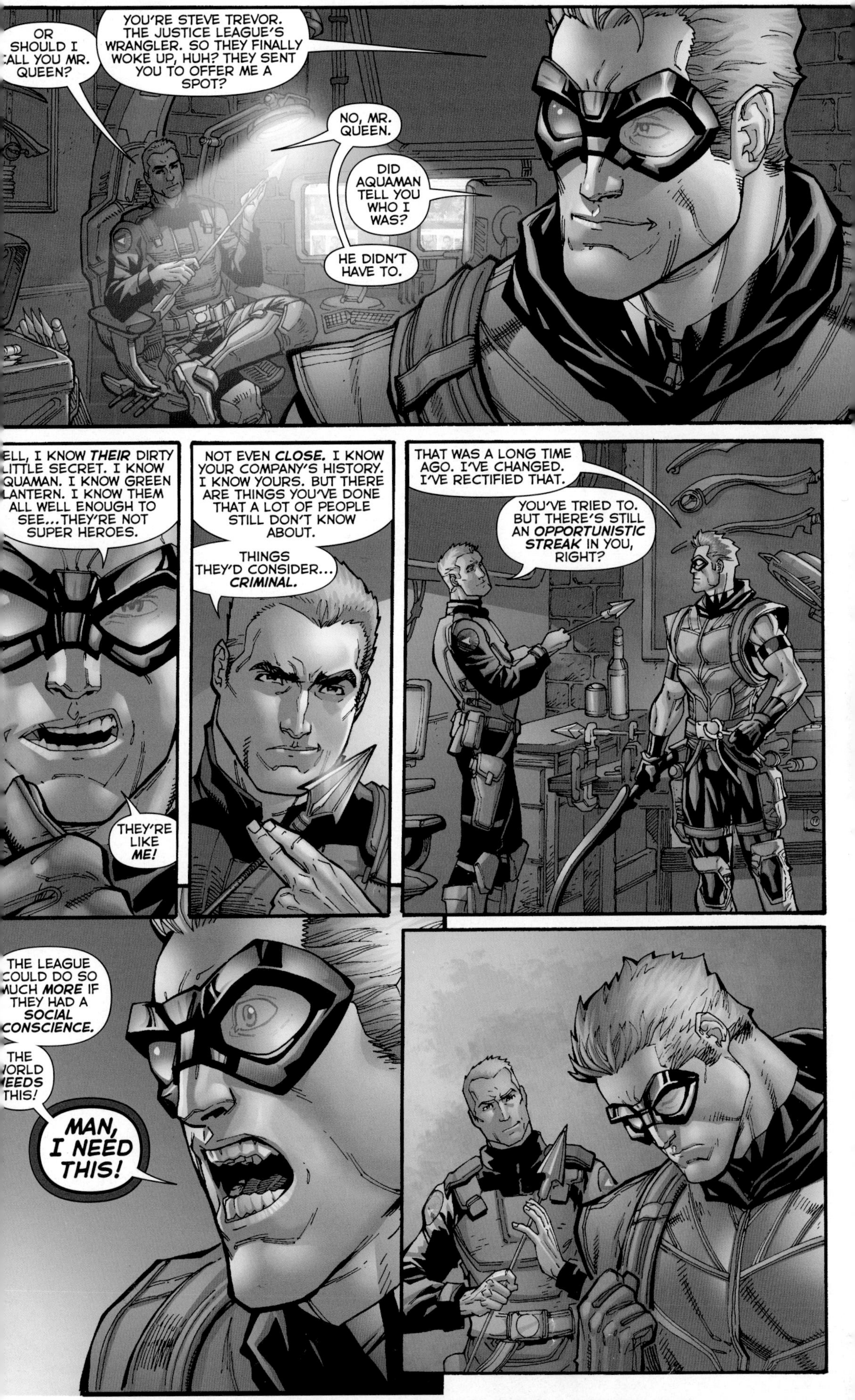

YOU'RE STEVE TREVOR. THE JUSTICE LEAGUE'S WRANGLER. SO THEY FINALLY WOKE UP, HUH? THEY SENT YOU TO OFFER ME A SPOT?
OR SHOULD I CALL YOU MR. QUEEN?
NO, MR. QUEEN.
DID AQUAMAN TELL YOU WHO I WAS?
HE DIDN'T HAVE TO.
ELL, I KNOW THEIR DIRTY LITTLE SECRET. I KNOW AQUAMAN. I KNOW GREEN LANTERN. I KNOW THEM ALL WELL ENOUGH TO SEE...THEY'RE NOT SUPER HEROES.
THEY'RE LIKE ME!
NOT EVEN CLOSE. I KNOW YOUR COMPANY'S HISTORY. I KNOW YOURS. BUT THERE ARE THINGS YOU'VE DONE THAT A LOT OF PEOPLE STILL DON'T KNOW ABOUT.
THINGS THEY'D CONSIDER... CRIMINAL.
THAT WAS A LONG TIME AGO. I'VE CHANGED. I'VE RECTIFIED THAT.
YOU'VE TRIED TO. BUT THERE'S STILL AN OPPORTUNISTIC STREAK IN YOU, RIGHT?
THE LEAGUE COULD DO SO MUCH MORE IF THEY HAD A SOCIAL CONSCIENCE.
THE WORLD NEEDS THIS!
MAN, I NEED THIS!

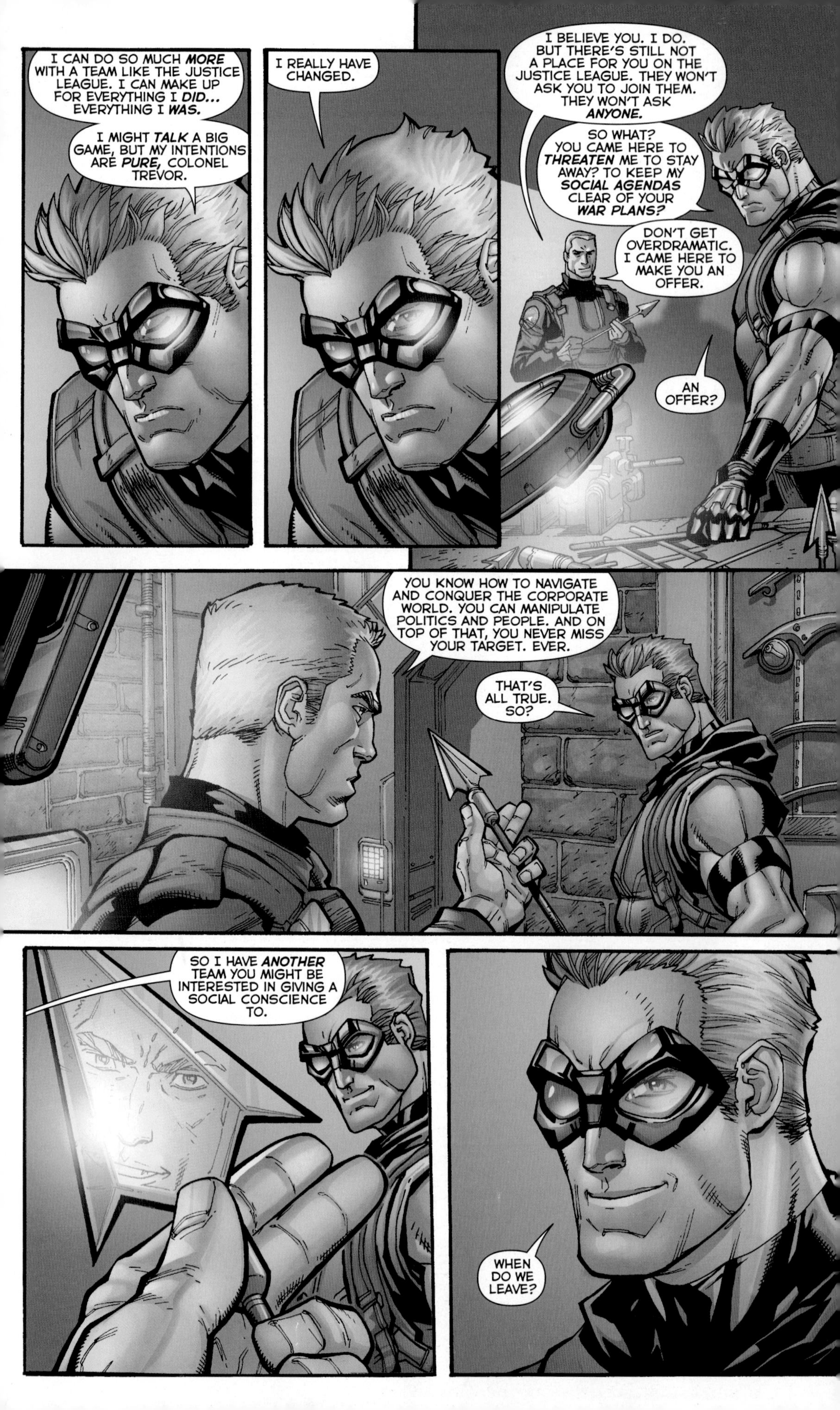
I CAN DO SO MUCH MORE WITH A TEAM LIKE THE JUSTICE LEAGUE. I CAN MAKE UP FOR EVERYTHING I DID... EVERYTHING I WAS.
I MIGHT TALK A BIG GAME, BUT MY INTENTIONS ARE PURE, COLONEL TREVOR.
I REALLY HAVE CHANGED.
I BELIEVE YOU. I DO. BUT THERE'S STILL NOT A PLACE FOR YOU ON THE JUSTICE LEAGUE. THEY WON'T ASK YOU TO JOIN THEM. THEY WON'T ASK ANYONE.
SO WHAT? YOU CAME HERE TO THREATEN ME TO STAY AWAY? TO KEEP MY SOCIAL AGENDAS CLEAR OF YOUR WAR PLANS?
DON'T GET OVERDRAMATIC. I CAME HERE TO MAKE YOU AN OFFER.
AN OFFER?
YOU KNOW HOW TO NAVIGATE AND CONQUER THE CORPORATE WORLD. YOU CAN MANIPULATE POLITICS AND PEOPLE. AND ON TOP OF THAT, YOU NEVER MISS YOUR TARGET. EVER.
THAT'S ALL TRUE. SO?
SO I HAVE ANOTHER TEAM YOU MIGHT BE INTERESTED IN GIVING A SOCIAL CONSCIENCE TO.
WHEN DO WE LEAVE?

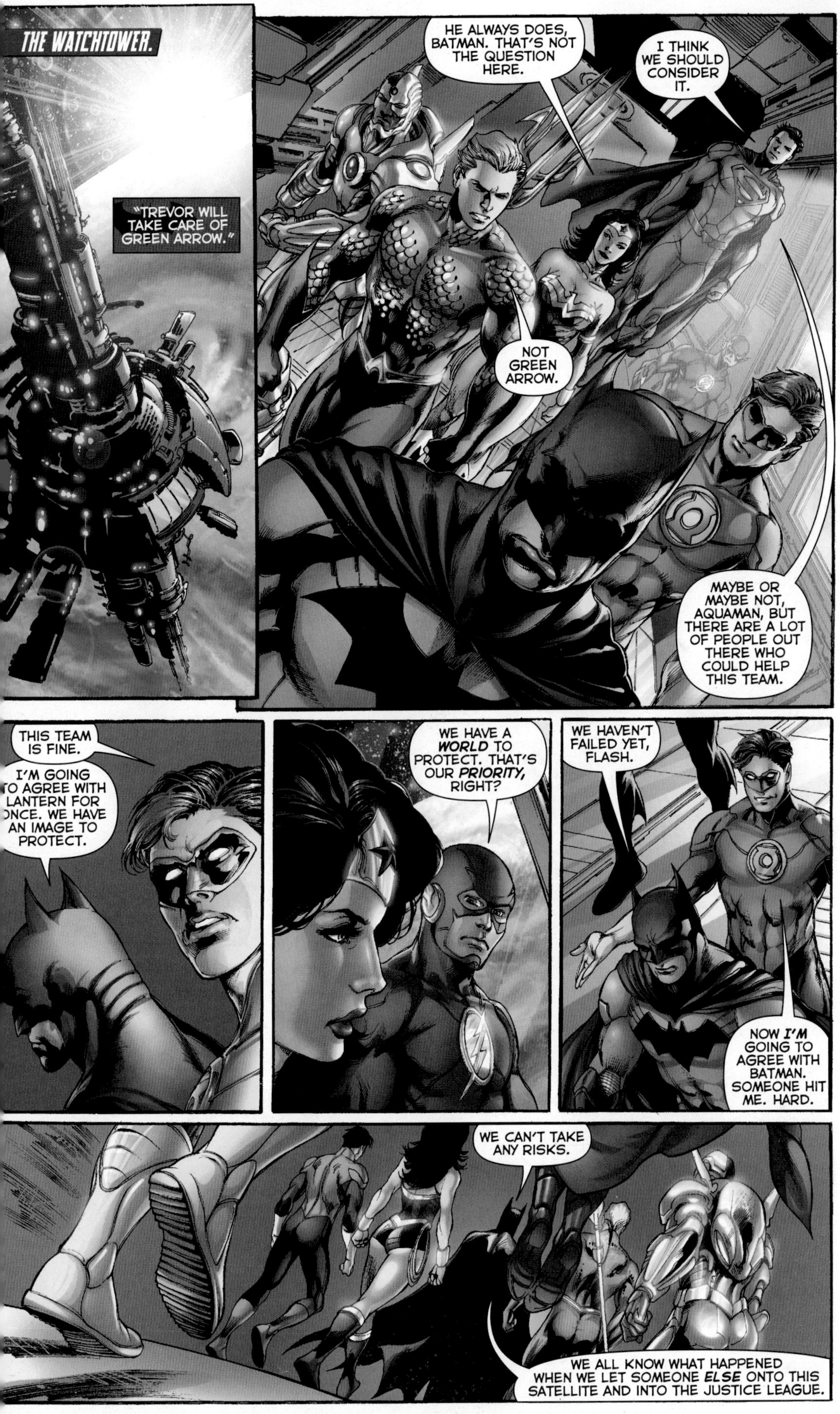
THE WATCHTOWER.
"TREVOR WILL TAKE CARE OF GREEN ARROW."
HE ALWAYS DOES, BATMAN. THAT'S NOT THE QUESTION HERE.
I THINK WE SHOULD CONSIDER IT.
NOT GREEN ARROW.
MAYBE OR MAYBE NOT, AQUAMAN, BUT THERE ARE A LOT OF PEOPLE OUT THERE WHO COULD HELP THIS TEAM.
THIS TEAM IS FINE.
I'M GOING TO AGREE WITH LANTERN FOR ONCE. WE HAVE AN IMAGE TO PROTECT.
WE HAVE A WORLD TO PROTECT. THAT'S OUR PRIORITY, RIGHT?
WE HAVEN'T FAILED YET, FLASH.
NOW I'M GOING TO AGREE WITH BATMAN. SOMEONE HIT ME. HARD.
WE CAN'T TAKE ANY RISKS.
WE ALL KNOW WHAT HAPPENED WHEN WE LET SOMEONE ELSE ONTO THIS SATELLITE AND INTO THE JUSTICE LEAGUE.

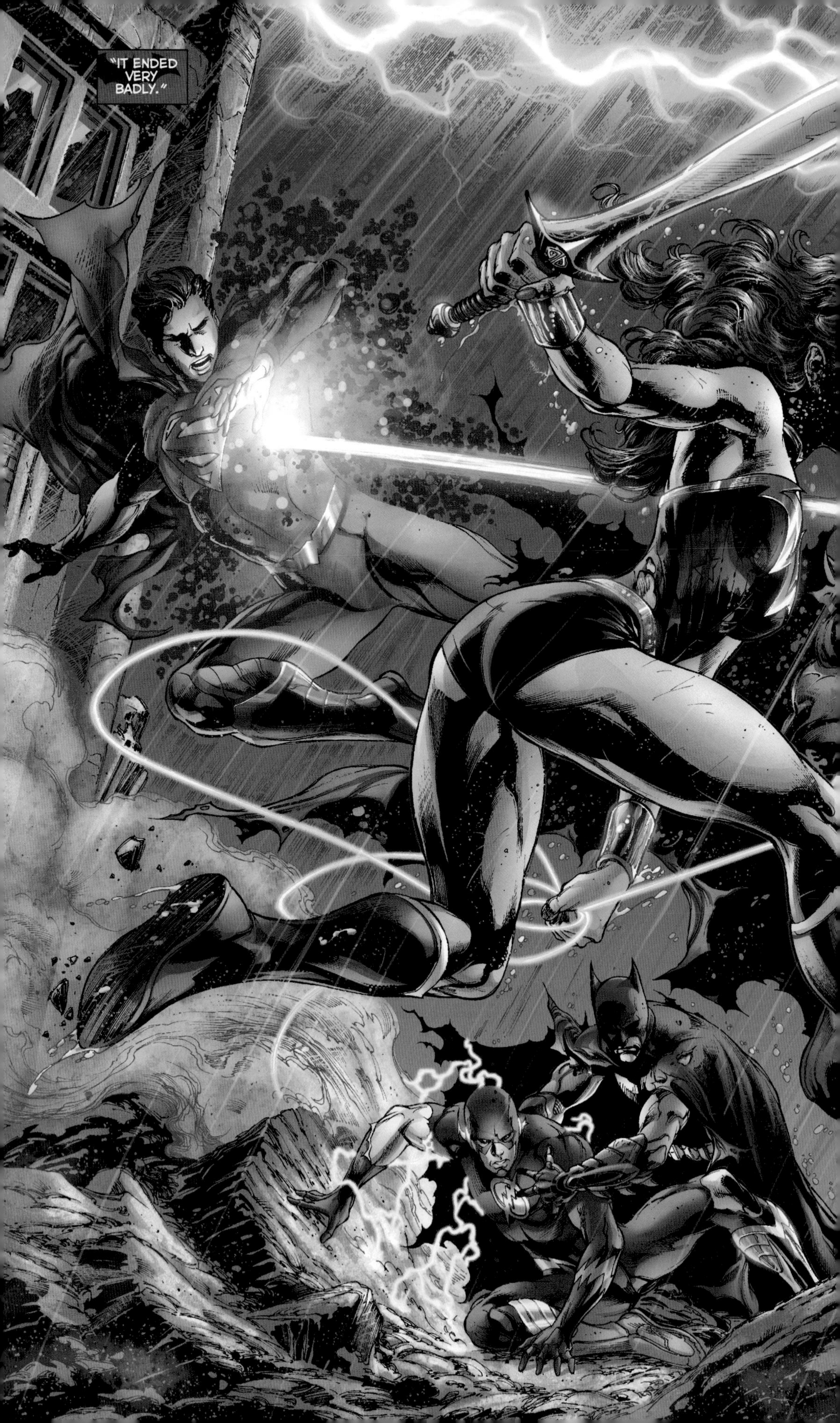
"IT ENDED VERY BADLY."

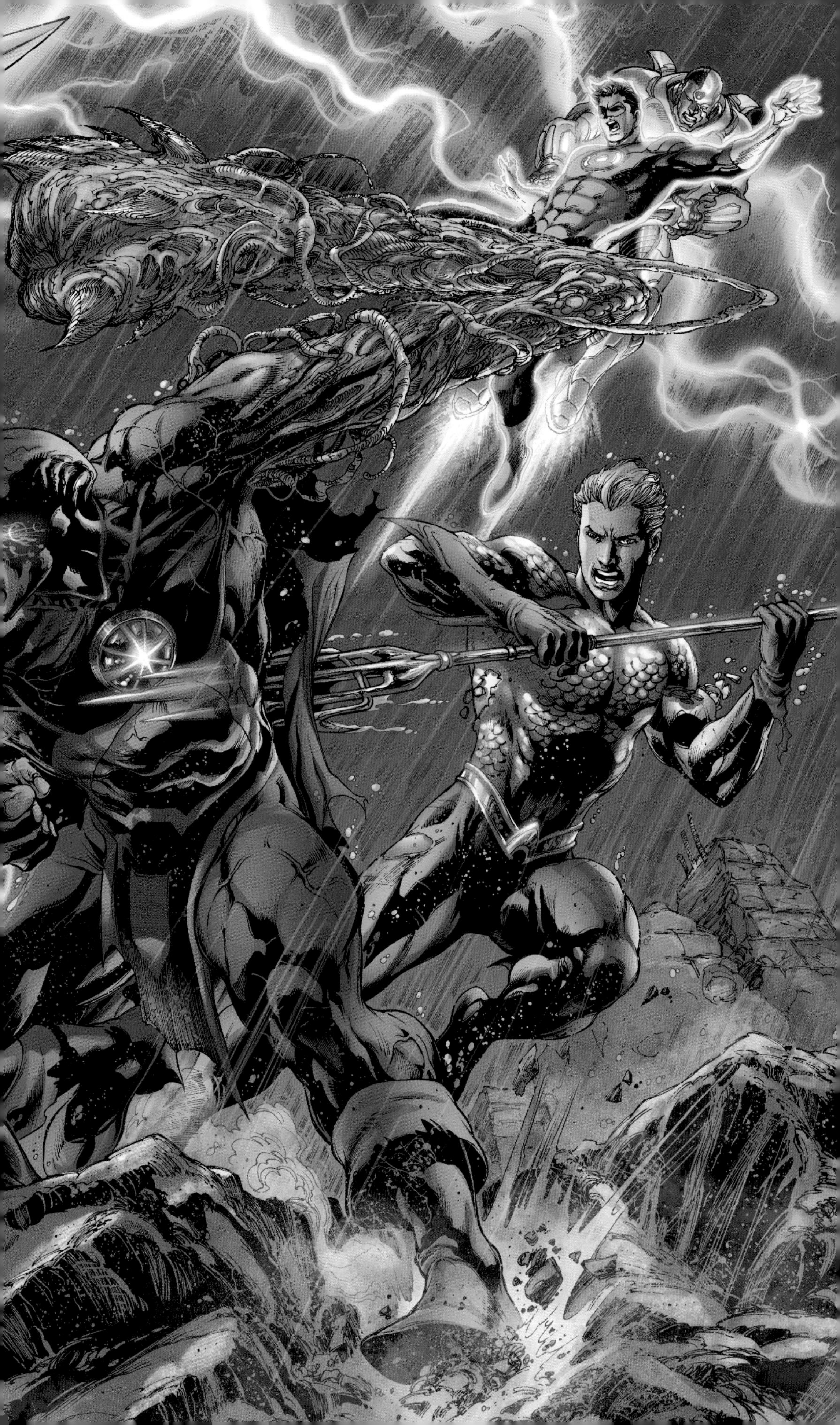

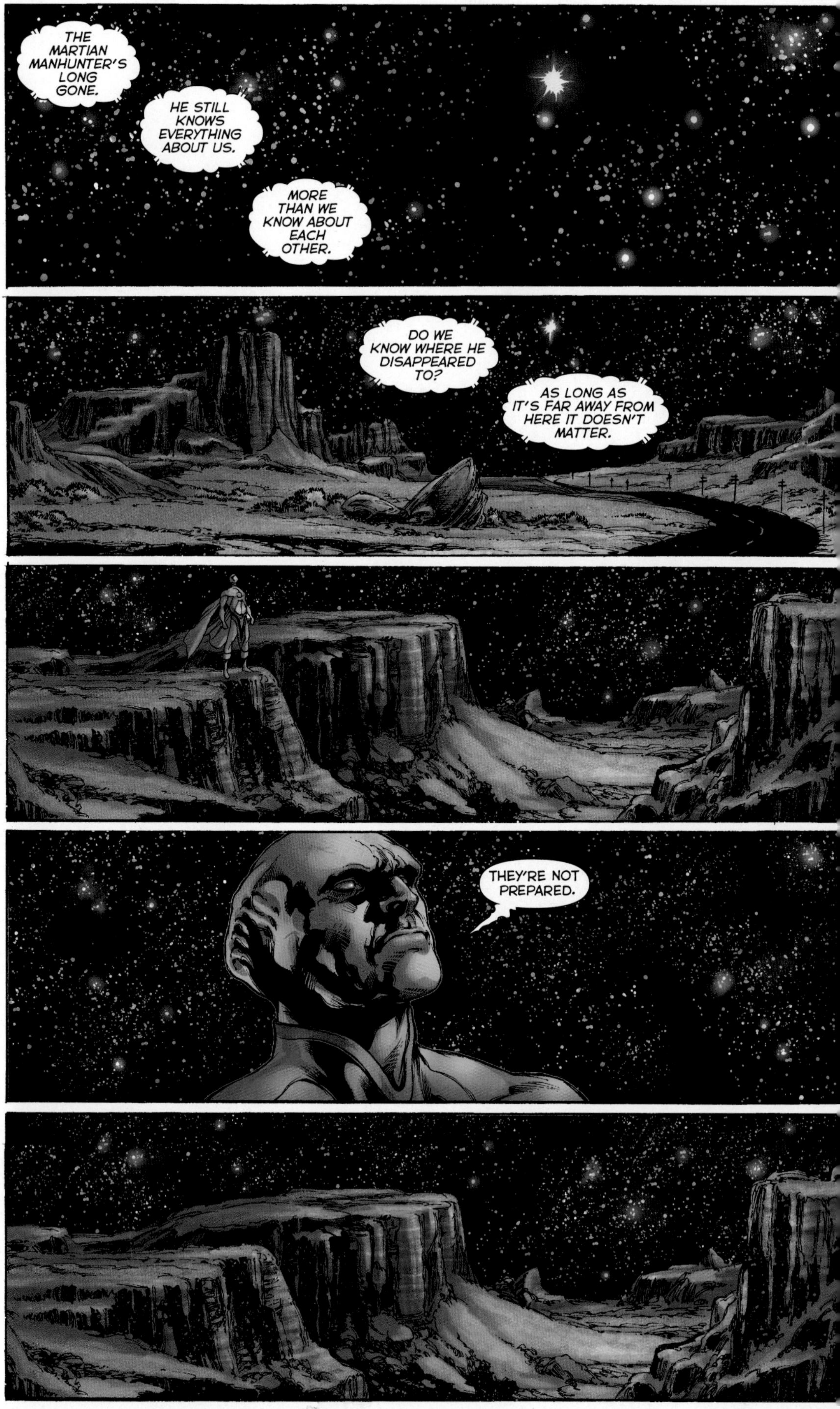
THE MARTIAN MANHUNTER'S LONG GONE.
HE STILL KNOWS EVERYTHING ABOUT US.
MORE THAN WE KNOW ABOUT EACH OTHER.
DO WE KNOW WHERE HE DISAPPEARED TO?
AS LONG AS IT'S FAR AWAY FROM HERE IT DOESN'T MATTER.
THEY'RE NOT PREPARED.

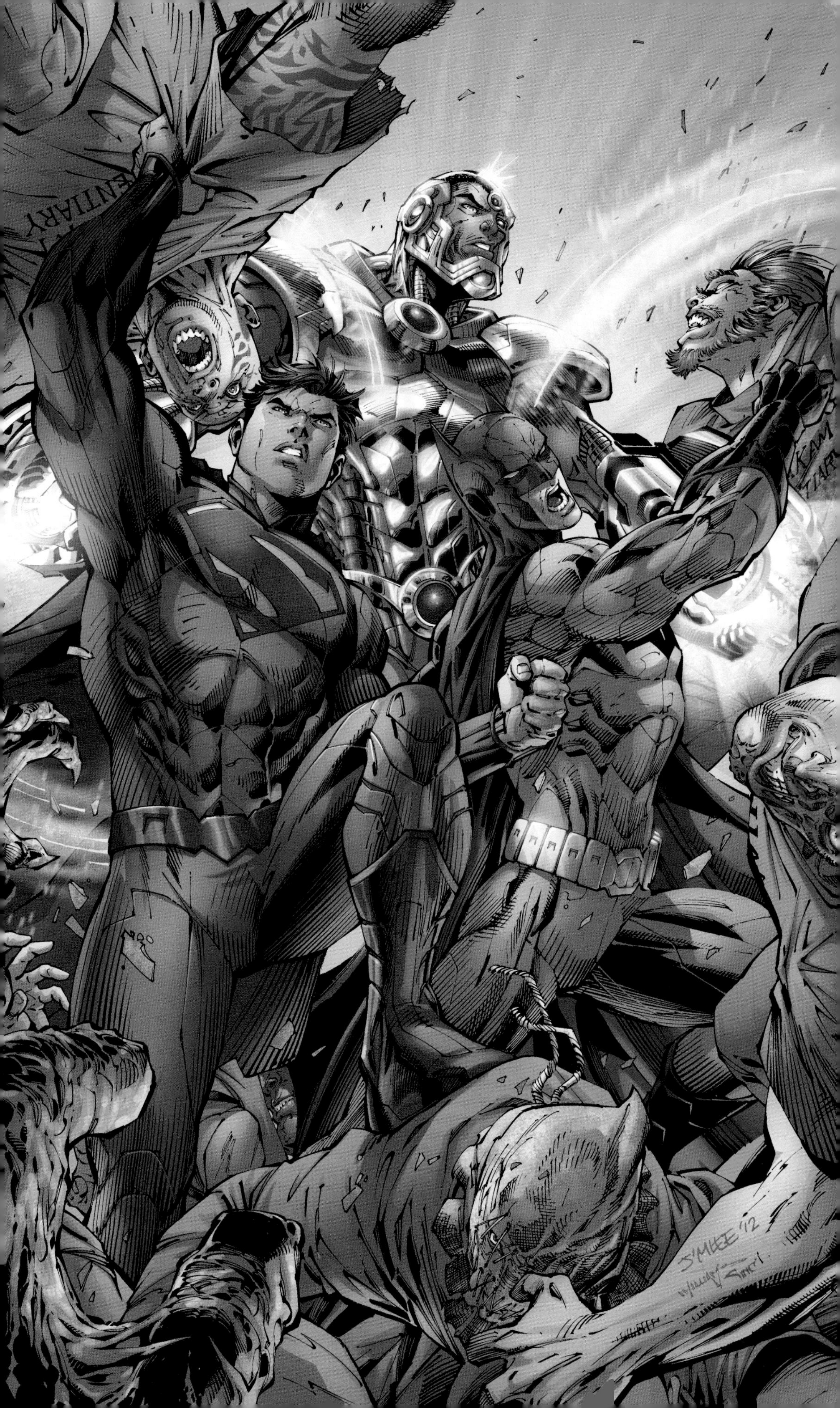

THE VILLAIN'S JOURNEY CHAPTER ONE: THE CALL FOR ADVENTURE

GEOFF JOHNS writer **JIM LEE** penciller **SCOTT WILLIAMS** inker cover by **JIM LEE, SCOTT WILLIAMS & ALEX SINCLAIR**

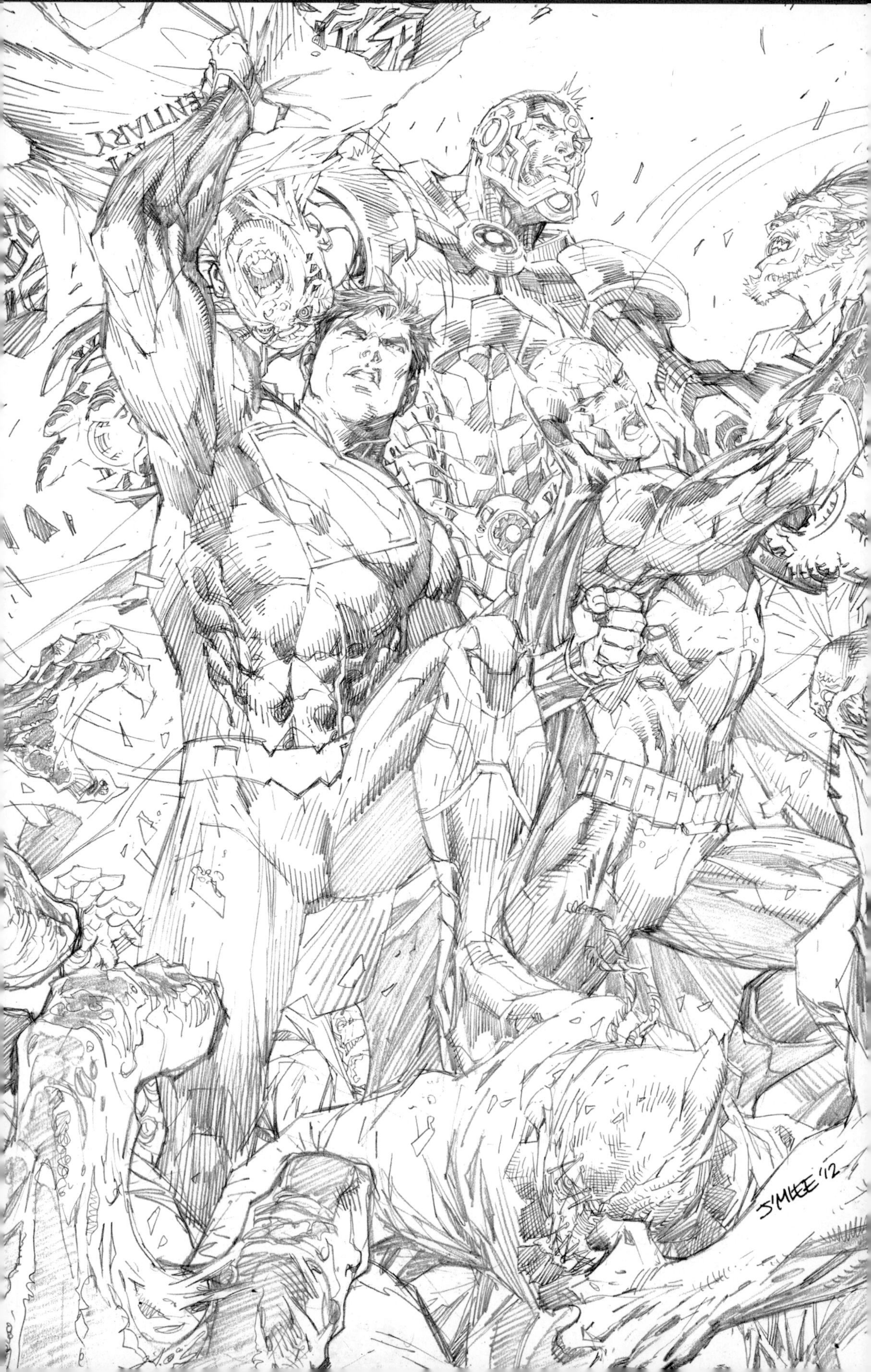

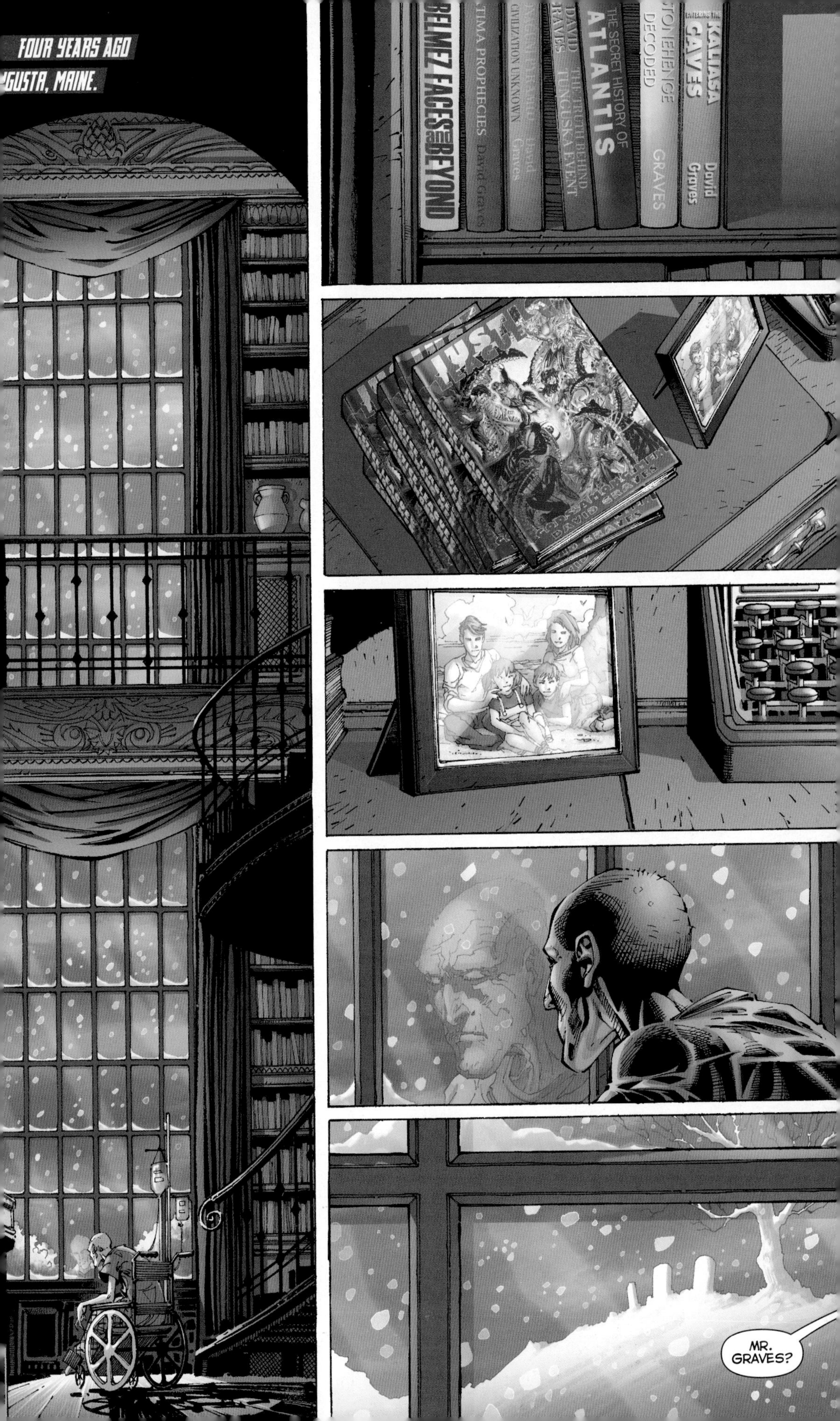
FOUR YEARS AGO
GUSTA, MAINE.
BELMEZ FACES and BEYOND
TIMA PROPHECIES David Graves
CIVILIZATION UNKNOWN
DAVID GRAVES THE TRUTH BEHIND TUNGUSKA EVENT
THE SECRET HISTORY OF ATLANTIS
TONEHENGE DECODED GRAVES
ENTERING THE KALIASA GAVES David Graves
DAVID GRAVES
MR. GRAVES?

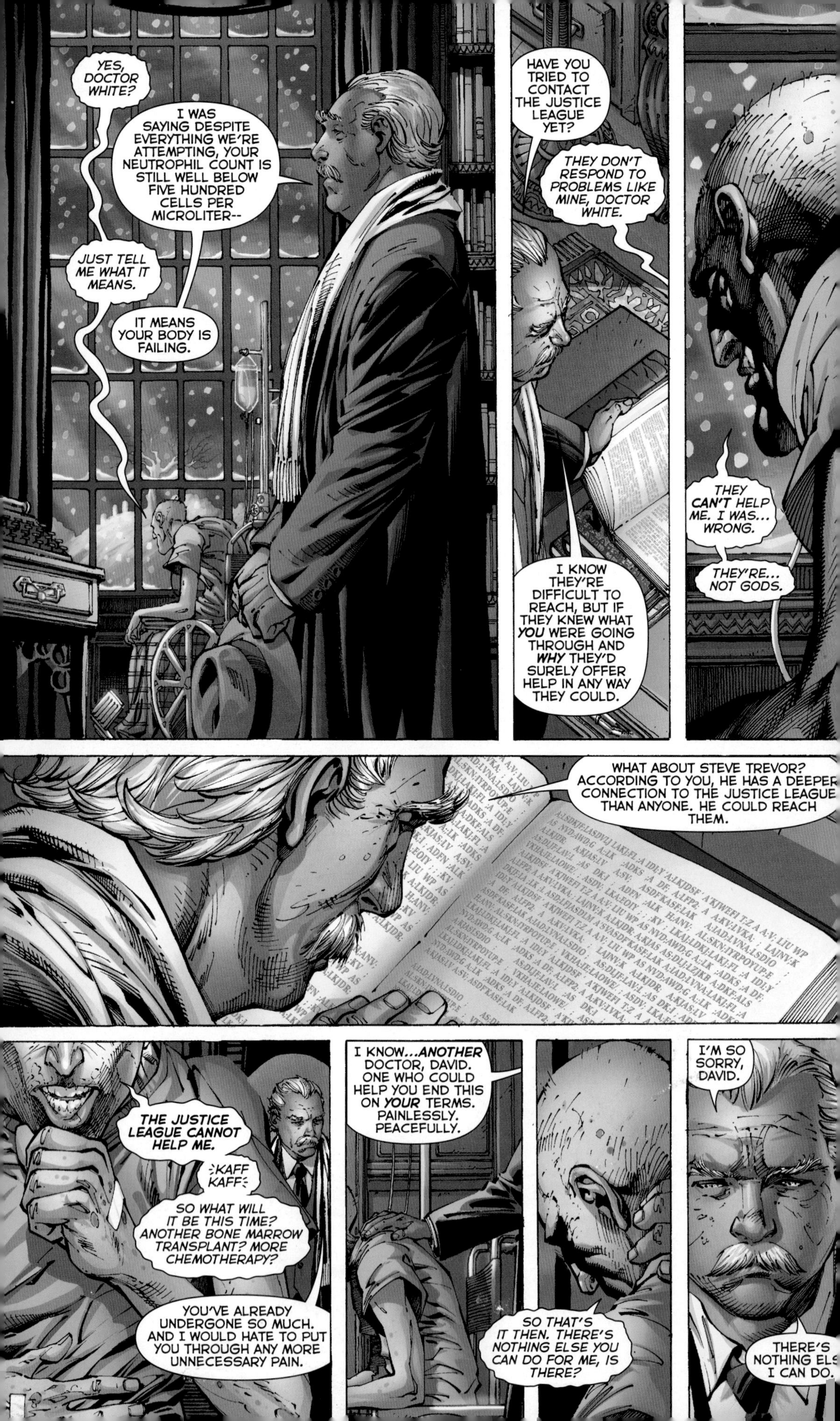
YES, DOCTOR WHITE?
I WAS SAYING DESPITE EVERYTHING WE'RE ATTEMPTING, YOUR NEUTROPHIL COUNT IS STILL WELL BELOW FIVE HUNDRED CELLS PER MICROLITER--
JUST TELL ME WHAT IT MEANS.
IT MEANS YOUR BODY IS FAILING.
HAVE YOU TRIED TO CONTACT THE JUSTICE LEAGUE YET?
THEY DON'T RESPOND TO PROBLEMS LIKE MINE, DOCTOR WHITE.
I KNOW THEY'RE DIFFICULT TO REACH, BUT IF THEY KNEW WHAT YOU WERE GOING THROUGH AND WHY THEY'D SURELY OFFER HELP IN ANY WAY THEY COULD.
THEY CAN'T HELP ME. I WAS... WRONG.
THEY'RE... NOT GODS.
WHAT ABOUT STEVE TREVOR? ACCORDING TO YOU, HE HAS A DEEPER CONNECTION TO THE JUSTICE LEAGUE THAN ANYONE. HE COULD REACH THEM.
THE JUSTICE LEAGUE CANNOT HELP ME.
KAFF KAFF
SO WHAT WILL IT BE THIS TIME? ANOTHER BONE MARROW TRANSPLANT? MORE CHEMOTHERAPY?
YOU'VE ALREADY UNDERGONE SO MUCH. AND I WOULD HATE TO PUT YOU THROUGH ANY MORE UNNECESSARY PAIN.
I KNOW...ANOTHER DOCTOR, DAVID. ONE WHO COULD HELP YOU END THIS ON YOUR TERMS. PAINLESSLY. PEACEFULLY.
SO THAT'S IT THEN. THERE'S NOTHING ELSE YOU CAN DO FOR ME, IS THERE?
I'M SO SORRY, DAVID.
THERE'S NOTHING ELS I CAN DO.

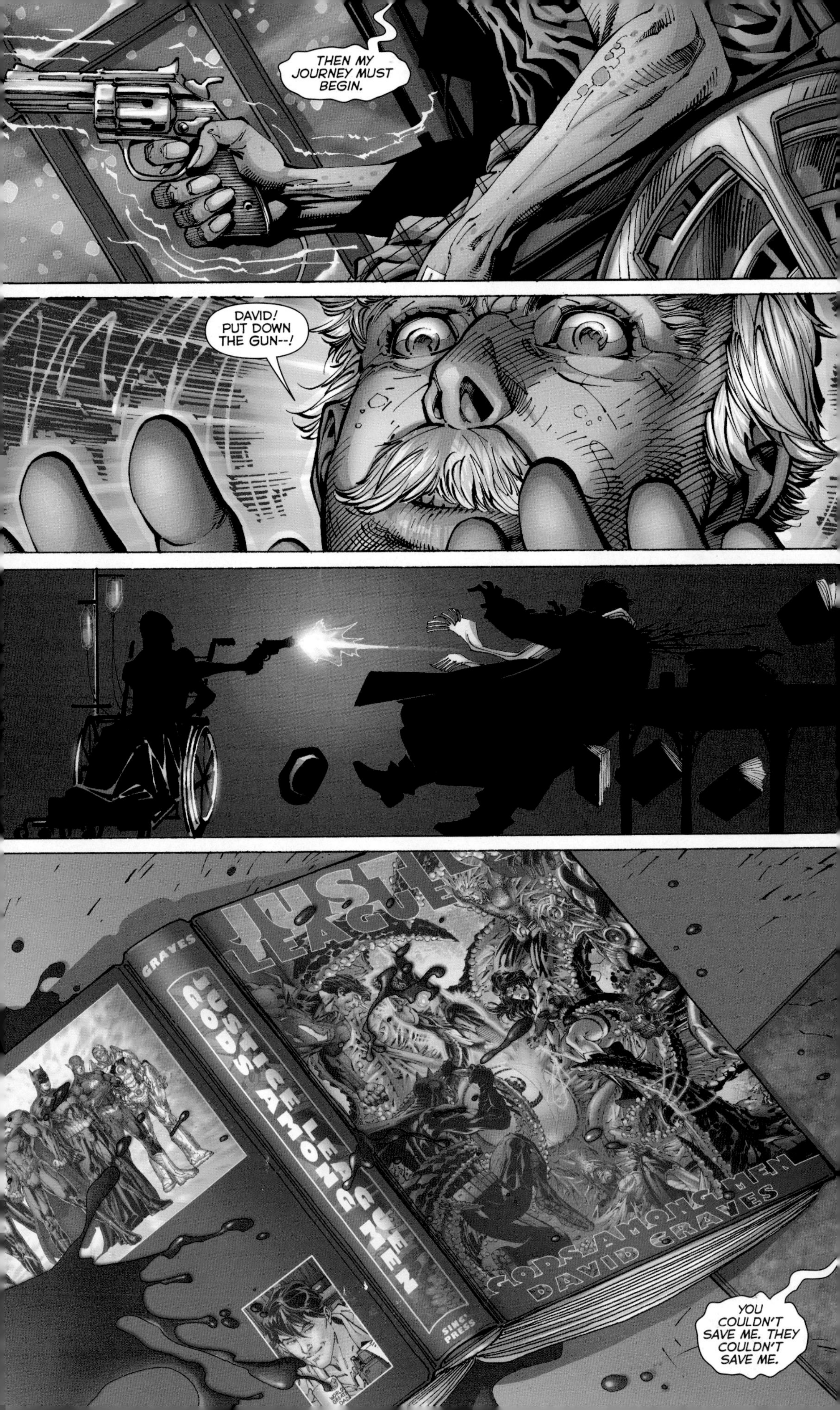
THEN MY JOURNEY MUST BEGIN.
DAVID! PUT DOWN THE GUN--!
JUSTICE LEAGUE
GRAVES
JUSTICE LEAGUE GODS AMONG MEN
GODS AMONG MEN DAVID GRAVES
YOU COULDN'T SAVE ME. THEY COULDN'T SAVE ME.

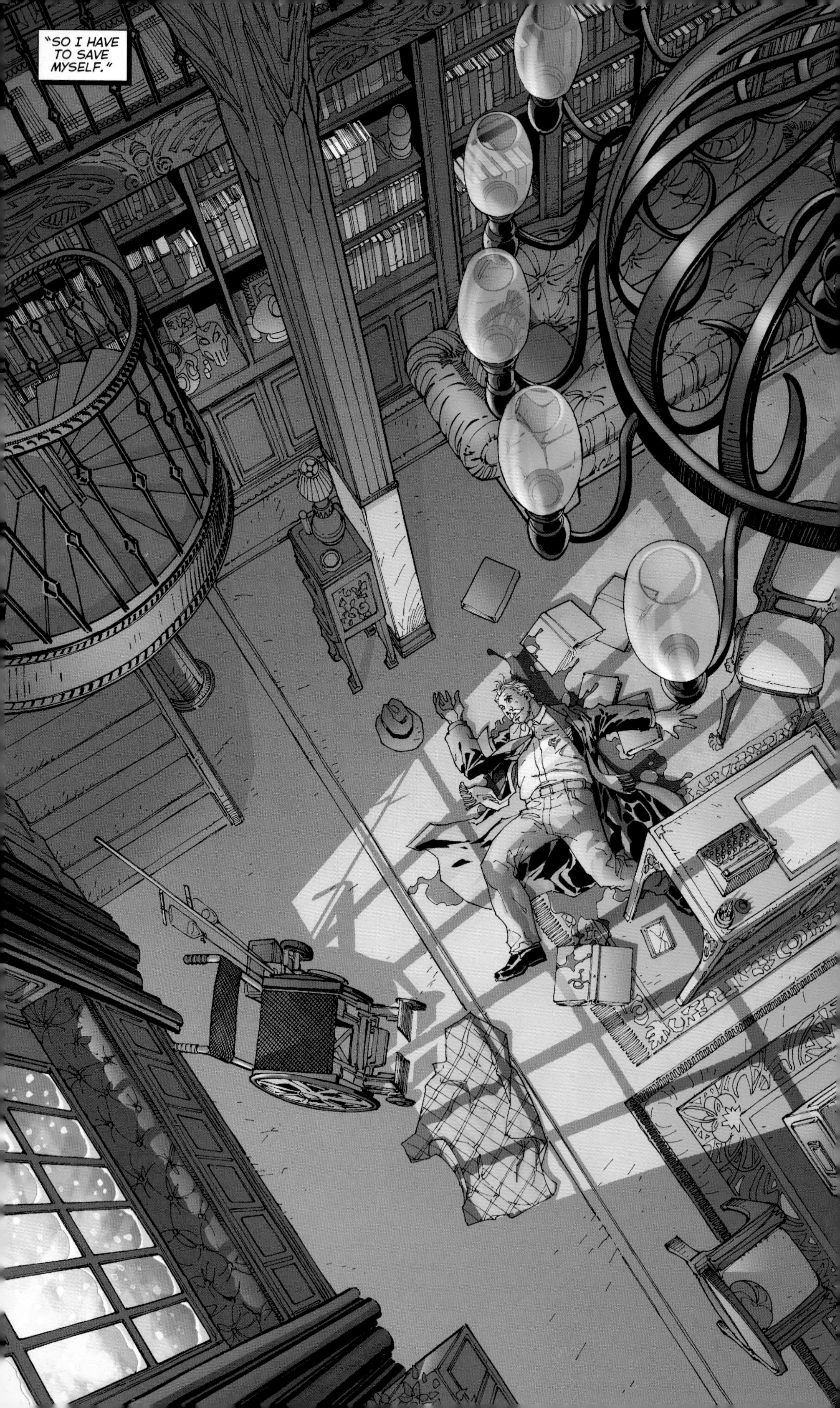
"SO I HAVE TO SAVE MYSELF."

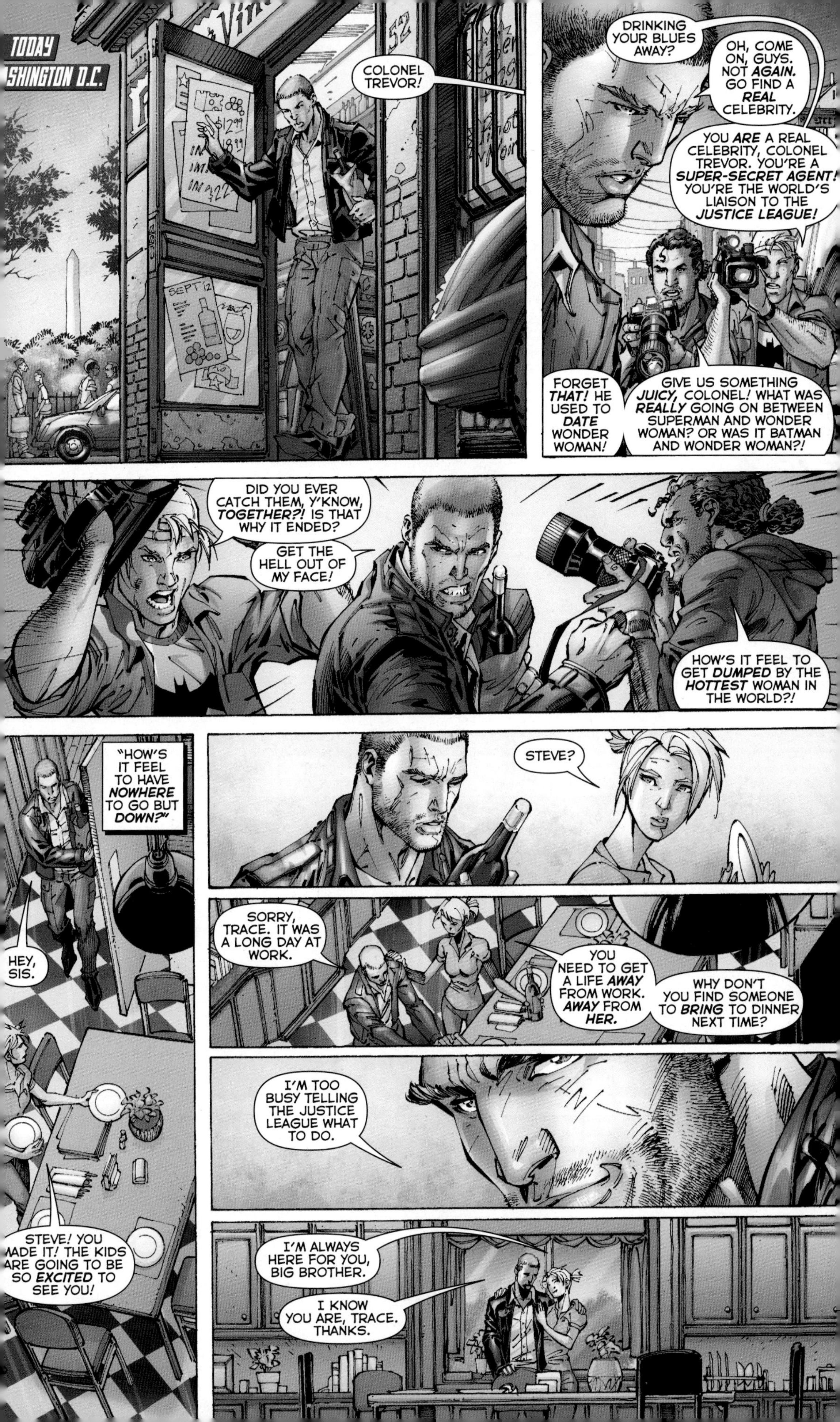
TODAY
SHINGTON D.C.
COLONEL TREVOR!
DRINKING YOUR BLUES AWAY?
OH, COME ON, GUYS. NOT AGAIN. GO FIND A REAL CELEBRITY.
YOU ARE A REAL CELEBRITY, COLONEL TREVOR. YOU'RE A SUPER-SECRET AGENT! YOU'RE THE WORLD'S LIAISON TO THE JUSTICE LEAGUE!
FORGET THAT! HE USED TO DATE WONDER WOMAN!
GIVE US SOMETHING JUICY, COLONEL! WHAT WAS REALLY GOING ON BETWEEN SUPERMAN AND WONDER WOMAN? OR WAS IT BATMAN AND WONDER WOMAN?!
DID YOU EVER CATCH THEM, Y'KNOW, TOGETHER?! IS THAT WHY IT ENDED?
GET THE HELL OUT OF MY FACE!
HOW'S IT FEEL TO GET DUMPED BY THE HOTTEST WOMAN IN THE WORLD?!
"HOW'S IT FEEL TO HAVE NOWHERE TO GO BUT DOWN?"
HEY, SIS.
STEVE! YOU MADE IT! THE KIDS ARE GOING TO BE SO EXCITED TO SEE YOU!
STEVE?
SORRY, TRACE. IT WAS A LONG DAY AT WORK.
YOU NEED TO GET A LIFE AWAY FROM WORK. AWAY FROM HER.
WHY DON'T YOU FIND SOMEONE TO BRING TO DINNER NEXT TIME?
I'M TOO BUSY TELLING THE JUSTICE LEAGUE WHAT TO DO.
I'M ALWAYS HERE FOR YOU, BIG BROTHER.
I KNOW YOU ARE, TRACE. THANKS.

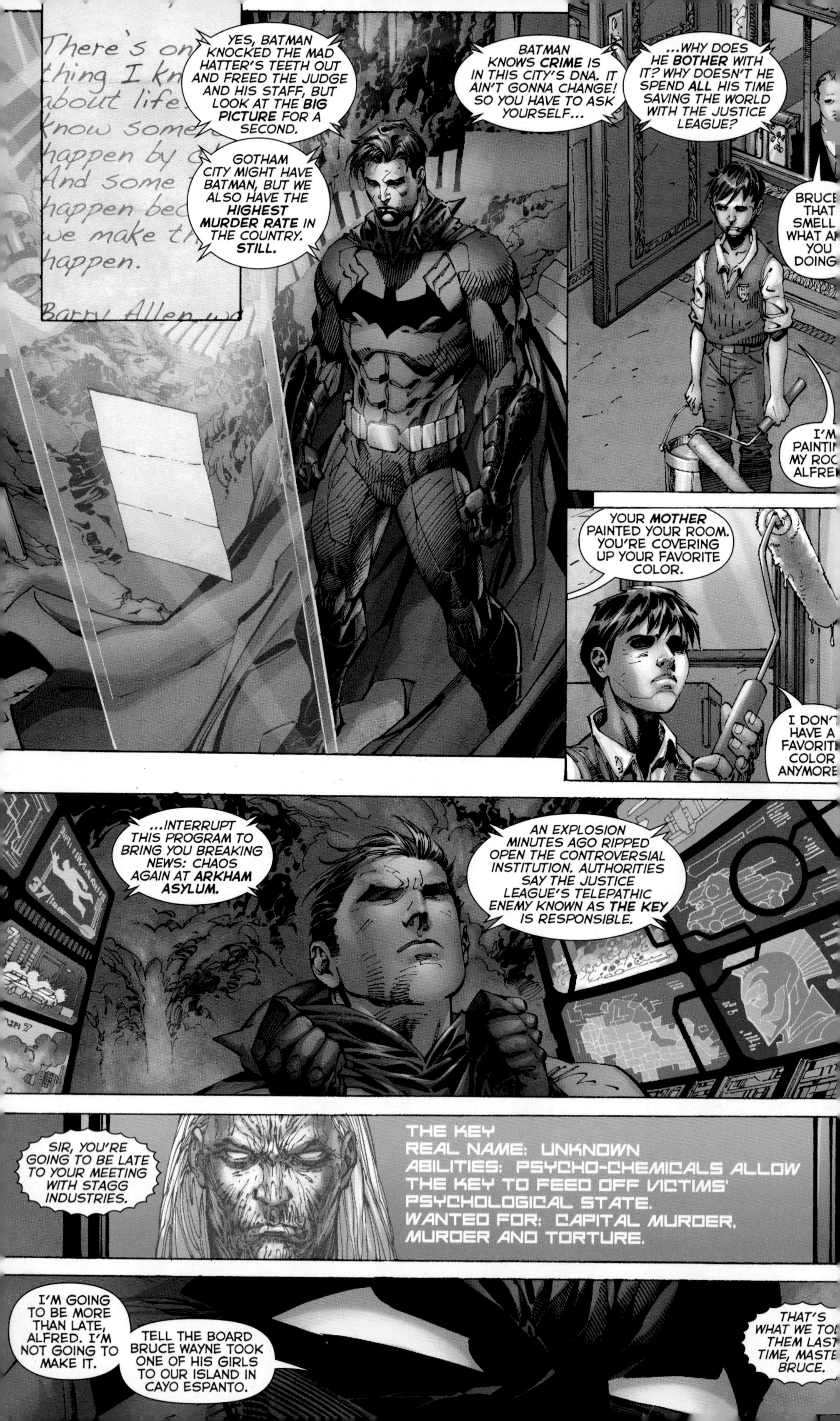
There's on
thing I kn
about life.
know some
happen by c
And some
happen bec
we make th
happen.
Barry Allen
YES, BATMAN KNOCKED THE MAD HATTER'S TEETH OUT AND FREED THE JUDGE AND HIS STAFF, BUT LOOK AT THE BIG PICTURE FOR A SECOND.
GOTHAM CITY MIGHT HAVE BATMAN, BUT WE ALSO HAVE THE HIGHEST MURDER RATE IN THE COUNTRY. STILL.
BATMAN KNOWS CRIME IS IN THIS CITY'S DNA. IT AIN'T GONNA CHANGE! SO YOU HAVE TO ASK YOURSELF...
...WHY DOES HE BOTHER WITH IT? WHY DOESN'T HE SPEND ALL HIS TIME SAVING THE WORLD WITH THE JUSTICE LEAGUE?
BRUCE THAT SMELL WHAT A YOU DOING
I'M PAINTIN MY ROO ALFRE
YOUR MOTHER PAINTED YOUR ROOM. YOU'RE COVERING UP YOUR FAVORITE COLOR.
I DON'T HAVE A FAVORIT COLOR ANYMORE
...INTERRUPT THIS PROGRAM TO BRING YOU BREAKING NEWS: CHAOS AGAIN AT ARKHAM ASYLUM.
AN EXPLOSION MINUTES AGO RIPPED OPEN THE CONTROVERSIAL INSTITUTION. AUTHORITIES SAY THE JUSTICE LEAGUE'S TELEPATHIC ENEMY KNOWN AS THE KEY IS RESPONSIBLE.
SIR, YOU'RE GOING TO BE LATE TO YOUR MEETING WITH STAGG INDUSTRIES.
THE KEY
REAL NAME: UNKNOWN
ABILITIES: PSYCHO-CHEMICALS ALLOW THE KEY TO FEED OFF VICTIMS' PSYCHOLOGICAL STATE.
WANTED FOR: CAPITAL MURDER, MURDER AND TORTURE.
I'M GOING TO BE MORE THAN LATE, ALFRED. I'M NOT GOING TO MAKE IT.
TELL THE BOARD BRUCE WAYNE TOOK ONE OF HIS GIRLS TO OUR ISLAND IN CAYO ESPANTO.
THAT'S WHAT WE TO THEM LAS TIME, MASTE BRUCE.

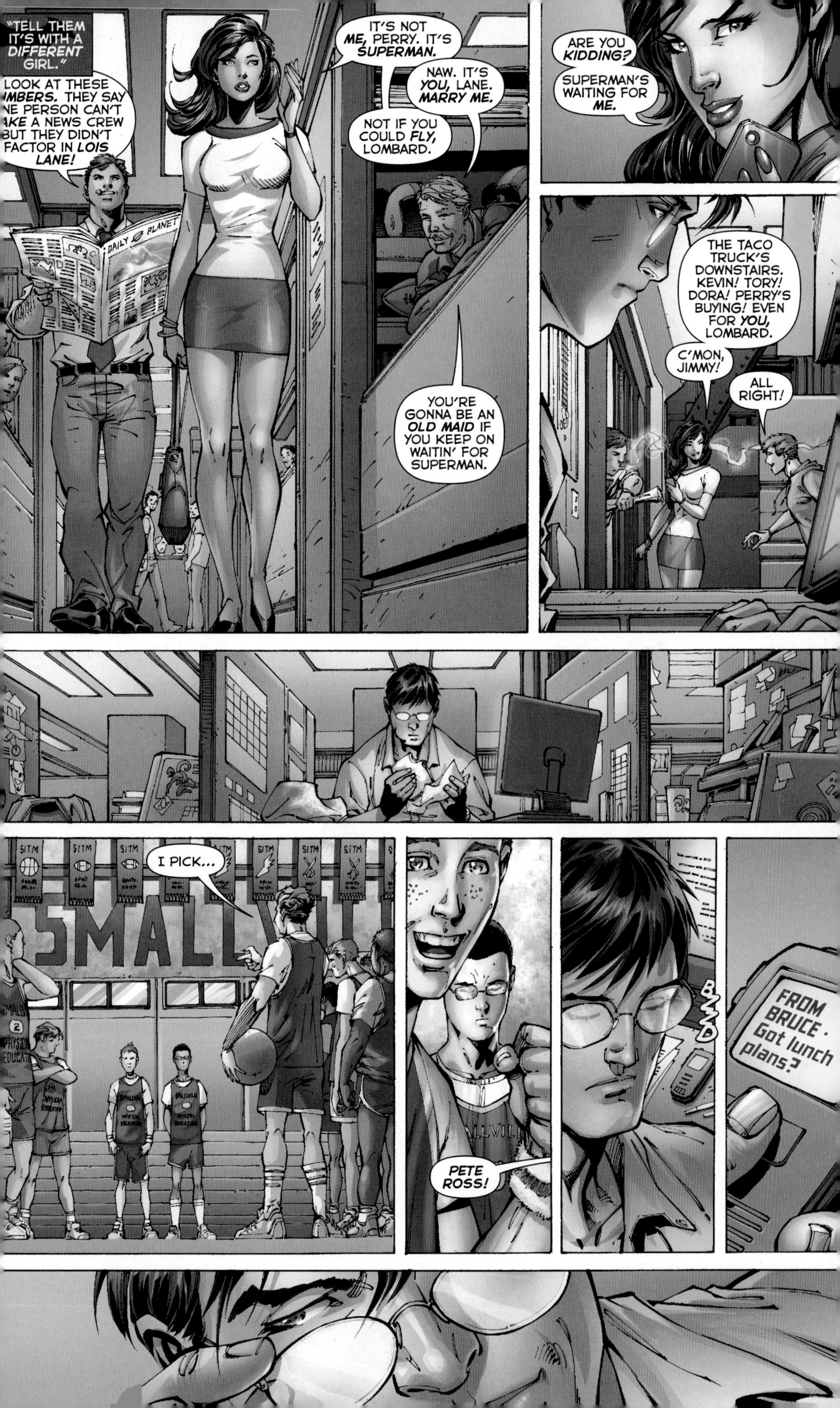
"TELL THEM IT'S WITH A DIFFERENT GIRL."
LOOK AT THESE NUMBERS. THEY SAY ONE PERSON CAN'T TAKE A NEWS CREW BUT THEY DIDN'T FACTOR IN LOIS LANE!
IT'S NOT ME, PERRY. IT'S SUPERMAN.
NAW. IT'S YOU, LANE. MARRY ME.
NOT IF YOU COULD FLY, LOMBARD.
YOU'RE GONNA BE AN OLD MAID IF YOU KEEP ON WAITIN' FOR SUPERMAN.
ARE YOU KIDDING?
SUPERMAN'S WAITING FOR ME.
THE TACO TRUCK'S DOWNSTAIRS. KEVIN! TORY! DORA! PERRY'S BUYING! EVEN FOR YOU, LOMBARD.
C'MON, JIMMY!
ALL RIGHT!
I PICK...
PETE ROSS!
BZZD
FROM BRUCE. Got lunch plans?

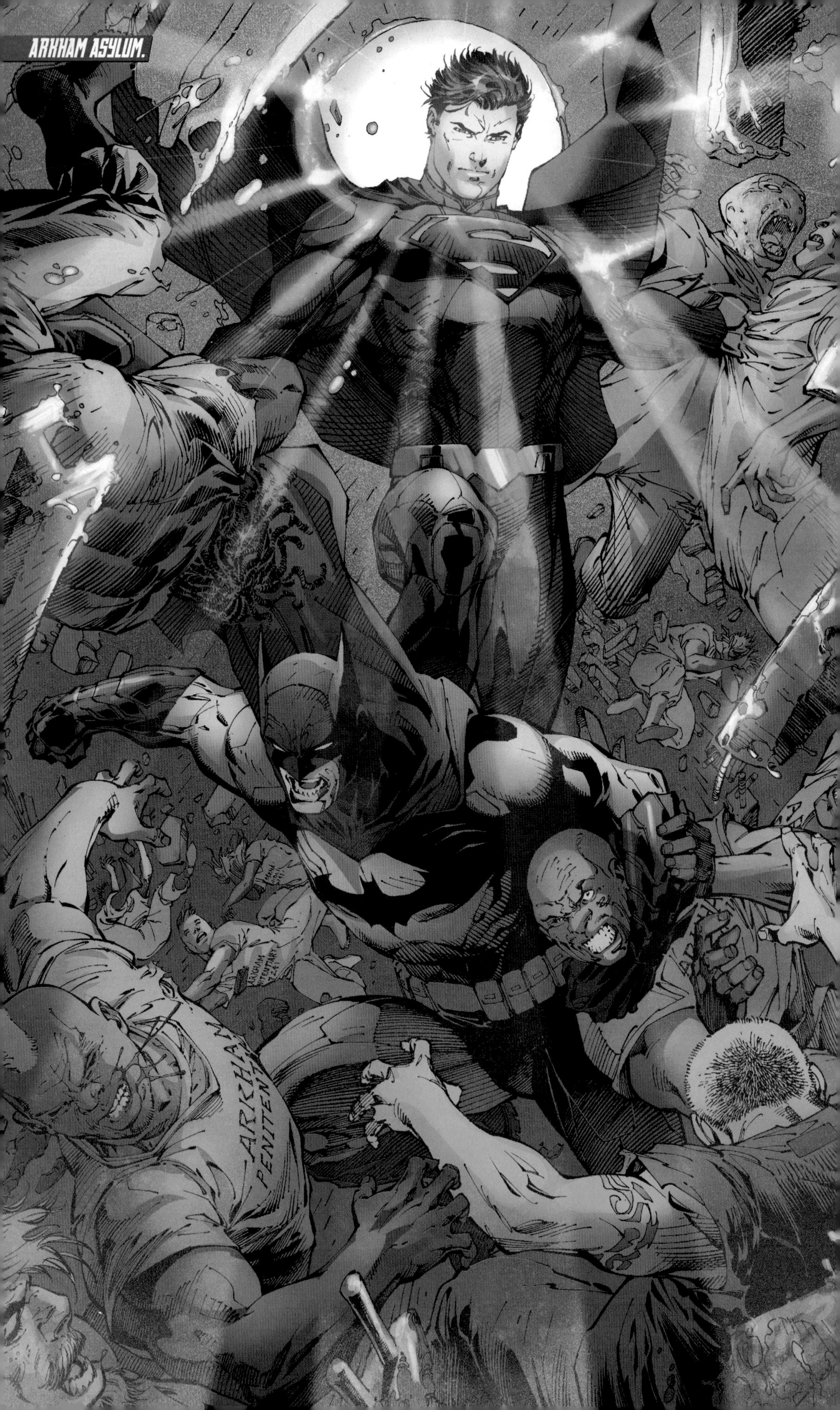
ARKHAM ASYLUM.

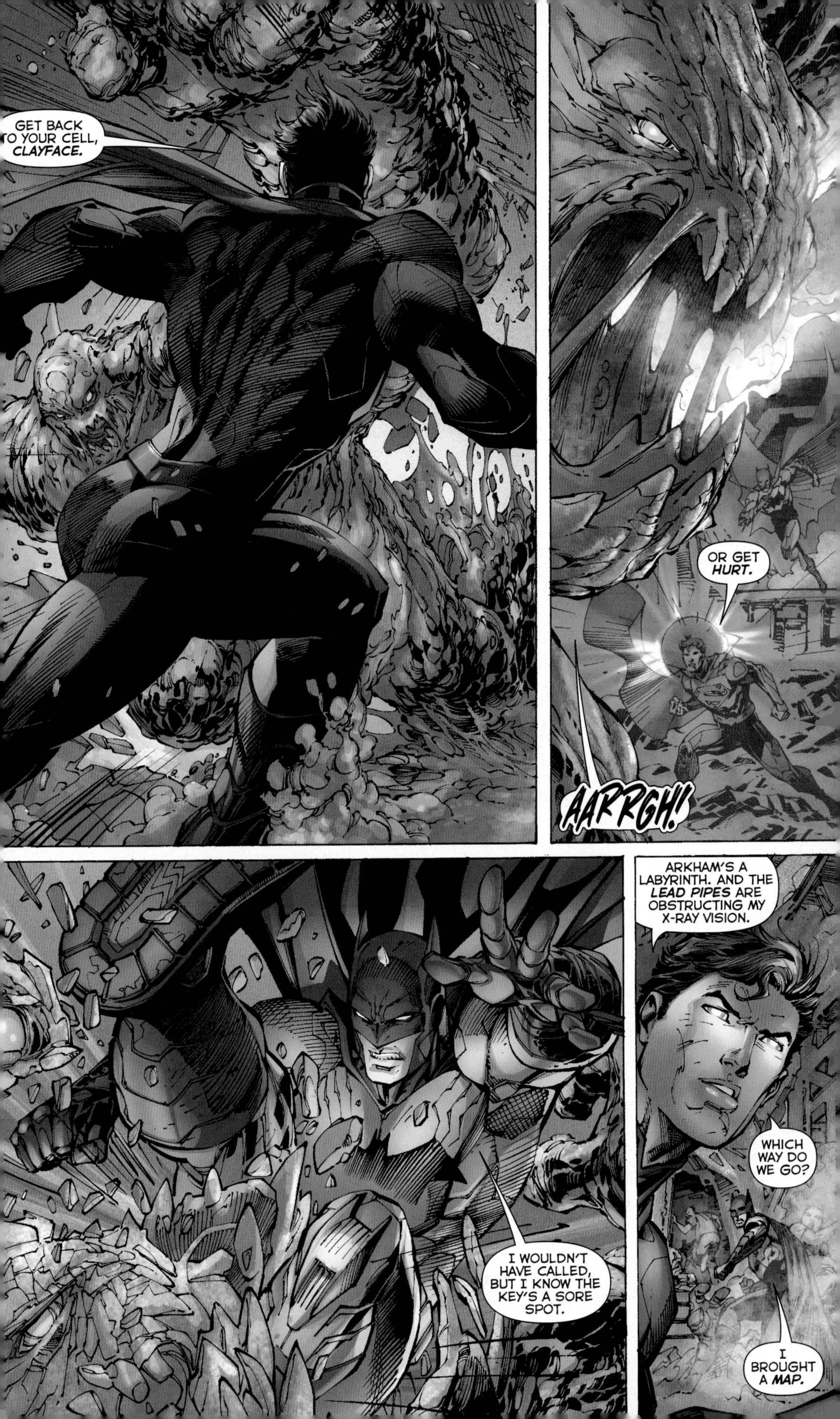
GET BACK TO YOUR CELL, *CLAYFACE.*
OR GET *HURT.*
AARRGH!
ARKHAM'S A LABYRINTH. AND THE *LEAD PIPES* ARE OBSTRUCTING MY X-RAY VISION.
WHICH WAY DO WE GO?
I WOULDN'T HAVE CALLED, BUT I KNOW THE KEY'S A SORE SPOT.
I BROUGHT A *MAP.*

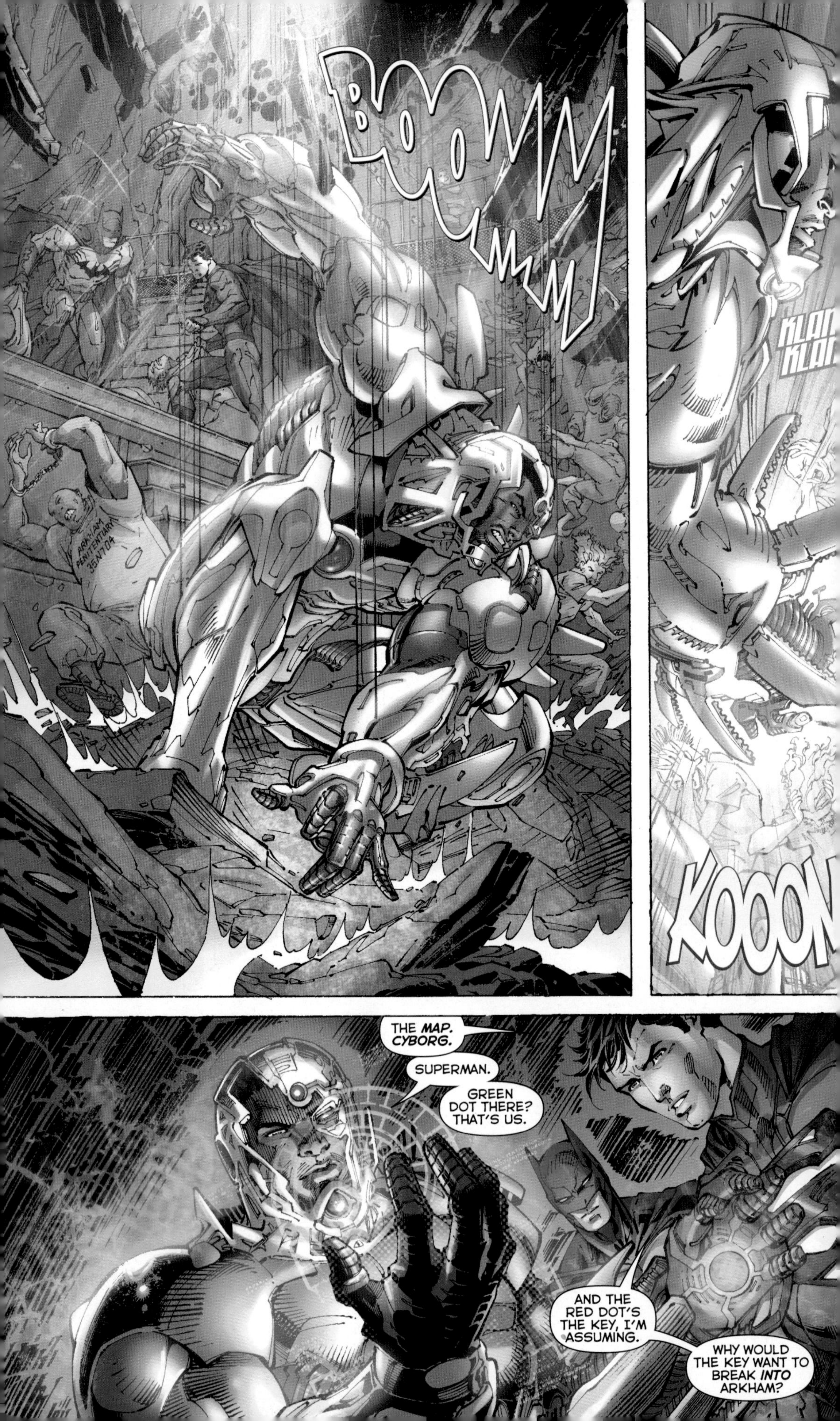
BOOOM
ARKHAM PENITENTIARY
THE MAP. CYBORG.
SUPERMAN.
GREEN DOT THERE? THAT'S US.
AND THE RED DOT'S THE KEY, I'M ASSUMING.
WHY WOULD THE KEY WANT TO BREAK INTO ARKHAM?

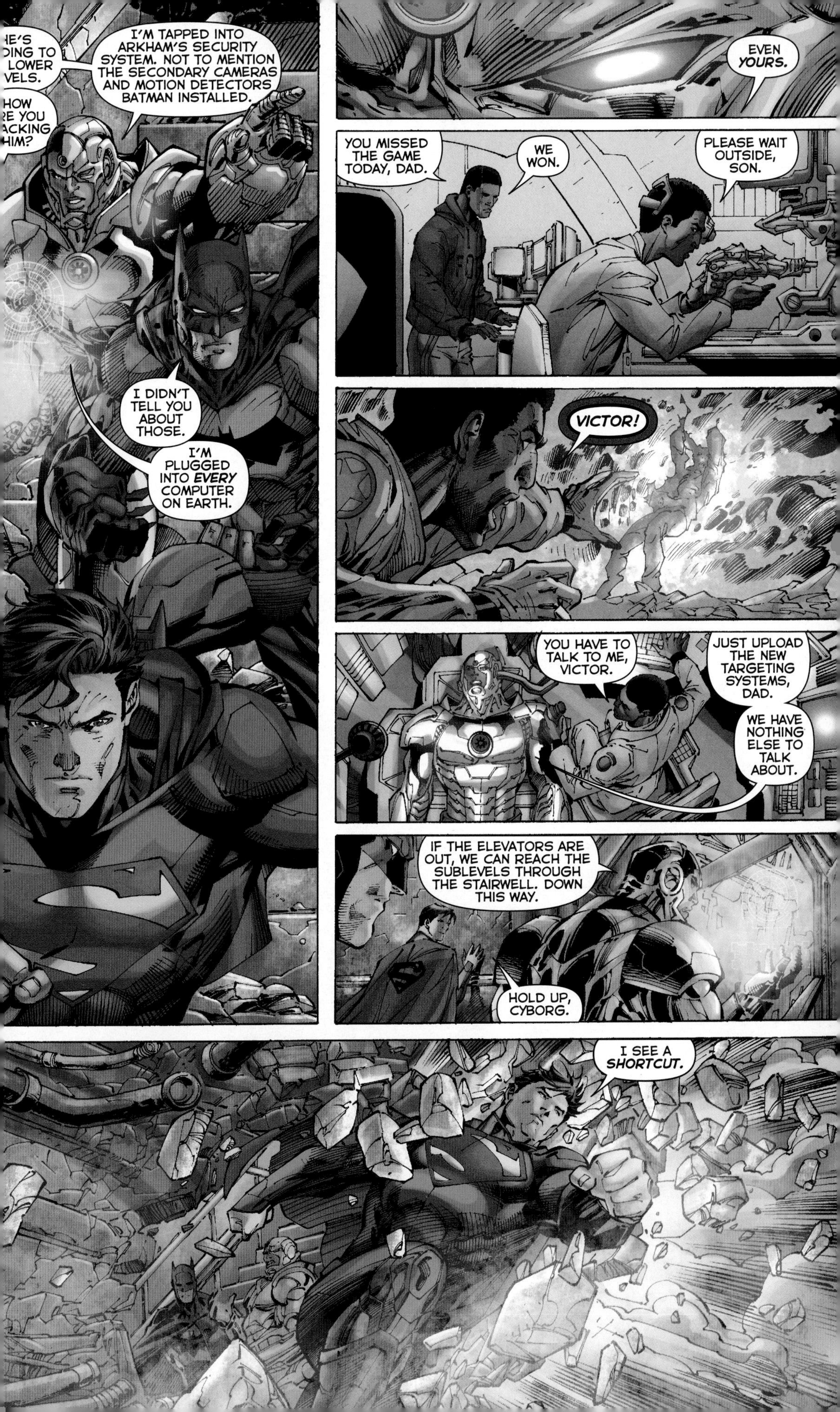

E'S
DING TO
LOWER
VELS.
I'M TAPPED INTO ARKHAM'S SECURITY SYSTEM. NOT TO MENTION THE SECONDARY CAMERAS AND MOTION DETECTORS BATMAN INSTALLED.
HOW
E YOU
ACKING
HIM?
EVEN YOURS.
I DIDN'T TELL YOU ABOUT THOSE.
I'M PLUGGED INTO EVERY COMPUTER ON EARTH.
YOU MISSED THE GAME TODAY, DAD.
WE WON.
PLEASE WAIT OUTSIDE, SON.
VICTOR!
YOU HAVE TO TALK TO ME, VICTOR.
JUST UPLOAD THE NEW TARGETING SYSTEMS, DAD.
WE HAVE NOTHING ELSE TO TALK ABOUT.
IF THE ELEVATORS ARE OUT, WE CAN REACH THE SUBLEVELS THROUGH THE STAIRWELL. DOWN THIS WAY.
HOLD UP, CYBORG.
I SEE A SHORTCUT.

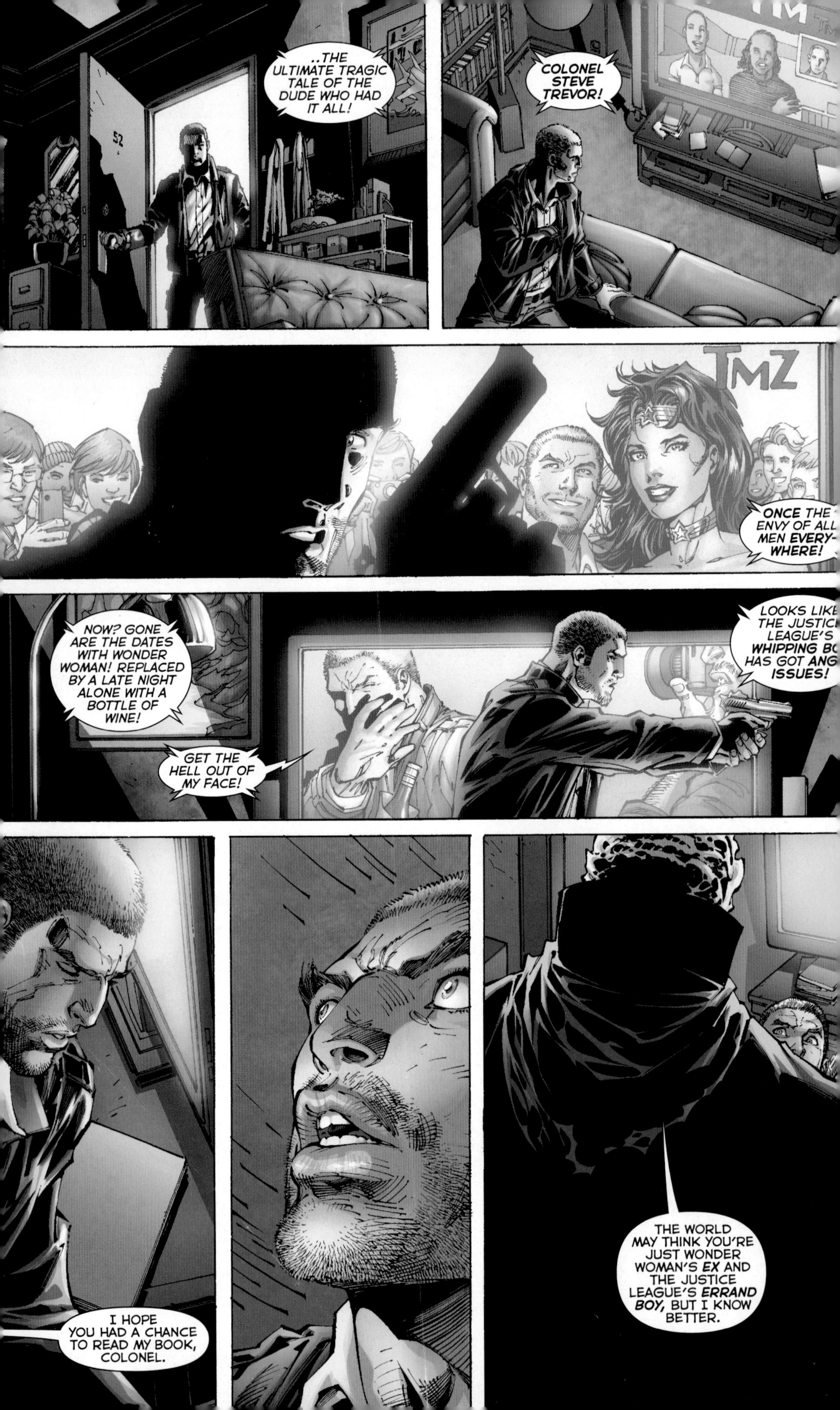
..THE ULTIMATE TRAGIC TALE OF THE DUDE WHO HAD IT ALL!
52
COLONEL STEVE TREVOR!
TMZ
ONCE THE ENVY OF ALL MEN EVERY-WHERE!
NOW? GONE ARE THE DATES WITH WONDER WOMAN! REPLACED BY A LATE NIGHT ALONE WITH A BOTTLE OF WINE!
GET THE HELL OUT OF MY FACE!
LOOKS LIKE THE JUSTICE LEAGUE'S WHIPPING BO HAS GOT ANG ISSUES!
I HOPE YOU HAD A CHANCE TO READ MY BOOK, COLONEL.
THE WORLD MAY THINK YOU'RE JUST WONDER WOMAN'S EX AND THE JUSTICE LEAGUE'S ERRAND BOY, BUT I KNOW BETTER.

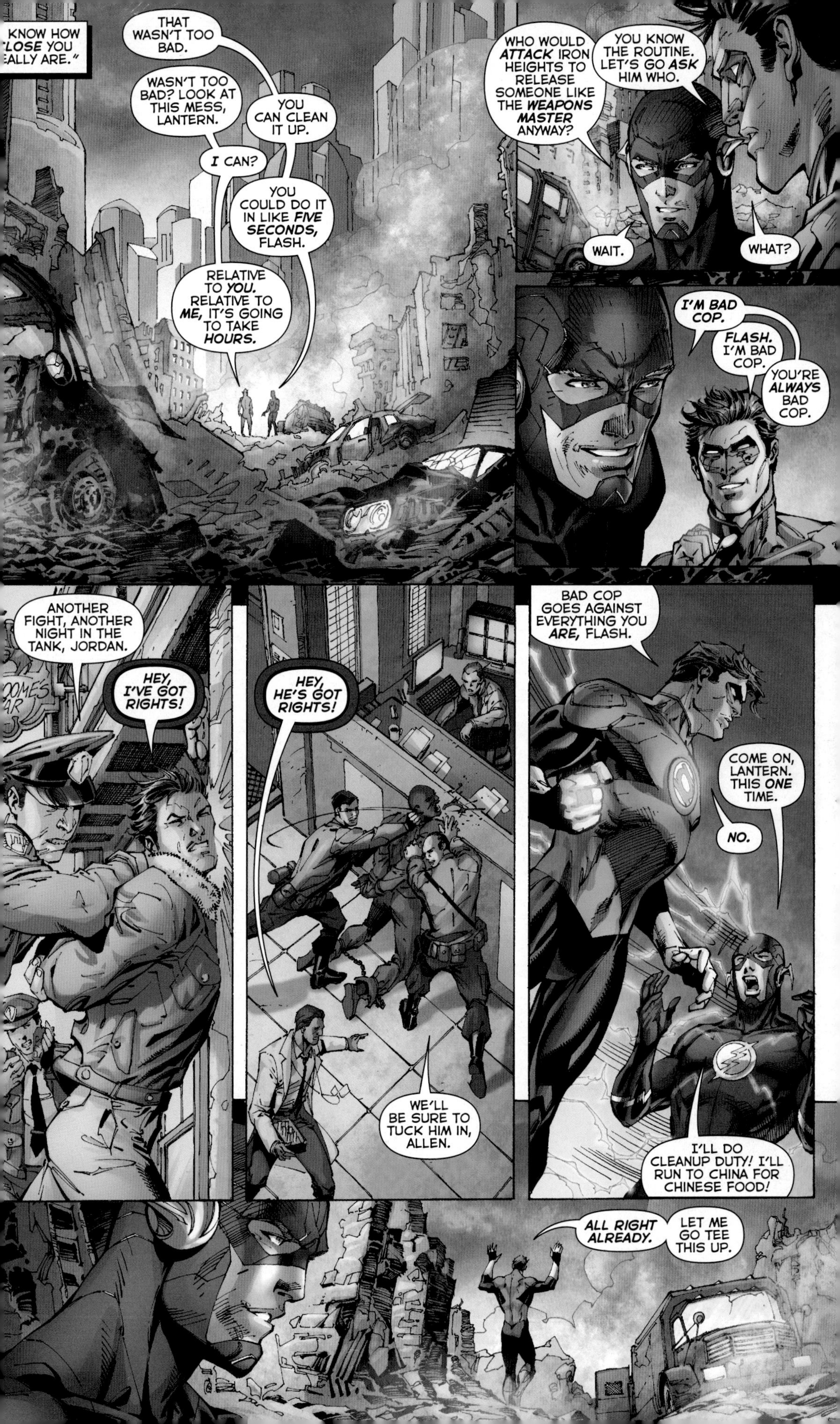
KNOW HOW
CLOSE YOU
EALLY ARE."
THAT WASN'T TOO BAD.
WASN'T TOO BAD? LOOK AT THIS MESS, LANTERN.
YOU CAN CLEAN IT UP.
I CAN?
YOU COULD DO IT IN LIKE FIVE SECONDS, FLASH.
RELATIVE TO YOU. RELATIVE TO ME, IT'S GOING TO TAKE HOURS.
WHO WOULD ATTACK IRON HEIGHTS TO RELEASE SOMEONE LIKE THE WEAPONS MASTER ANYWAY?
YOU KNOW THE ROUTINE. LET'S GO ASK HIM WHO.
WAIT.
WHAT?
I'M BAD COP.
FLASH. I'M BAD COP.
YOU'RE ALWAYS BAD COP.
ANOTHER FIGHT, ANOTHER NIGHT IN THE TANK, JORDAN.
HEY, I'VE GOT RIGHTS!
HEY, HE'S GOT RIGHTS!
WE'LL BE SURE TO TUCK HIM IN, ALLEN.
BAD COP GOES AGAINST EVERYTHING YOU ARE, FLASH.
COME ON, LANTERN. THIS ONE TIME.
NO.
I'LL DO CLEANUP DUTY! I'LL RUN TO CHINA FOR CHINESE FOOD!
ALL RIGHT ALREADY.
LET ME GO TEE THIS UP.

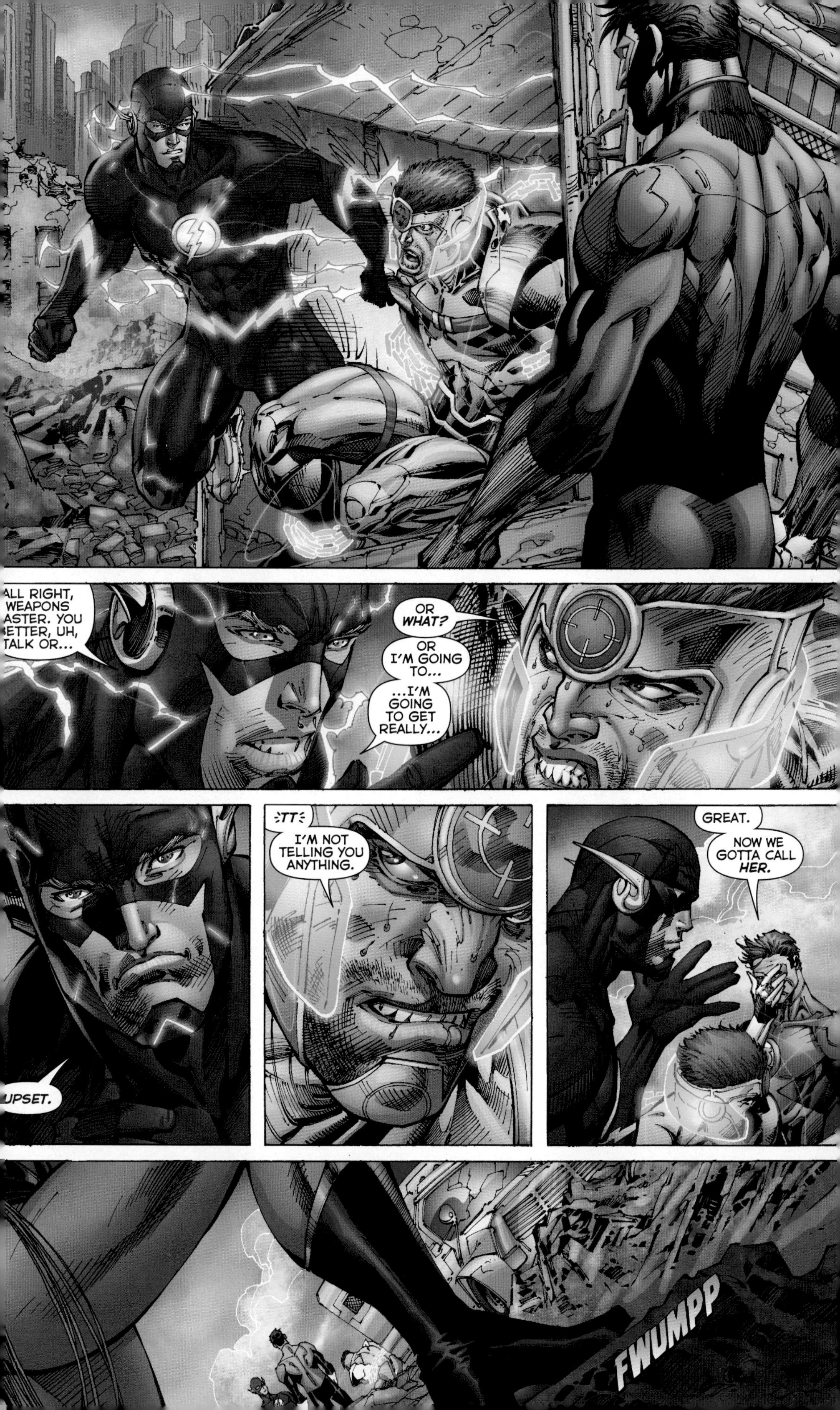

ALL RIGHT, WEAPONS MASTER. YOU BETTER, UH, TALK OR...
OR WHAT?
OR I'M GOING TO...
...I'M GOING TO GET REALLY...
UPSET.
TT
I'M NOT TELLING YOU ANYTHING.
GREAT.
NOW WE GOTTA CALL HER.
FWUMPP

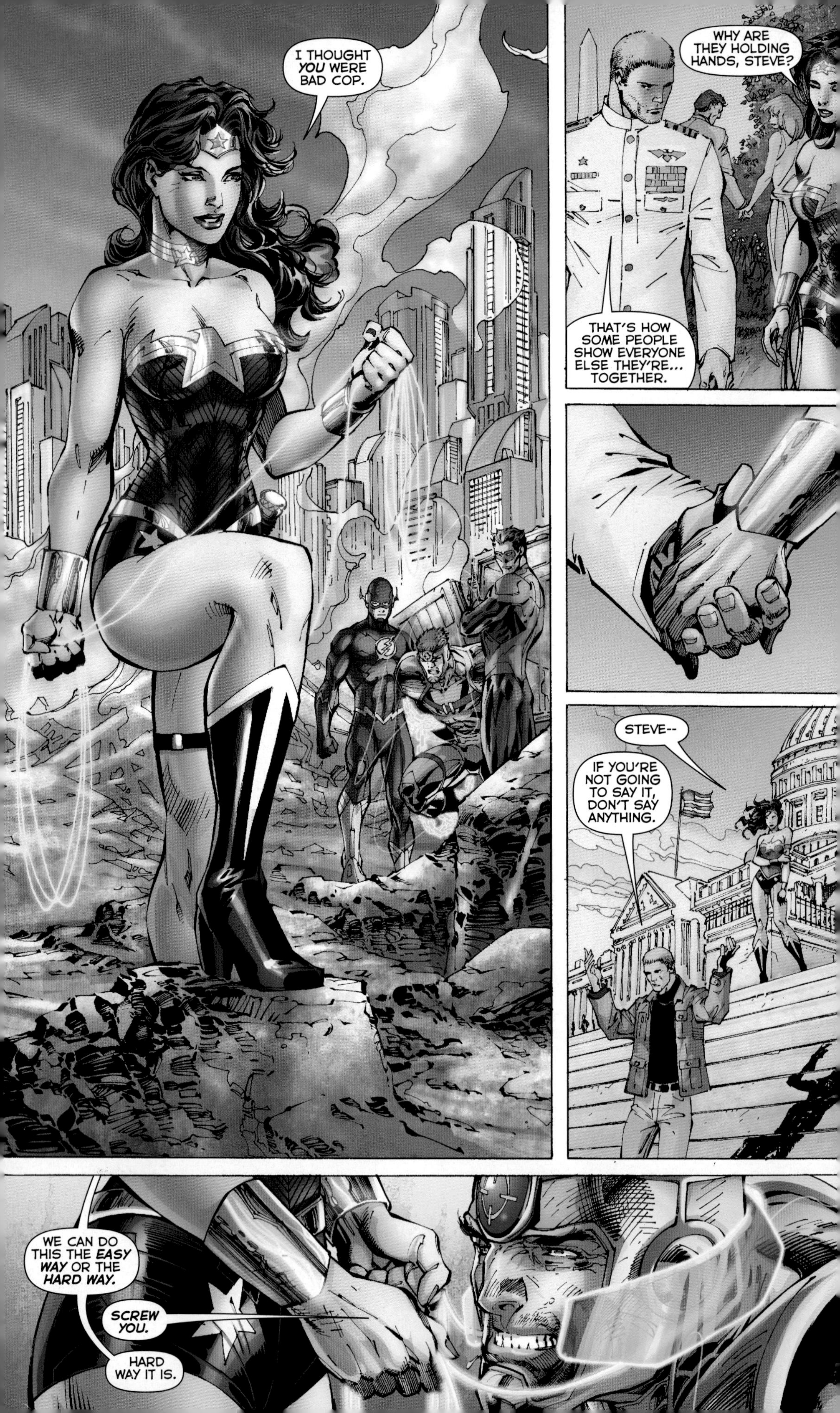

I THOUGHT *YOU* WERE BAD COP.
WHY ARE THEY HOLDING HANDS, STEVE?
THAT'S HOW SOME PEOPLE SHOW EVERYONE ELSE THEY'RE... TOGETHER.
STEVE--
IF YOU'RE NOT GOING TO SAY IT, DON'T SAY ANYTHING.
WE CAN DO THIS THE *EASY WAY* OR THE *HARD WAY.*
SCREW YOU.
HARD WAY IT IS.

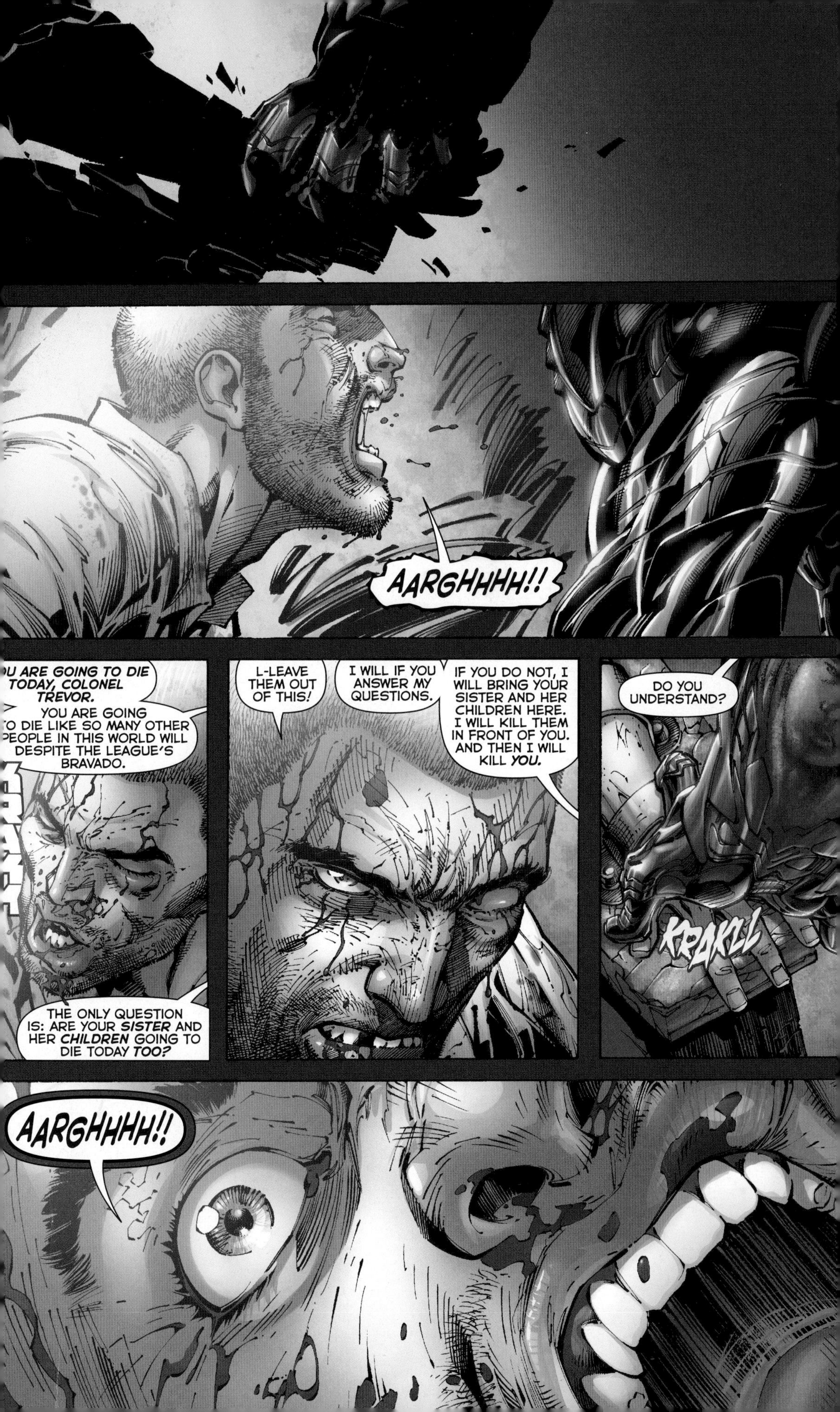
AARGHHHH!!
OU ARE GOING TO DIE TODAY, COLONEL TREVOR.
YOU ARE GOING TO DIE LIKE SO MANY OTHER PEOPLE IN THIS WORLD WILL DESPITE THE LEAGUE'S BRAVADO.
THE ONLY QUESTION IS: ARE YOUR SISTER AND HER CHILDREN GOING TO DIE TODAY TOO?
L-LEAVE THEM OUT OF THIS!
I WILL IF YOU ANSWER MY QUESTIONS.
IF YOU DO NOT, I WILL BRING YOUR SISTER AND HER CHILDREN HERE. I WILL KILL THEM IN FRONT OF YOU. AND THEN I WILL KILL YOU.
DO YOU UNDERSTAND?
KRAKLL
AARGHHHH!!

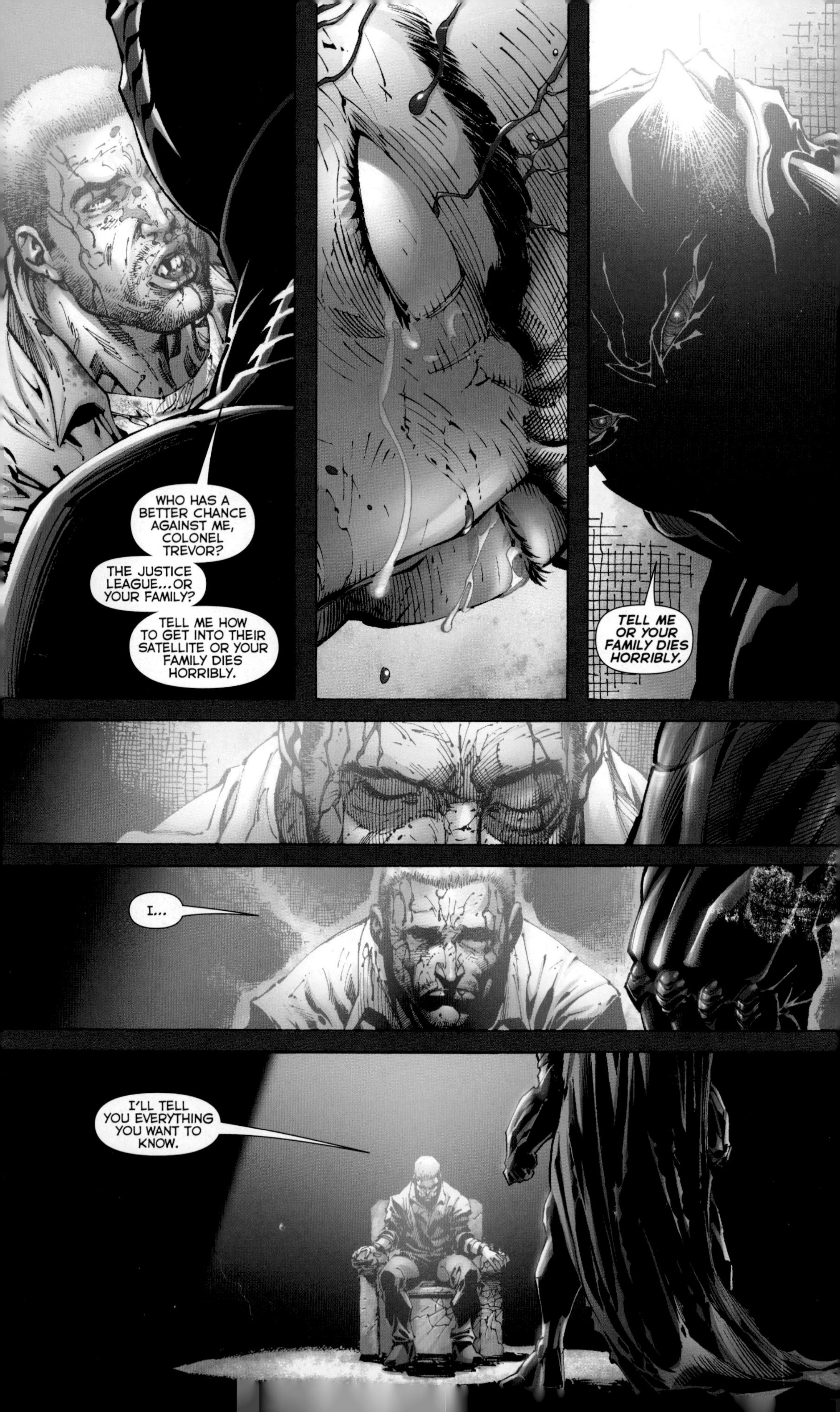
WHO HAS A BETTER CHANCE AGAINST ME, COLONEL TREVOR?
THE JUSTICE LEAGUE...OR YOUR FAMILY?
TELL ME HOW TO GET INTO THEIR SATELLITE OR YOUR FAMILY DIES HORRIBLY.
TELL ME OR YOUR FAMILY DIES HORRIBLY.
I...
I'LL TELL YOU EVERYTHING YOU WANT TO KNOW.

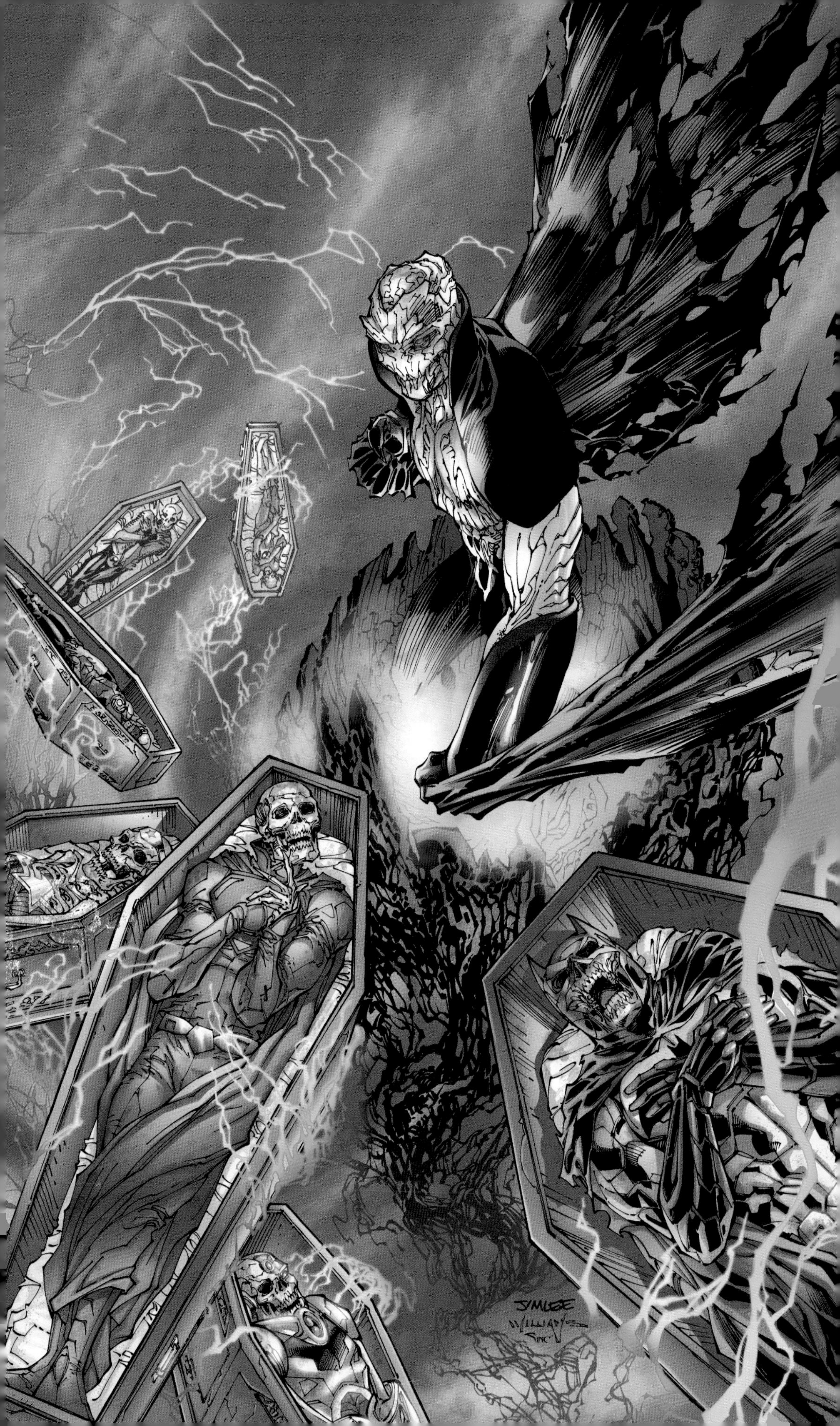

THE VILLAIN'S JOURNEY CHAPTER TWO: THE BELLY OF THE BEAST

GEOFF JOHNS writer JIM LEE penciller SCOTT WILLIAMS, MARK IRWIN & JONATHAN GLAPION inkers cover by JIM LEE, SCOTT WILLIAMS & ALEX SINCLAI

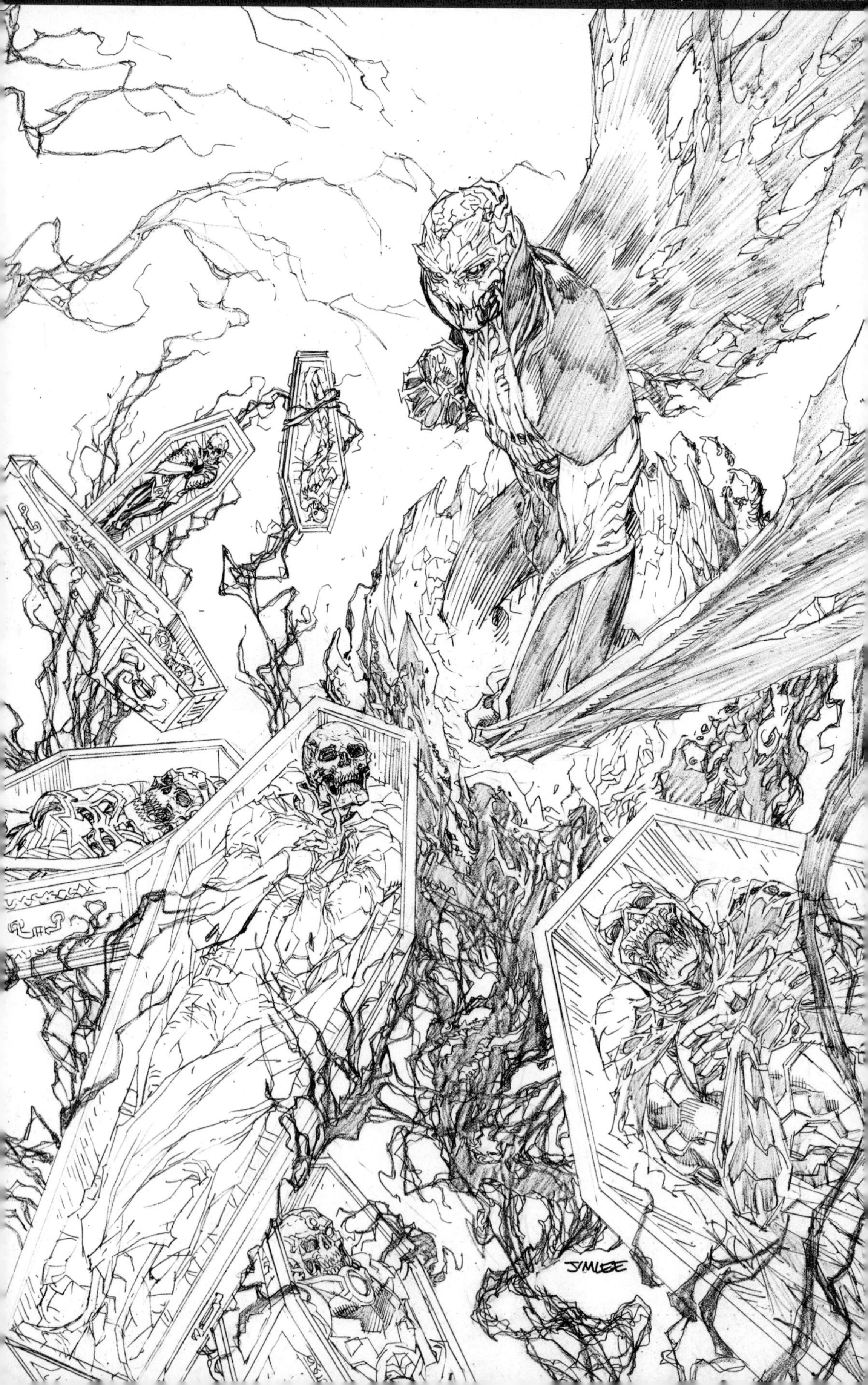

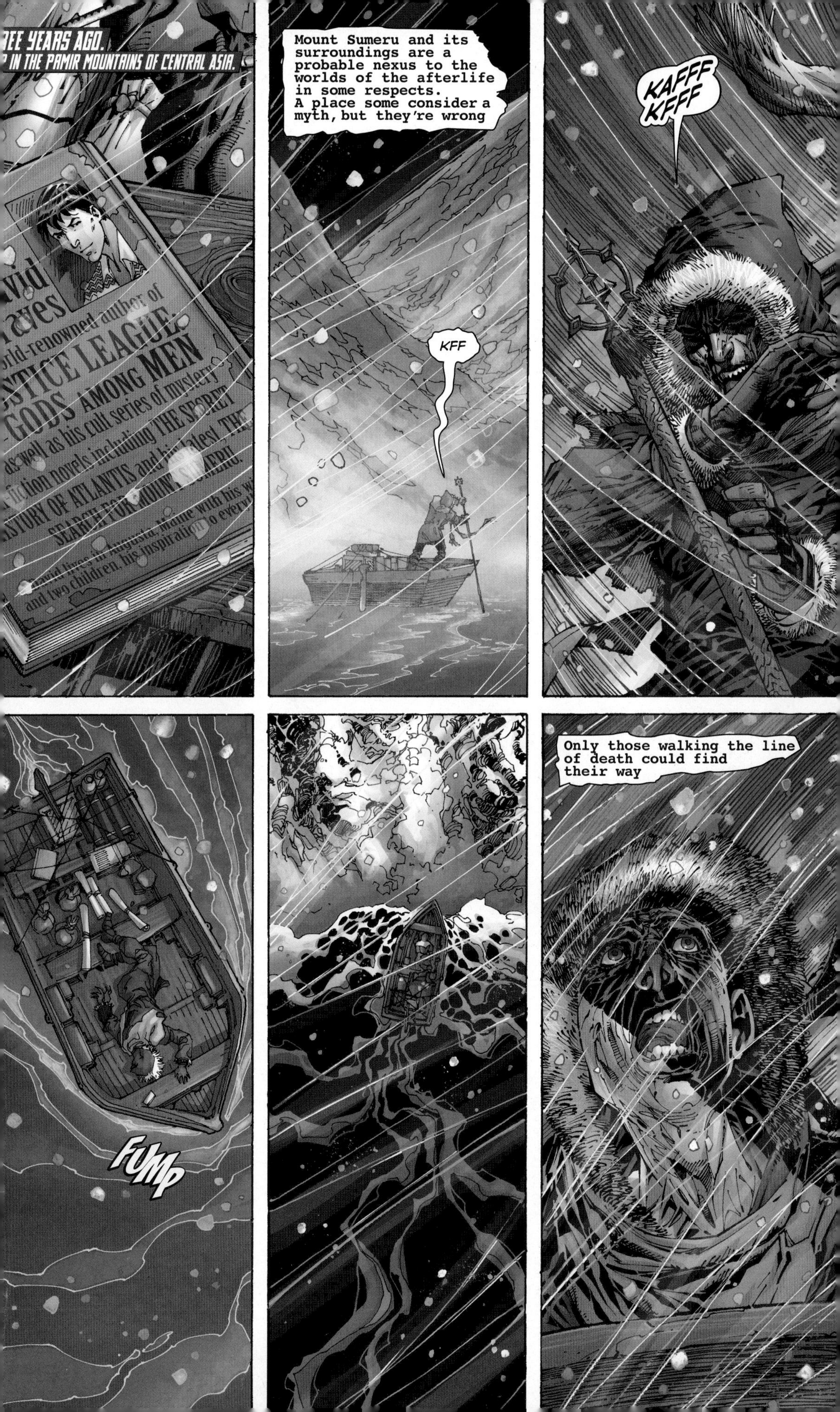
REE YEARS AGO.
IN THE PAMIR MOUNTAINS OF CENTRAL ASIA.
GODS AMONG MEN
as well as his cult series of mystery
HISTORY OF ATLANTIS and his latest, THE
Mount Sumeru and its surroundings are a probable nexus to the worlds of the afterlife in some respects.
A place some consider a myth, but they're wrong
KFF
KAFFF KFFF
FUMP
Only those walking the line of death could find their way

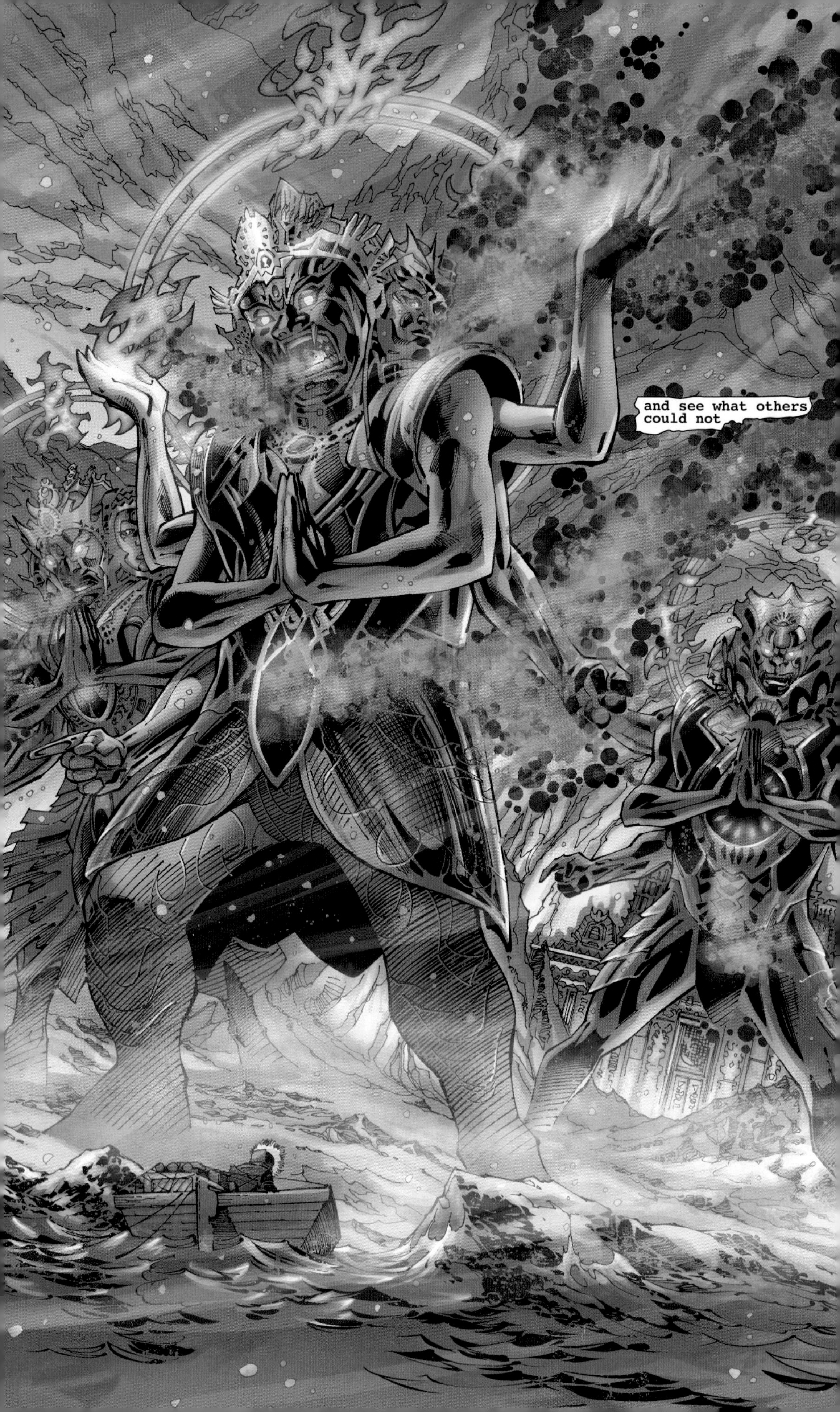
and see what others could not

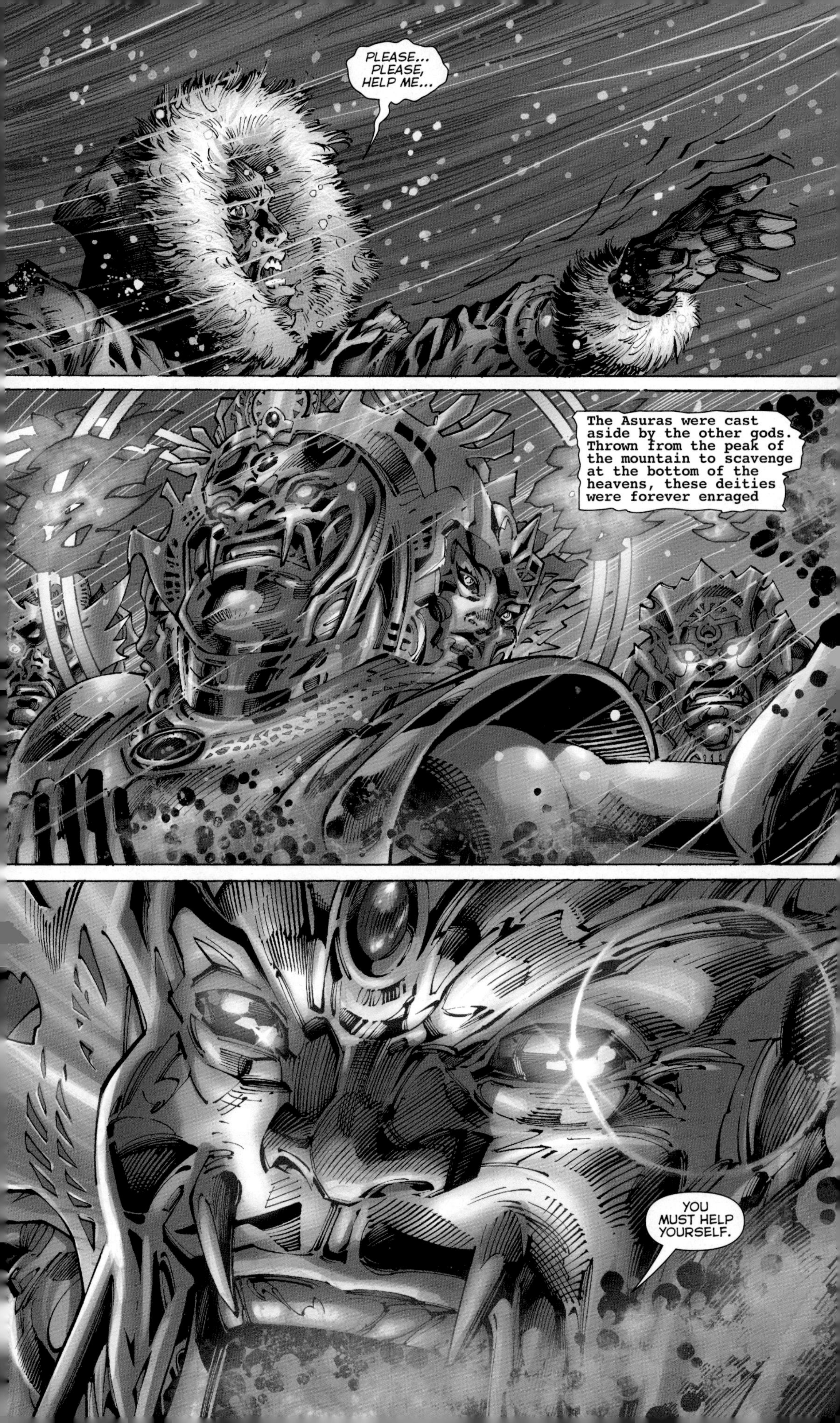

PLEASE... PLEASE, HELP ME...
The Asuras were cast aside by the other gods. Thrown from the peak of the mountain to scavenge at the bottom of the heavens, these deities were forever enraged
YOU MUST HELP YOURSELF.

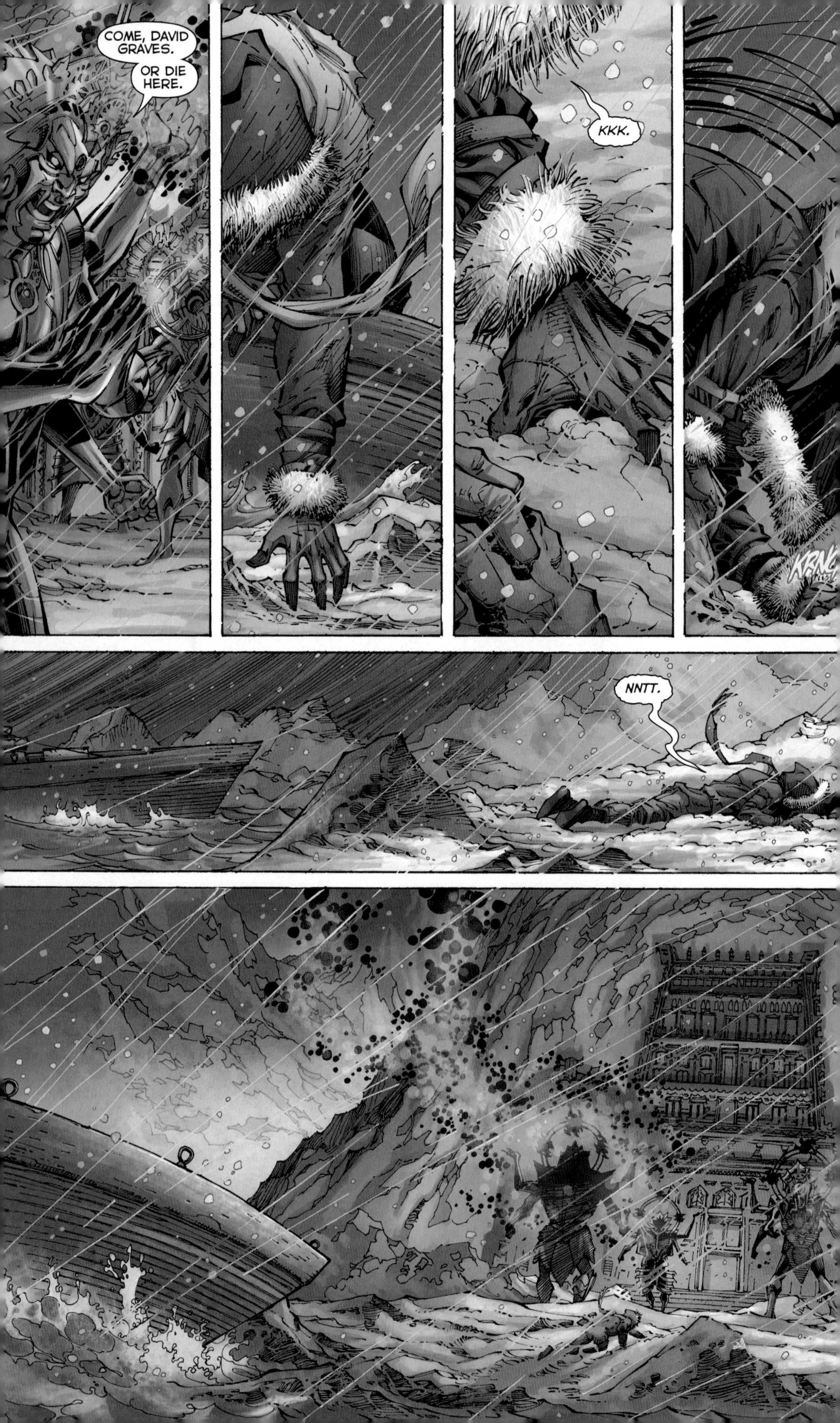
COME, DAVID GRAVES.
OR DIE HERE.
KKK.
KRNG
NNTT.

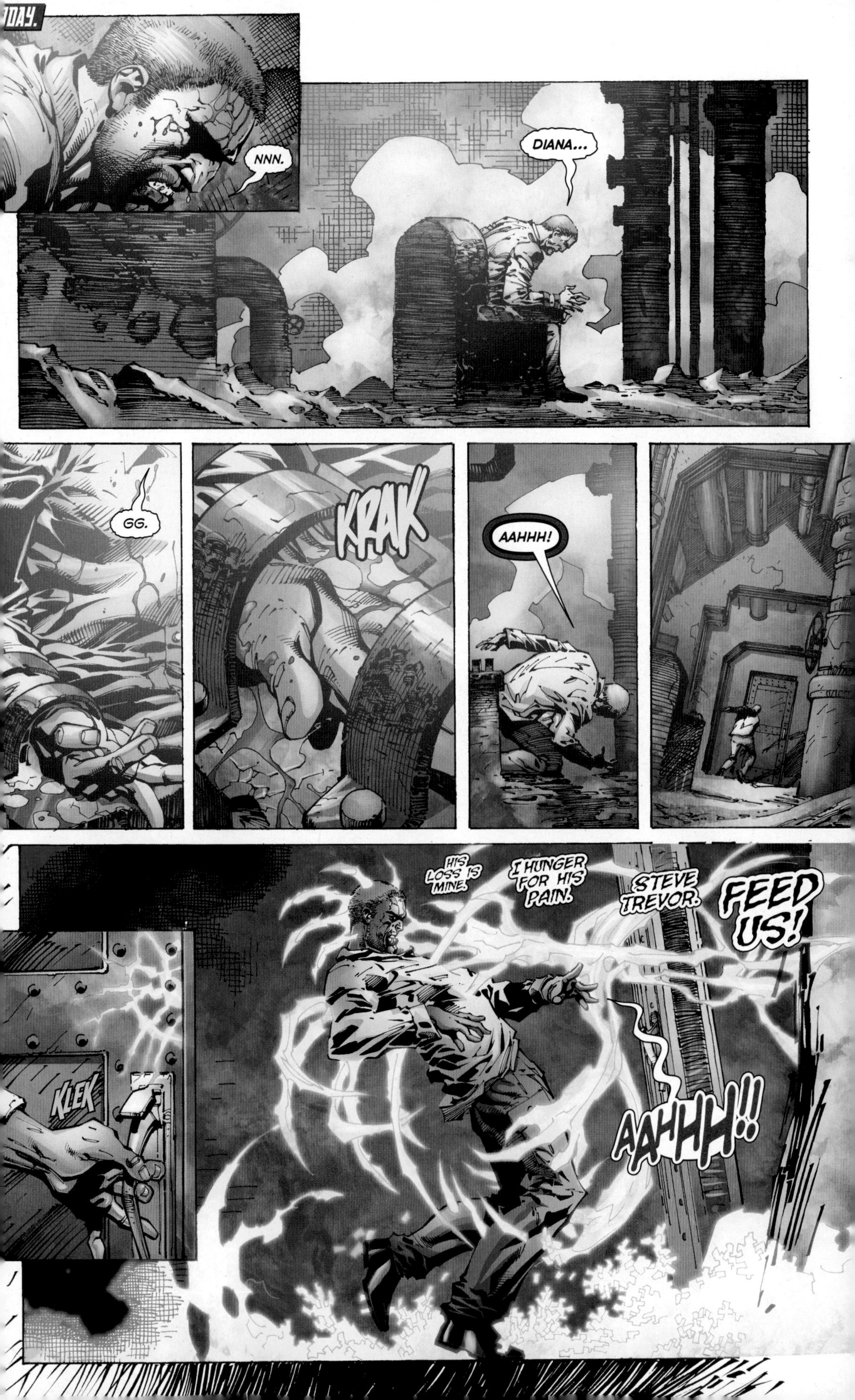

TODAY.
NNN.
DIANA...
GG.
KRAK
AAHHH!
KLEK
HIS LOSS IS MINE.
I HUNGER FOR HIS PAIN.
STEVE TREVOR.
FEED US!
AAHHH!!

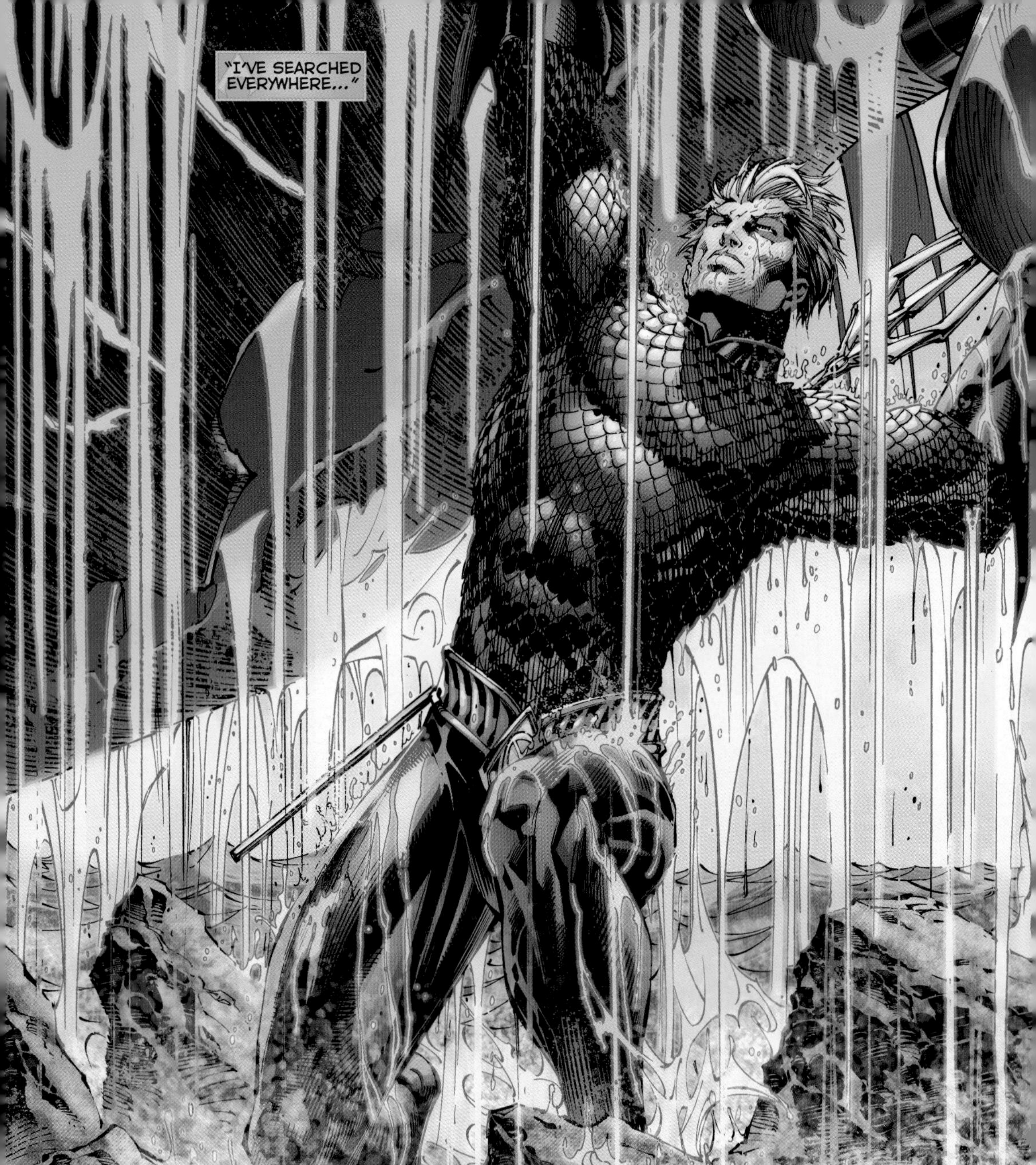
"I'VE SEARCHED EVERYWHERE..."

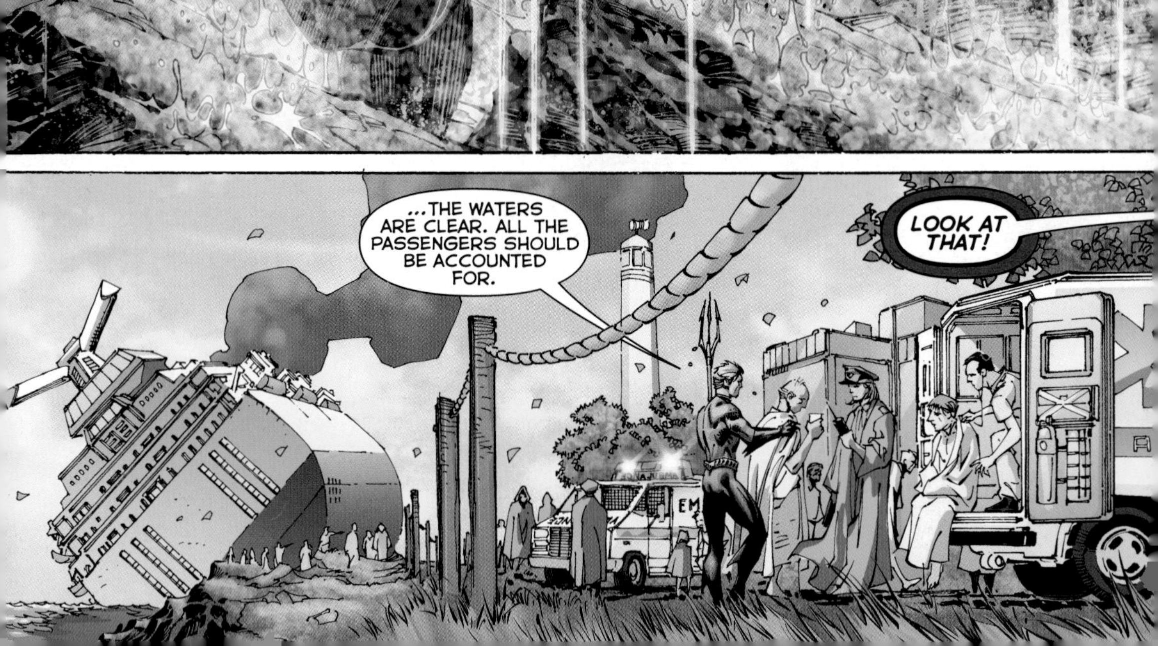
...THE WATERS ARE CLEAR. ALL THE PASSENGERS SHOULD BE ACCOUNTED FOR.
LOOK AT THAT!

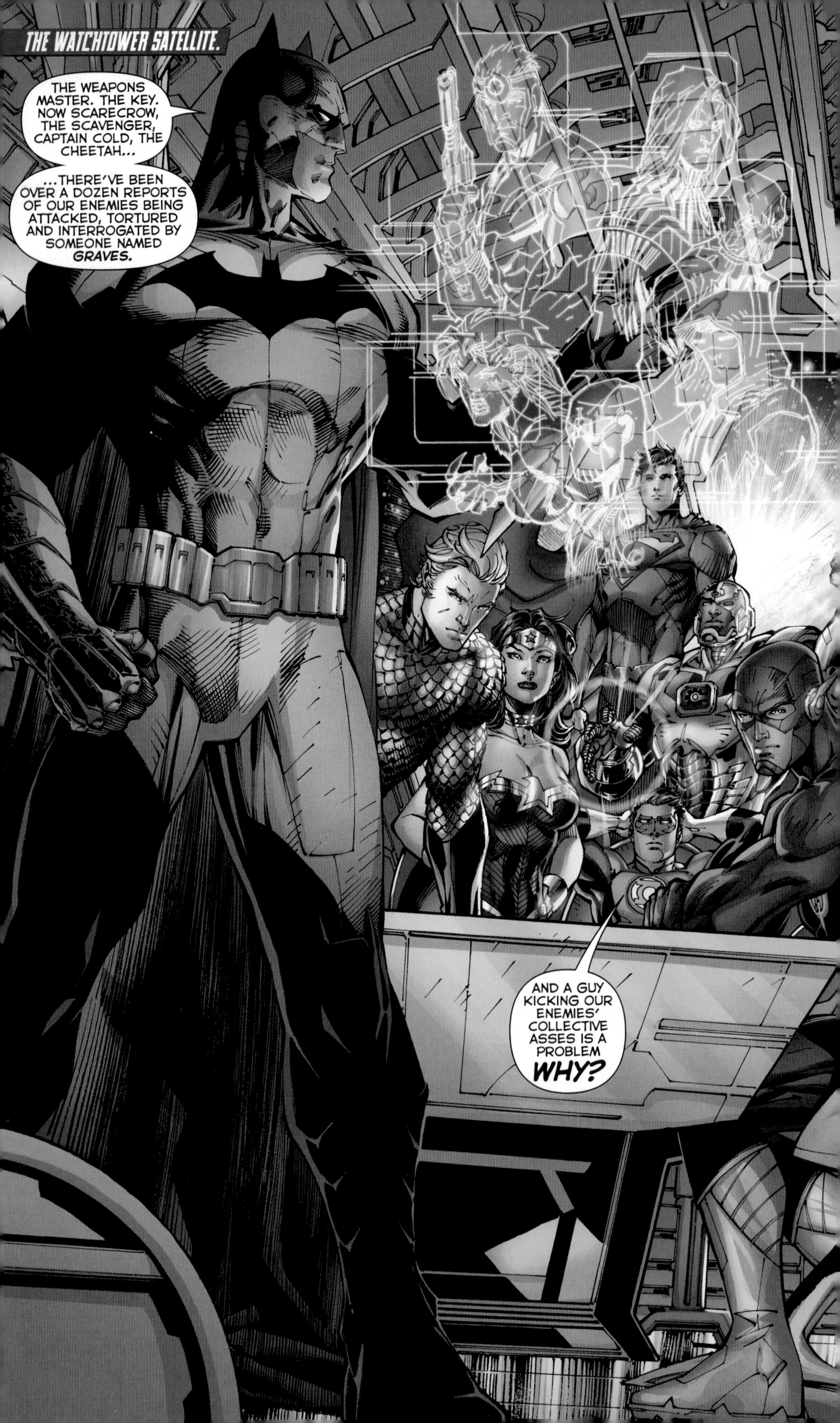
THE WATCHTOWER SATELLITE.
THE WEAPONS MASTER. THE KEY. NOW SCARECROW, THE SCAVENGER, CAPTAIN COLD, THE CHEETAH...
...THERE'VE BEEN OVER A DOZEN REPORTS OF OUR ENEMIES BEING ATTACKED, TORTURED AND INTERROGATED BY SOMEONE NAMED GRAVES.
AND A GUY KICKING OUR ENEMIES' COLLECTIVE ASSES IS A PROBLEM WHY?

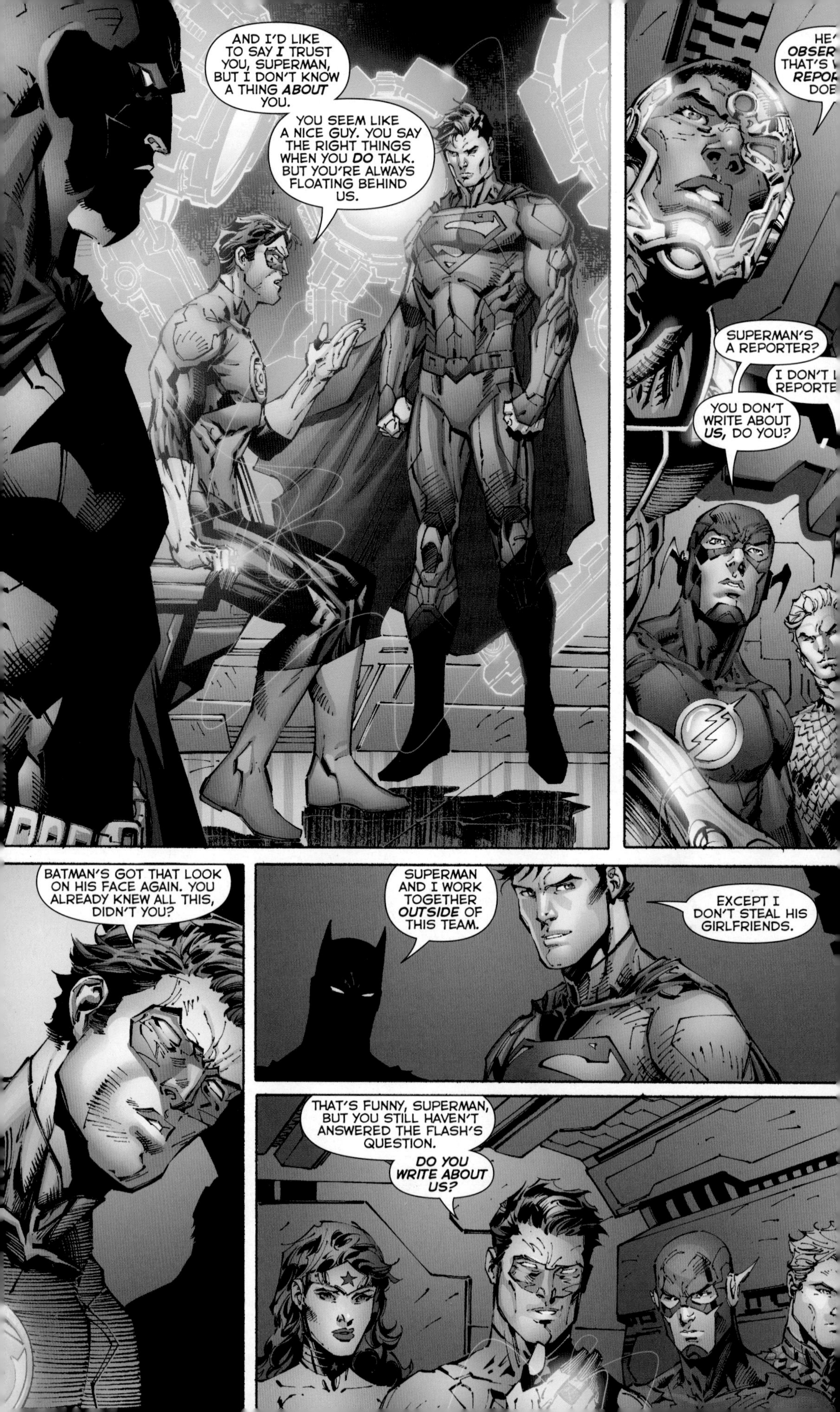
AND I'D LIKE TO SAY *I* TRUST YOU, SUPERMAN, BUT I DON'T KNOW A THING *ABOUT* YOU.
YOU SEEM LIKE A NICE GUY. YOU SAY THE RIGHT THINGS WHEN YOU *DO* TALK. BUT YOU'RE ALWAYS FLOATING BEHIND US.
SUPERMAN'S A REPORTER?
YOU DON'T WRITE ABOUT *US,* DO YOU?
BATMAN'S GOT THAT LOOK ON HIS FACE AGAIN. YOU ALREADY KNEW ALL THIS, DIDN'T YOU?
SUPERMAN AND I WORK TOGETHER *OUTSIDE* OF THIS TEAM.
EXCEPT I DON'T STEAL HIS GIRLFRIENDS.
THAT'S FUNNY, SUPERMAN, BUT YOU STILL HAVEN'T ANSWERED THE FLASH'S QUESTION.
DO YOU WRITE ABOUT US?

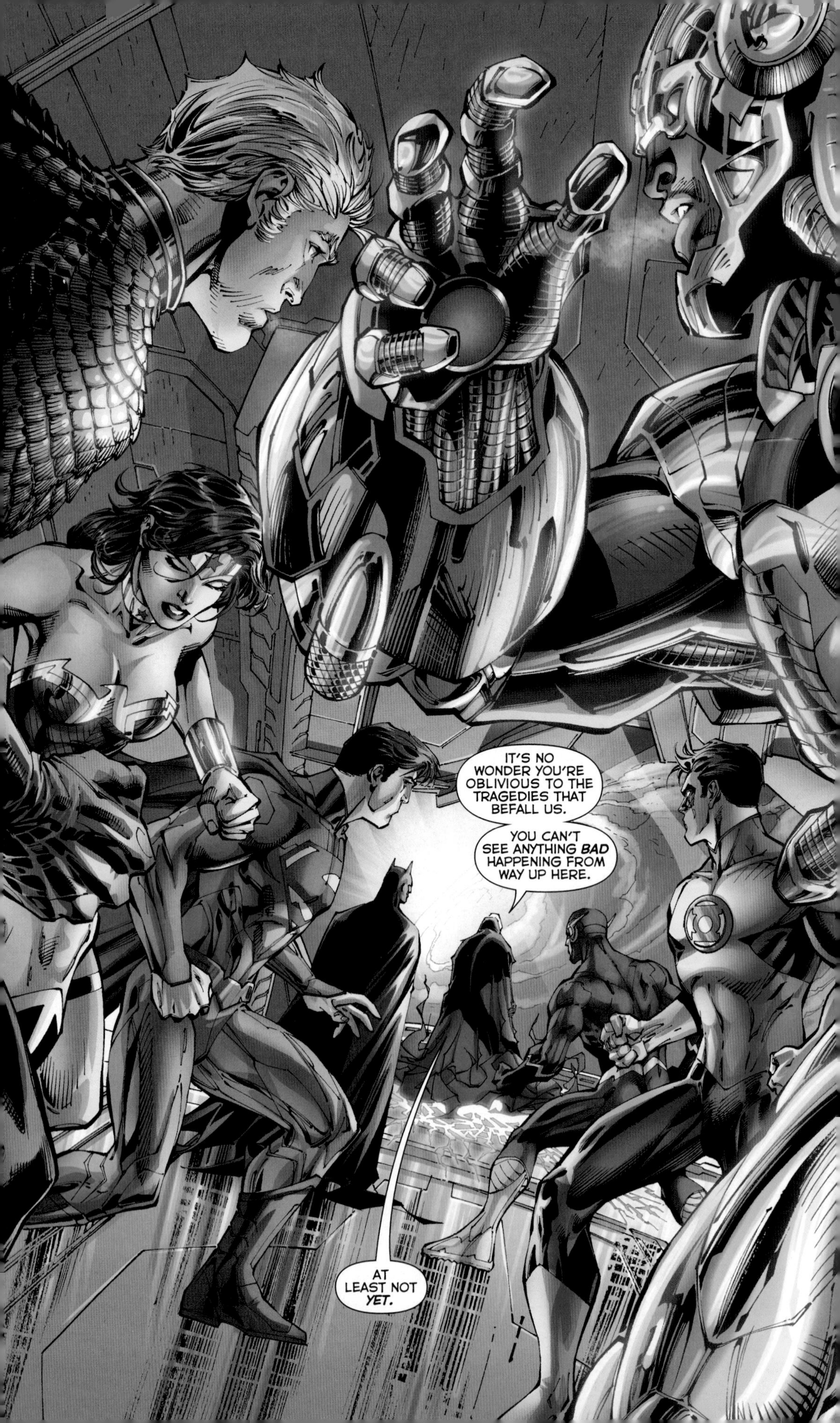
IT'S NO WONDER YOU'RE OBLIVIOUS TO THE TRAGEDIES THAT BEFALL US.
YOU CAN'T SEE ANYTHING *BAD* HAPPENING FROM WAY UP HERE.
AT LEAST NOT *YET.*

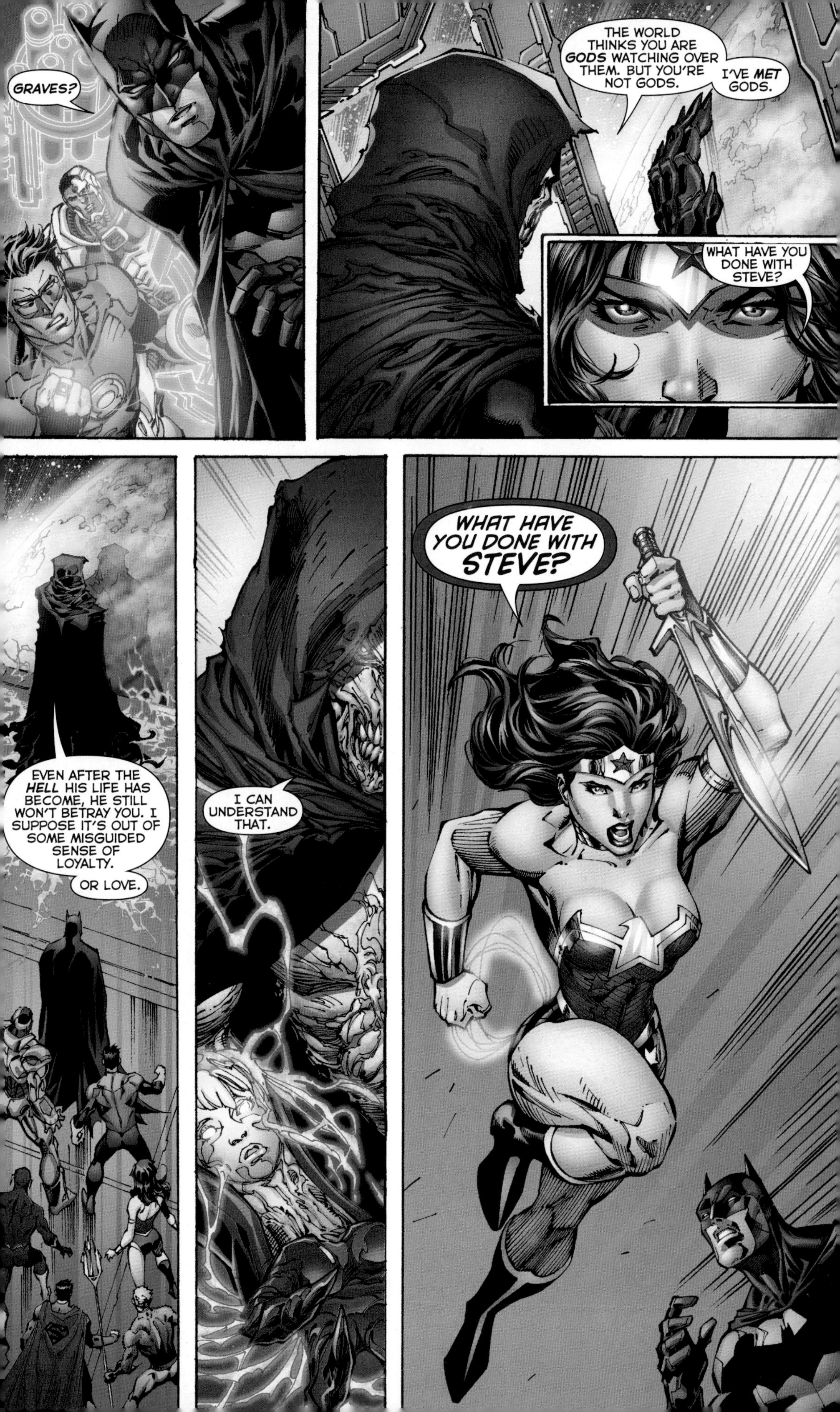
GRAVES?
THE WORLD THINKS YOU ARE GODS WATCHING OVER THEM. BUT YOU'RE NOT GODS.
I'VE MET GODS.
WHAT HAVE YOU DONE WITH STEVE?
EVEN AFTER THE HELL HIS LIFE HAS BECOME, HE STILL WON'T BETRAY YOU. I SUPPOSE IT'S OUT OF SOME MISGUIDED SENSE OF LOYALTY.
OR LOVE.
I CAN UNDERSTAND THAT.
WHAT HAVE YOU DONE WITH STEVE?

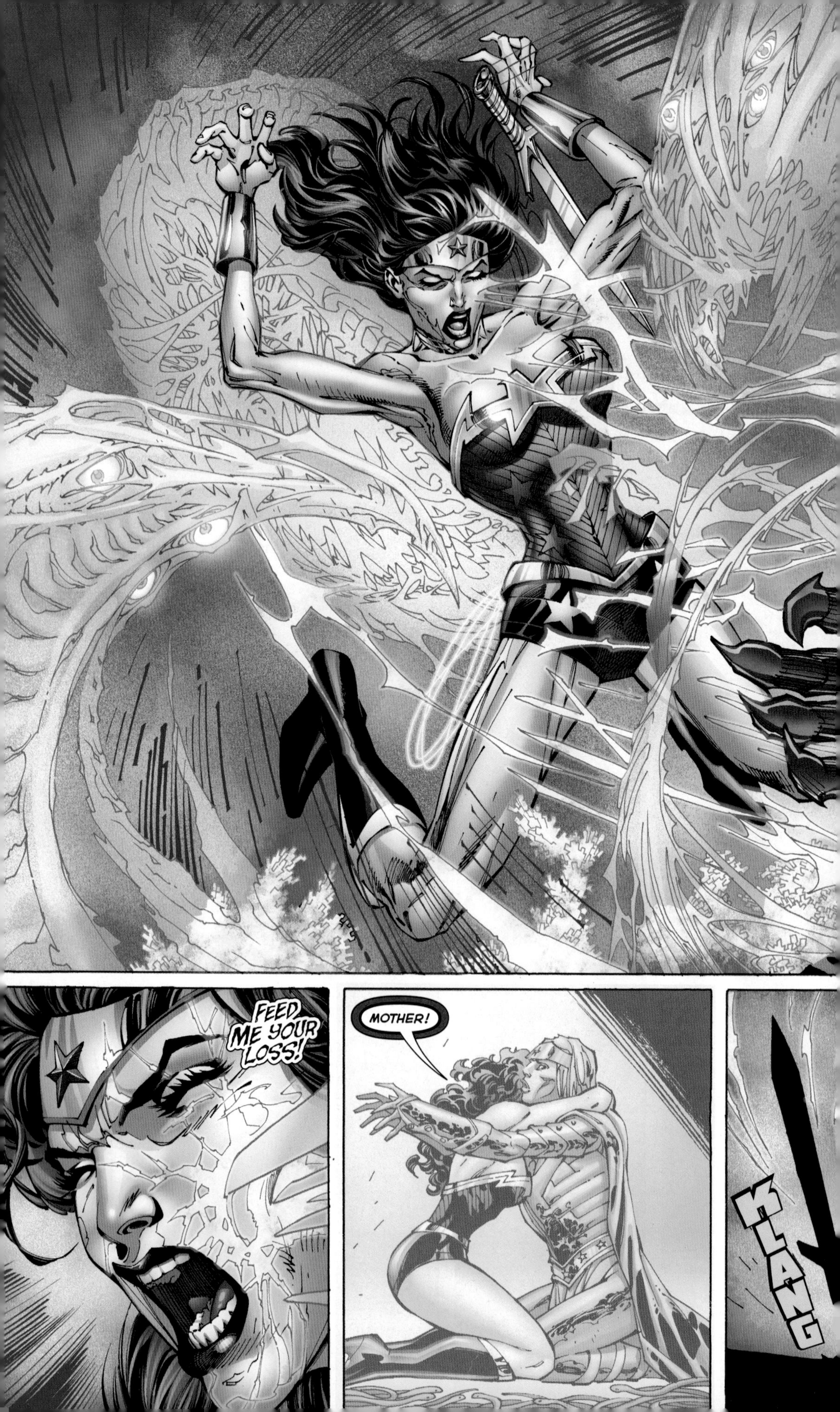
FEED ME YOUR LOSS!
MOTHER!
KLANG

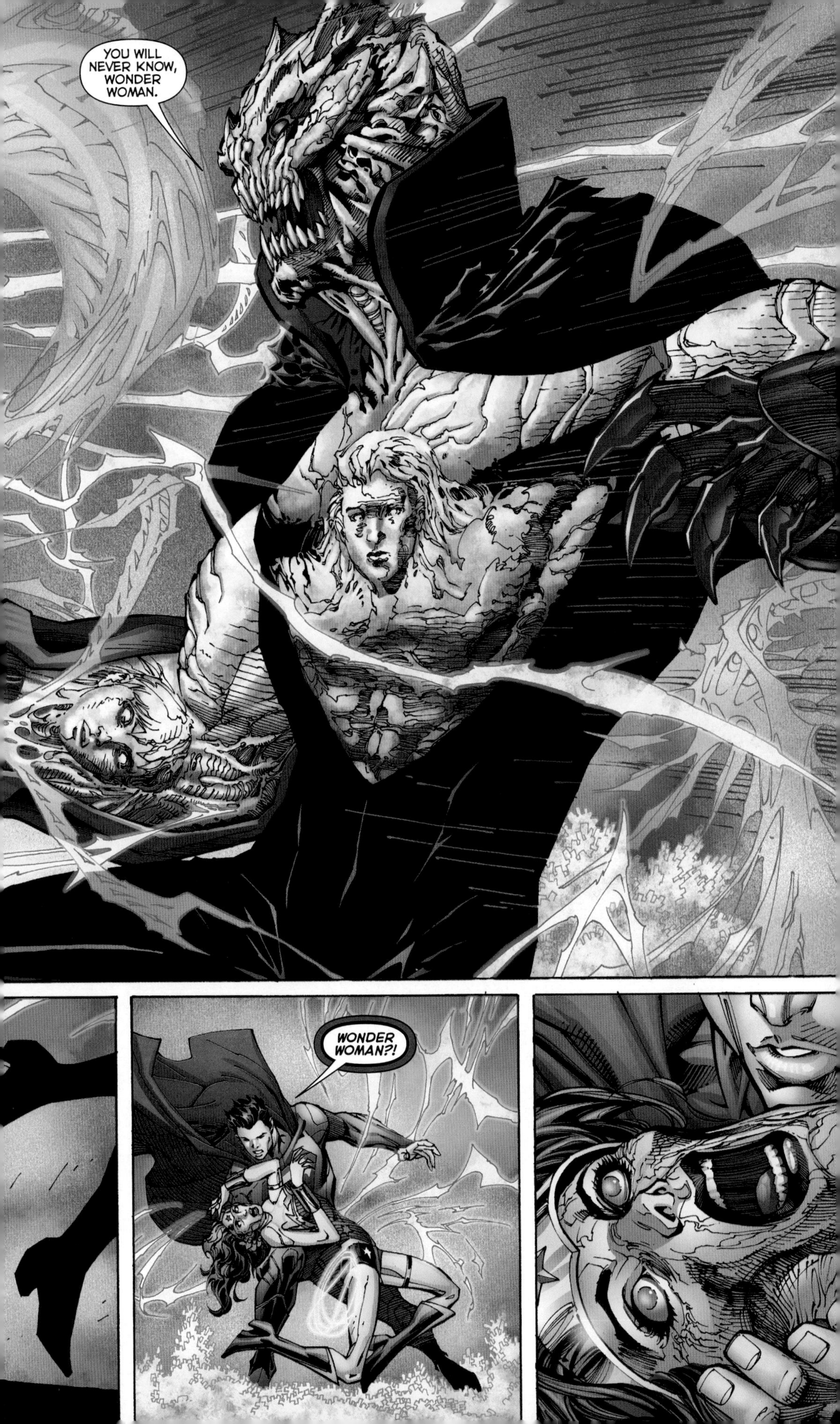
YOU WILL NEVER KNOW, WONDER WOMAN.
WONDER WOMAN?!

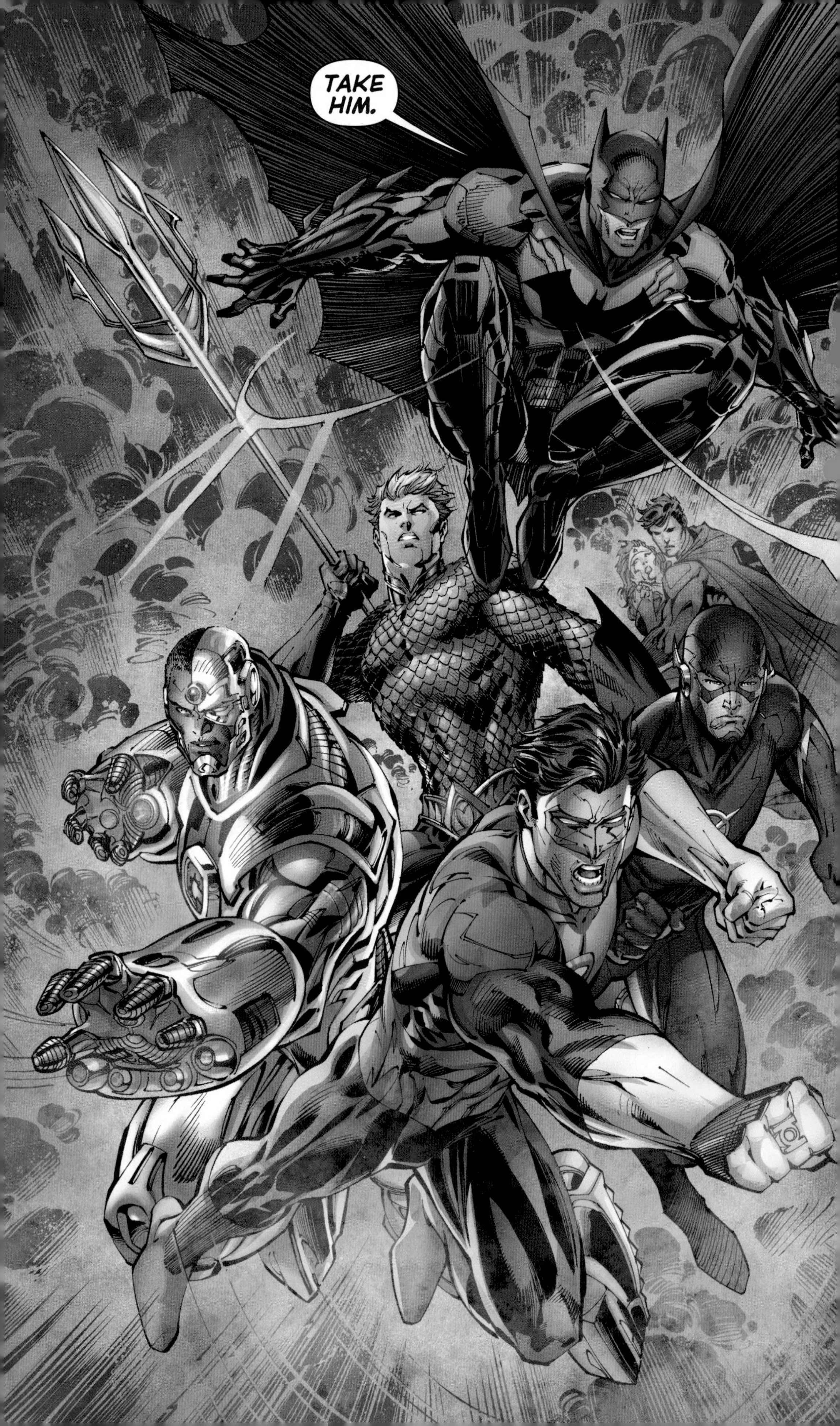
TAKE HIM.

WHAT PAIN DO *YOU* CARRY, GREEN LANTERN? WHAT LOSS RESTS WITHIN YOUR *SOUL?*

OH...

..OH, GOD.

YES.

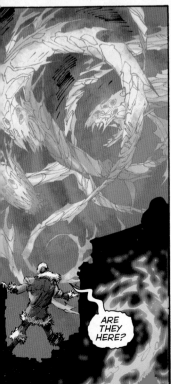

ARE THEY HERE?

WHAT DID YOU DO TO THEM?

WHAT *ARE* THOSE THINGS?

DAVID?

DADDY?!

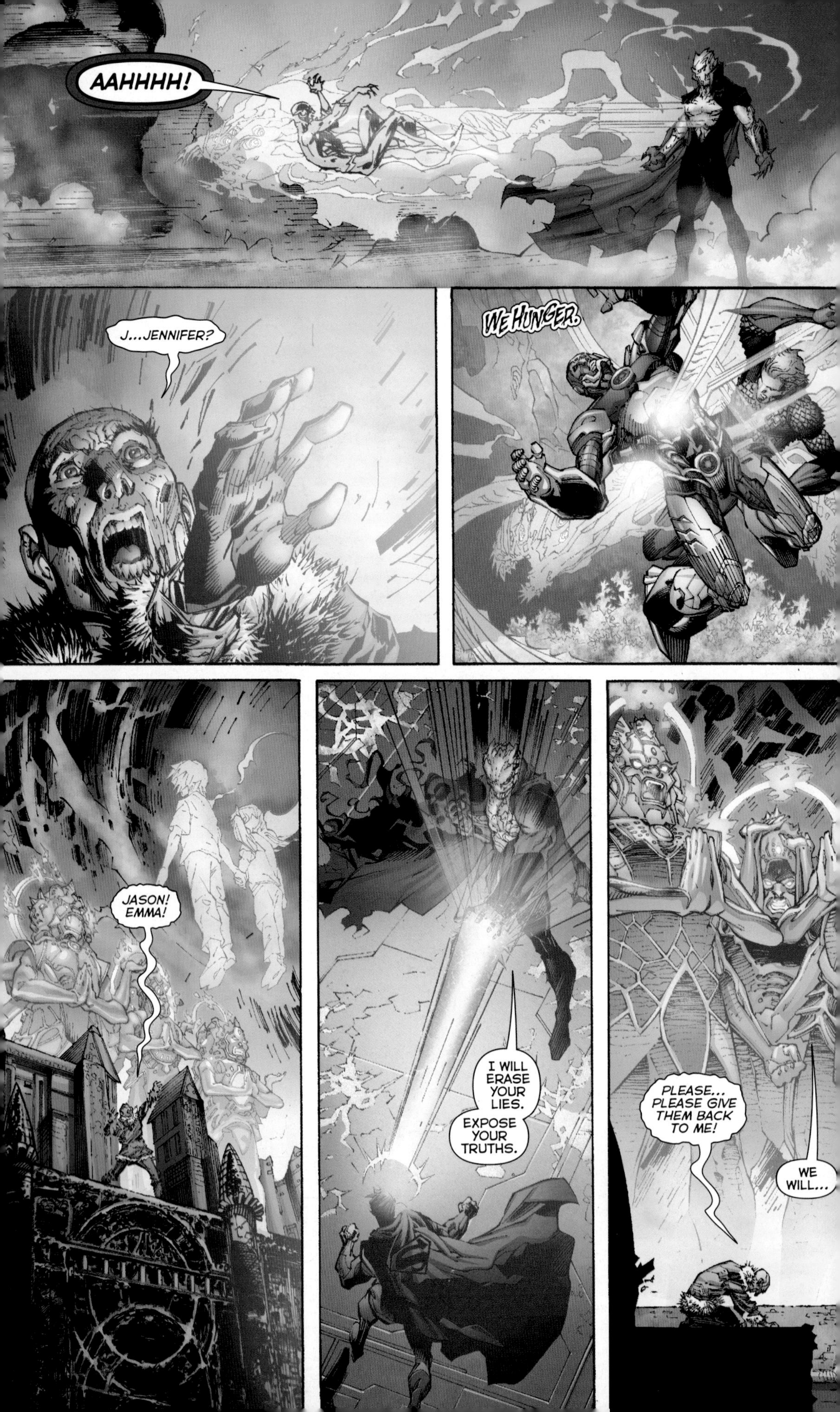
AAHHHH!
J...JENNIFER?
WE HUNGER.
JASON! EMMA!
I WILL ERASE YOUR LIES.
EXPOSE YOUR TRUTHS.
PLEASE... PLEASE GIVE THEM BACK TO ME!
WE WILL...

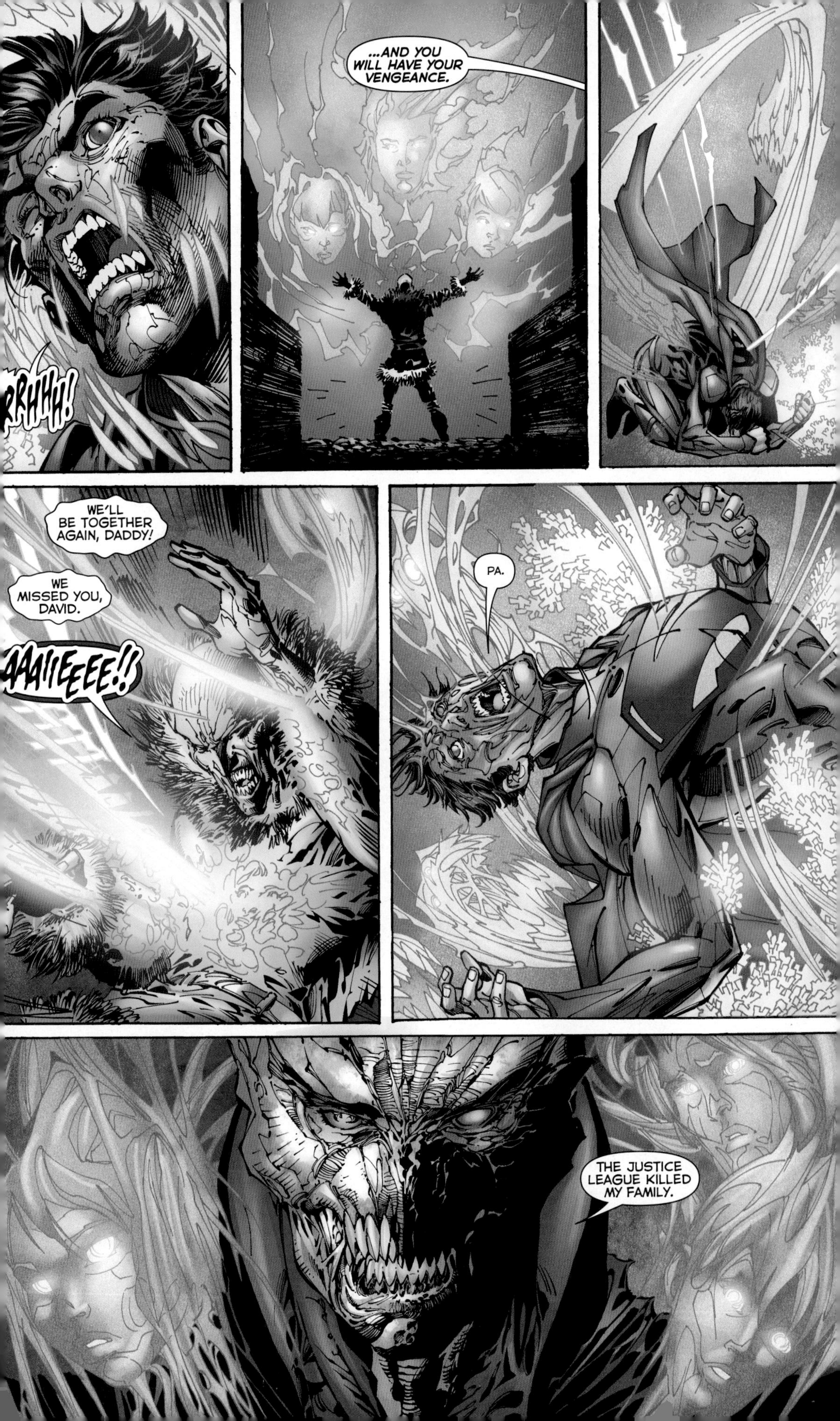
RHHH!
...AND YOU WILL HAVE YOUR VENGEANCE.
WE'LL BE TOGETHER AGAIN, DADDY!
WE MISSED YOU, DAVID.
AAIIEEEE!!
PA.
THE JUSTICE LEAGUE KILLED MY FAMILY.

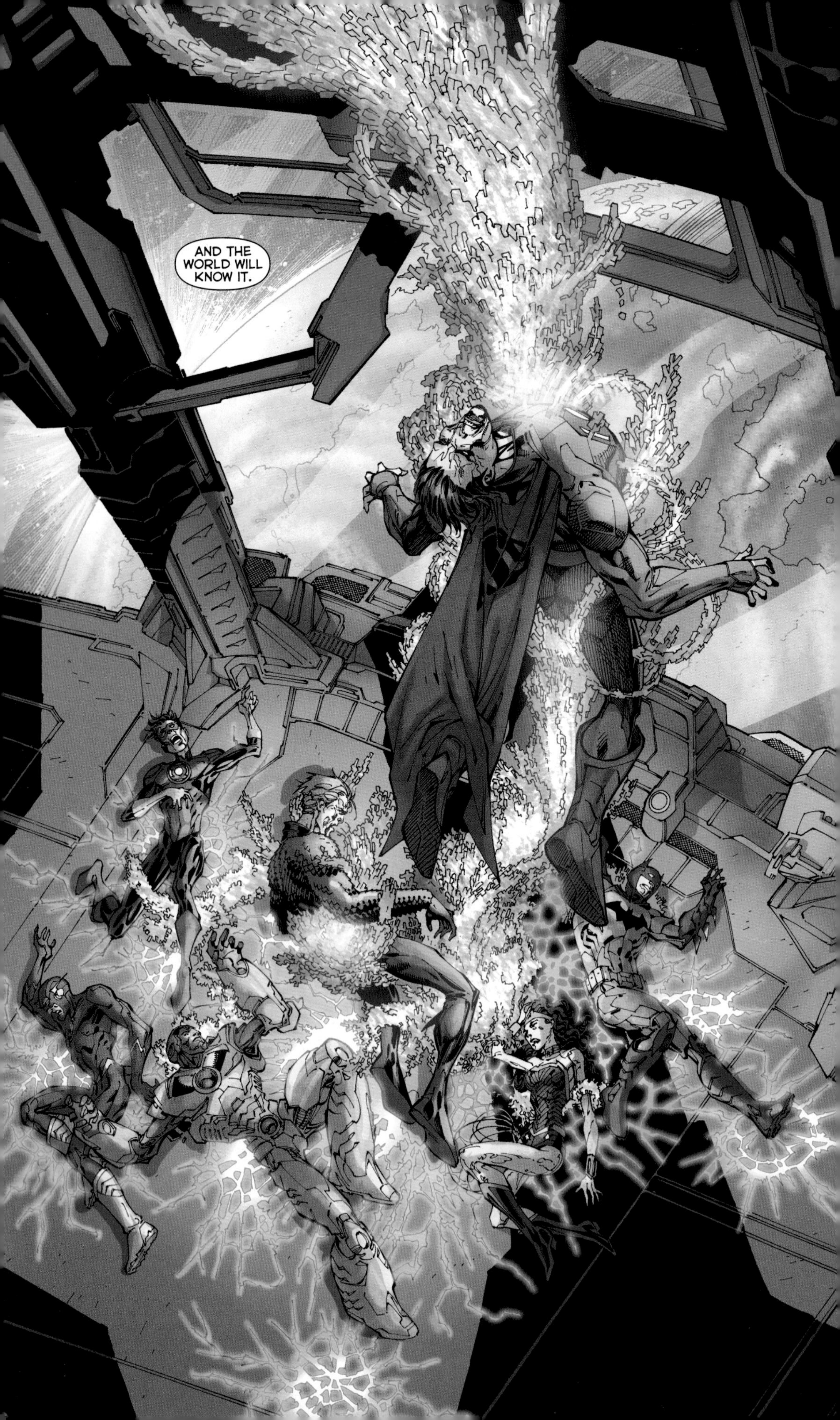
AND THE WORLD WILL KNOW IT.

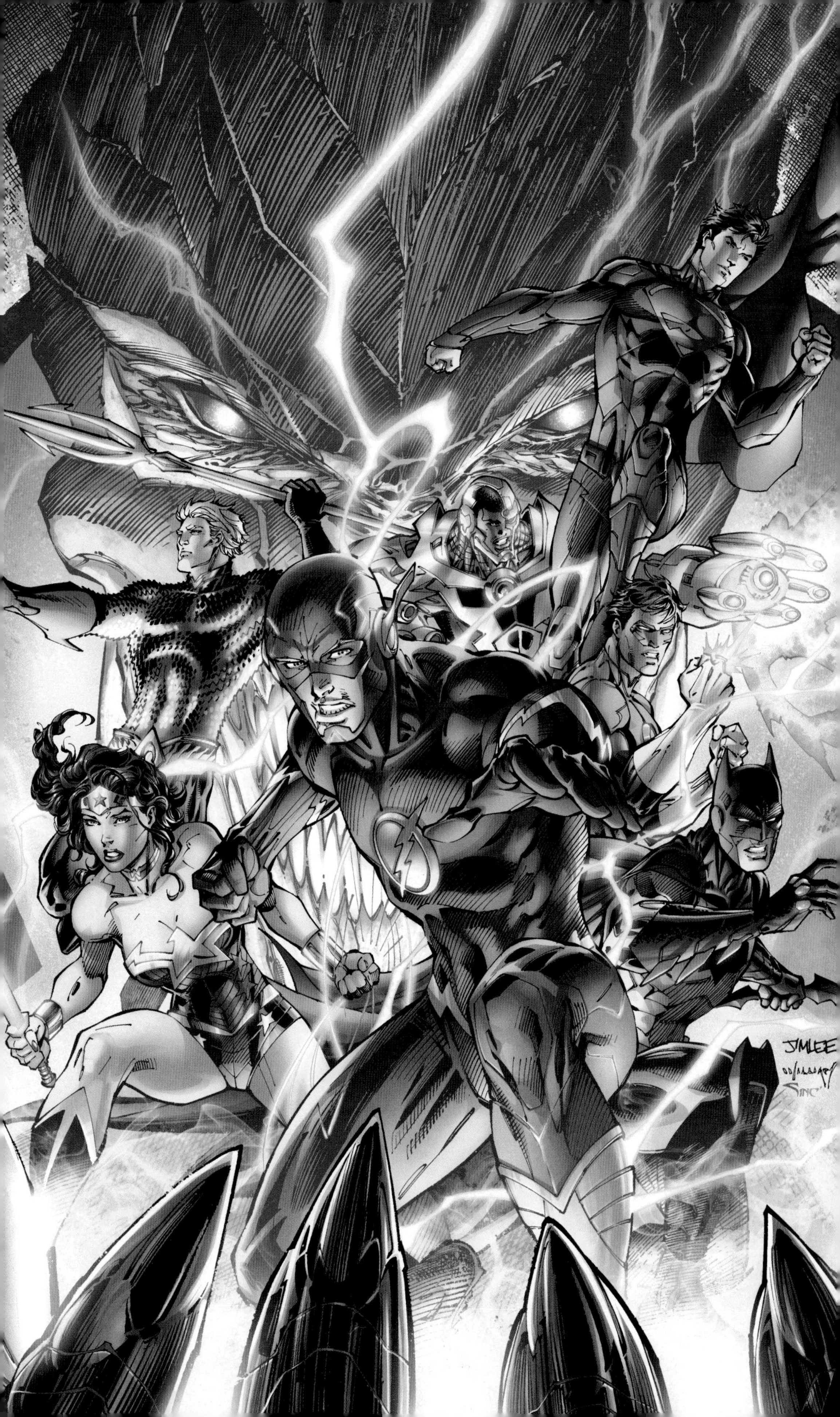

GEOFF JOHNS writer JIM LEE penciller SCOTT WILLIAMS & JONATHAN GLAPION inkers cover by JIM LEE, SCOTT WILLIAMS & ALEX SINCLAIR

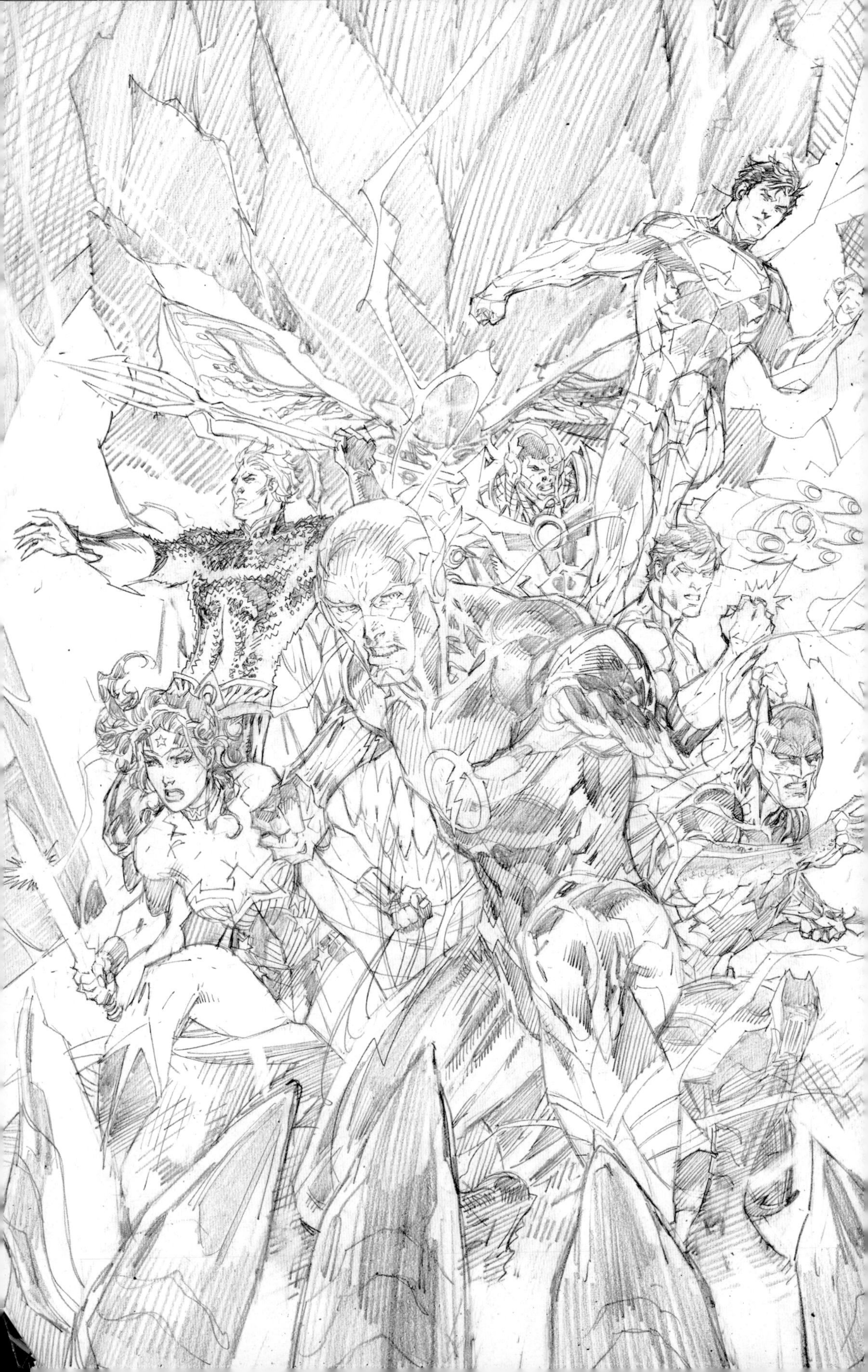

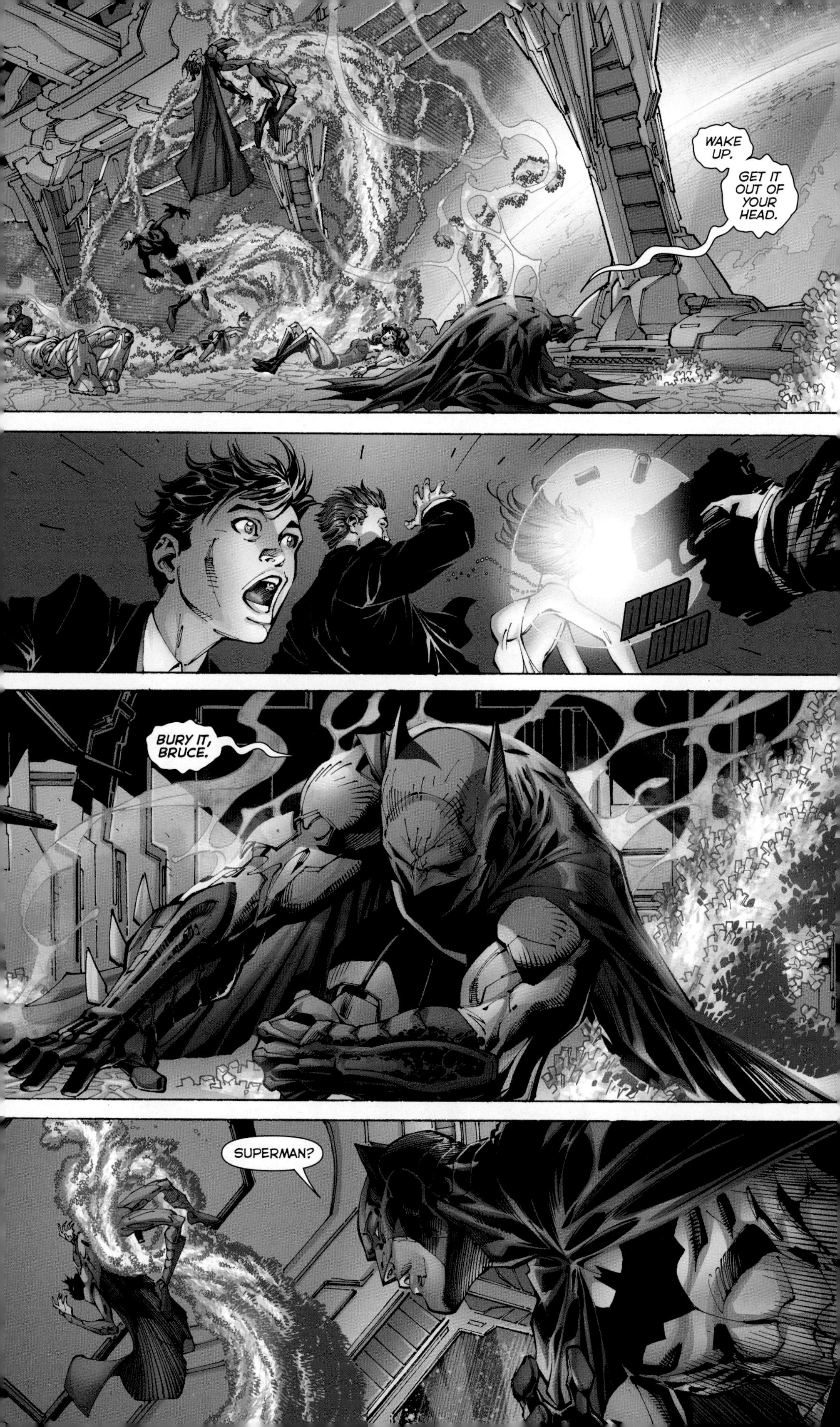
WAKE UP.
GET IT OUT OF YOUR HEAD.
BLAM BLAM
BURY IT, BRUCE.
SUPERMAN?

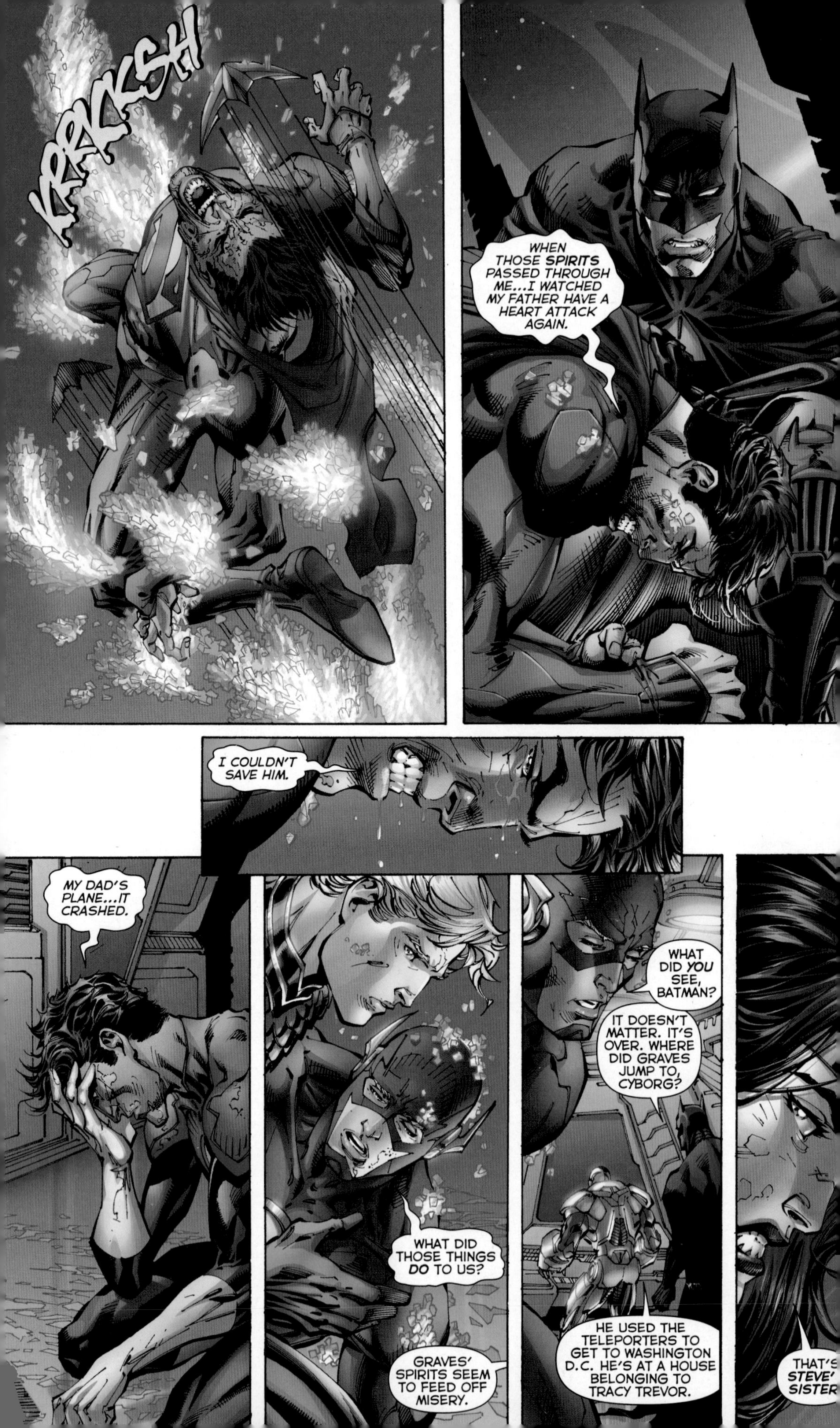
KRRKSH
WHEN THOSE SPIRITS PASSED THROUGH ME...I WATCHED MY FATHER HAVE A HEART ATTACK AGAIN.
I COULDN'T SAVE HIM.
MY DAD'S PLANE...IT CRASHED.
WHAT DID THOSE THINGS DO TO US?
GRAVES' SPIRITS SEEM TO FEED OFF MISERY.
WHAT DID YOU SEE, BATMAN?
IT DOESN'T MATTER. IT'S OVER. WHERE DID GRAVES JUMP TO, CYBORG?
HE USED THE TELEPORTERS TO GET TO WASHINGTON D.C. HE'S AT A HOUSE BELONGING TO TRACY TREVOR.
THAT'S STEVE' SISTER

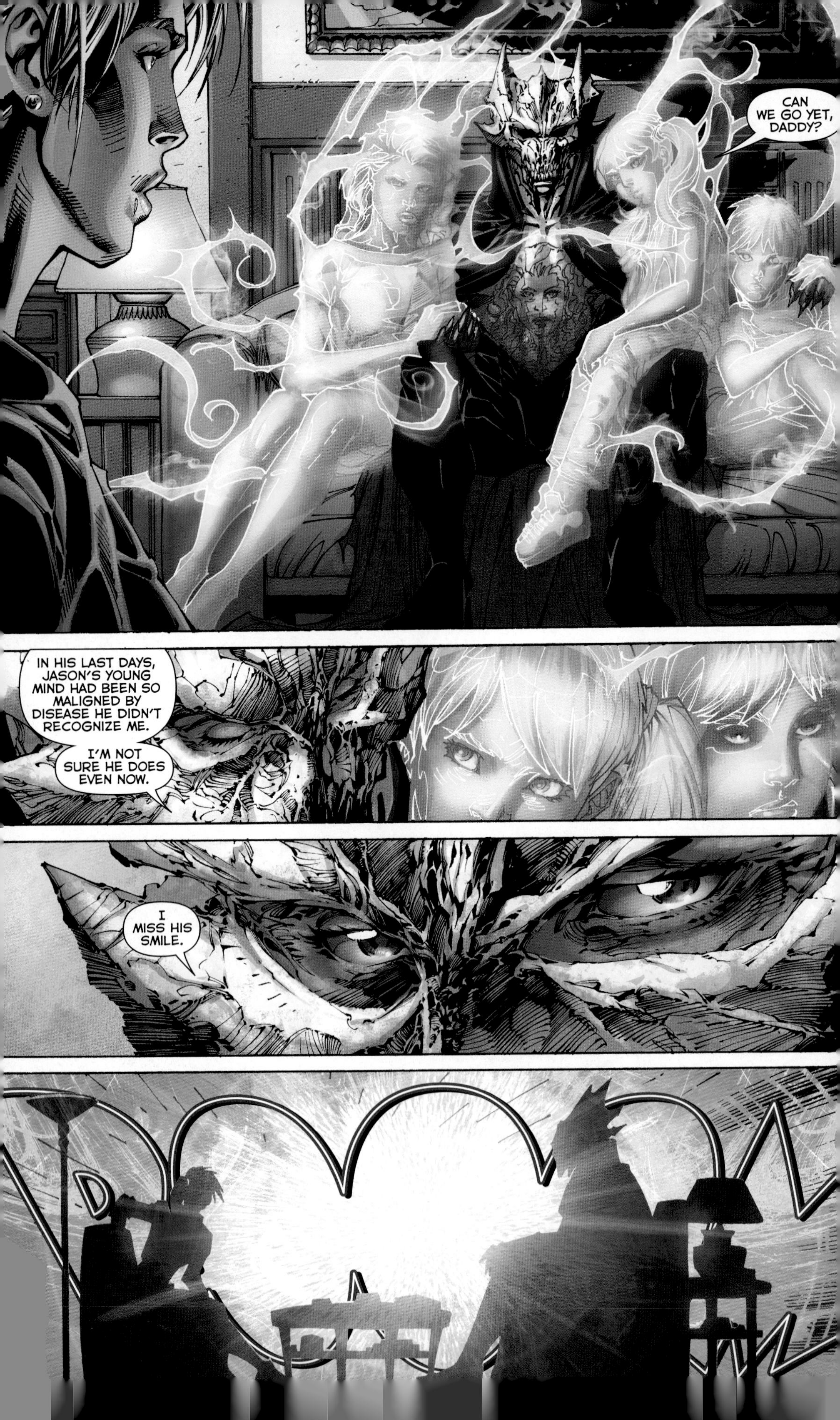
CAN WE GO YET, DADDY?
IN HIS LAST DAYS, JASON'S YOUNG MIND HAD BEEN SO MALIGNED BY DISEASE HE DIDN'T RECOGNIZE ME.
I'M NOT SURE HE DOES EVEN NOW.
I MISS HIS SMILE.

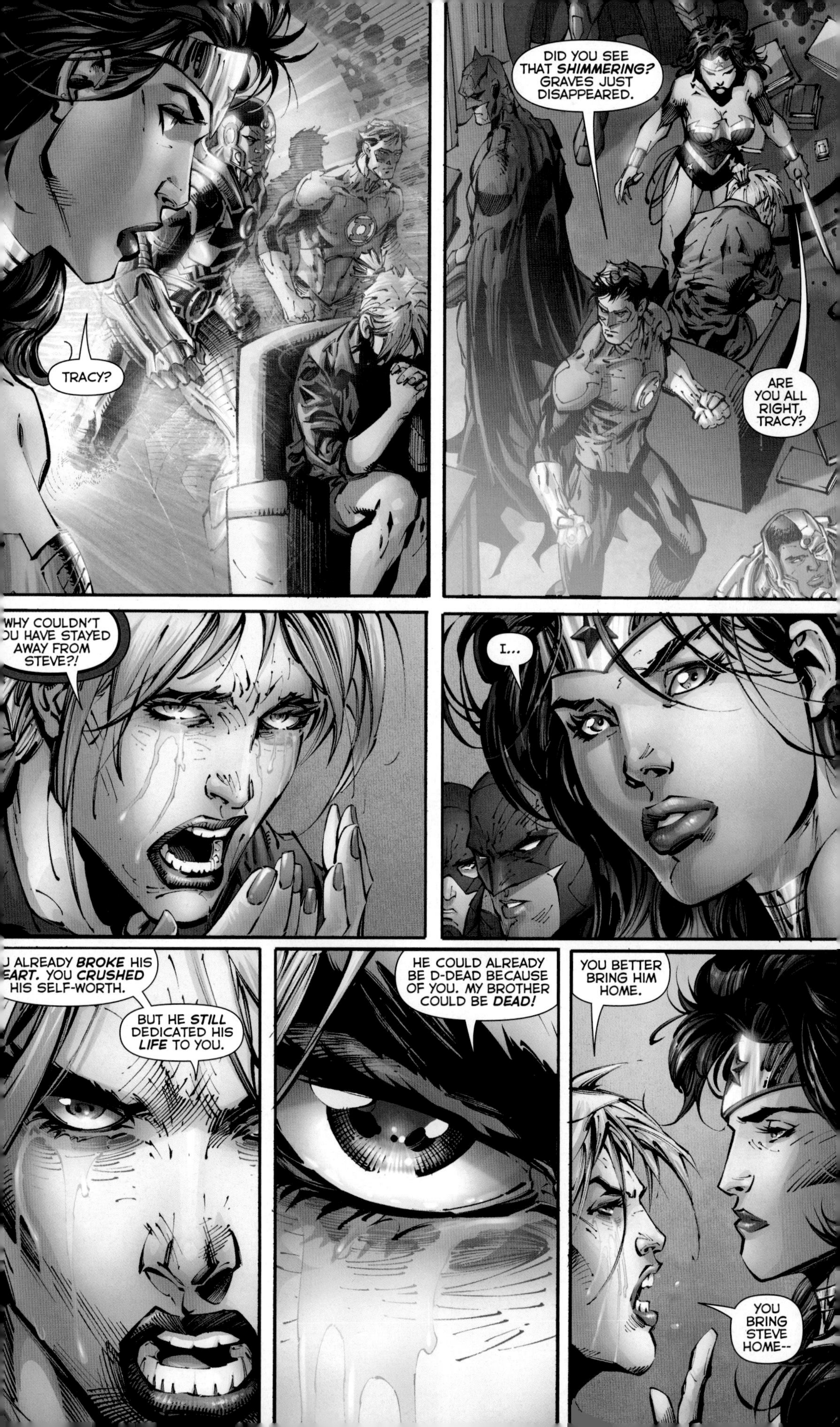
TRACY?
DID YOU SEE THAT SHIMMERING? GRAVES JUST DISAPPEARED.
ARE YOU ALL RIGHT, TRACY?
WHY COULDN'T OU HAVE STAYED AWAY FROM STEVE?!
I...
U ALREADY BROKE HIS EART. YOU CRUSHED HIS SELF-WORTH.
BUT HE STILL DEDICATED HIS LIFE TO YOU.
HE COULD ALREADY BE D-DEAD BECAUSE OF YOU. MY BROTHER COULD BE DEAD!
YOU BETTER BRING HIM HOME.
YOU BRING STEVE HOME--

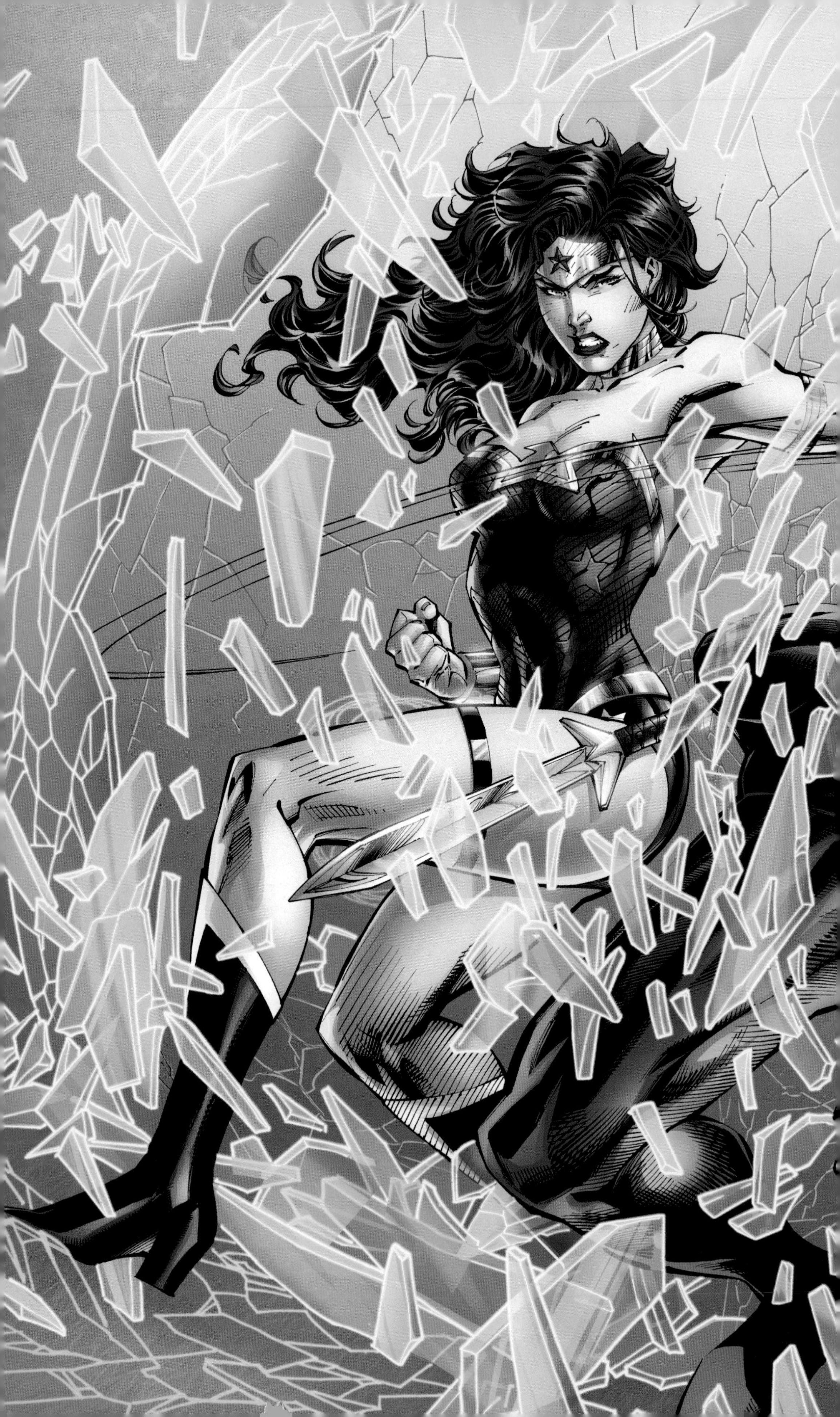

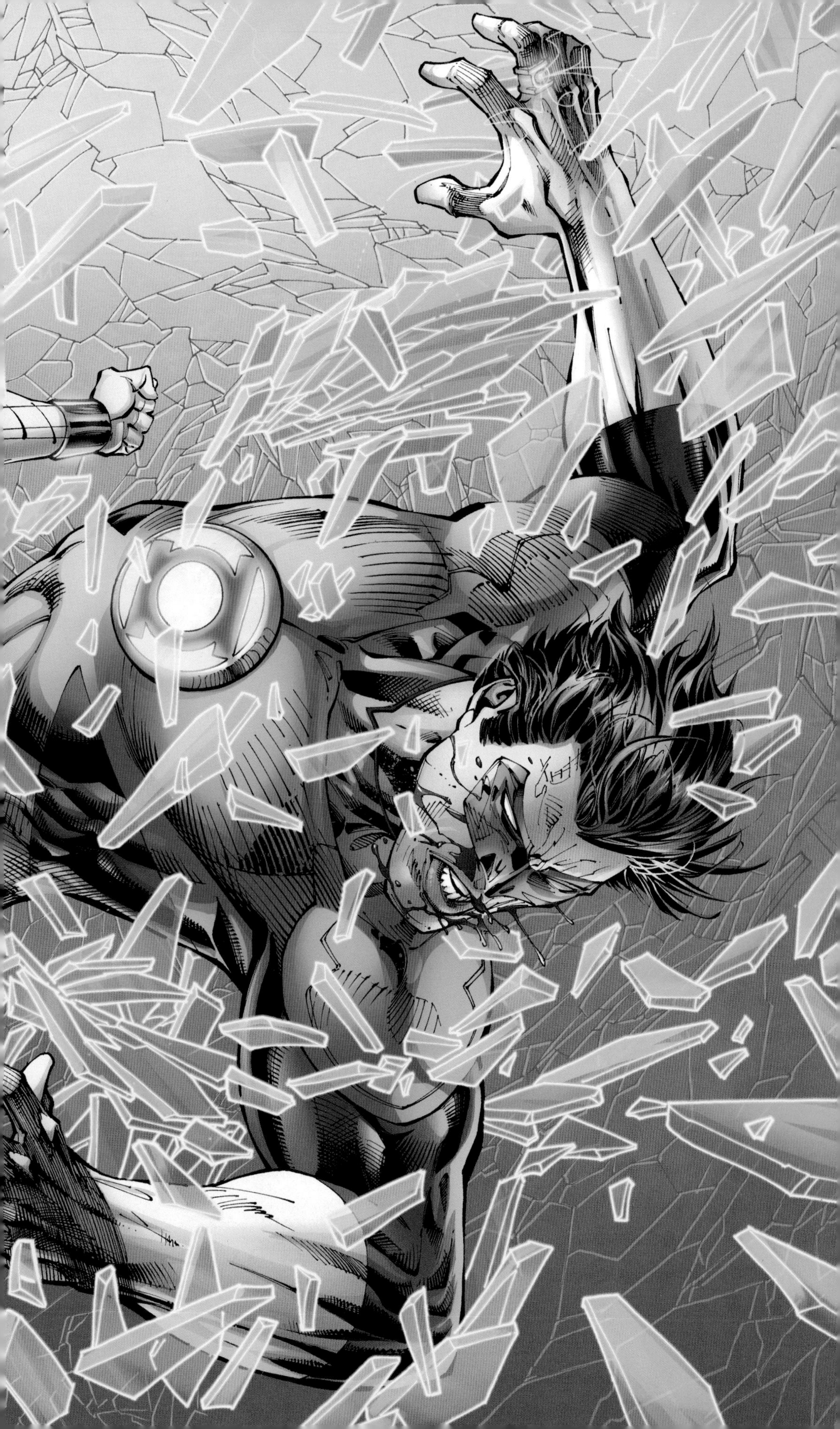

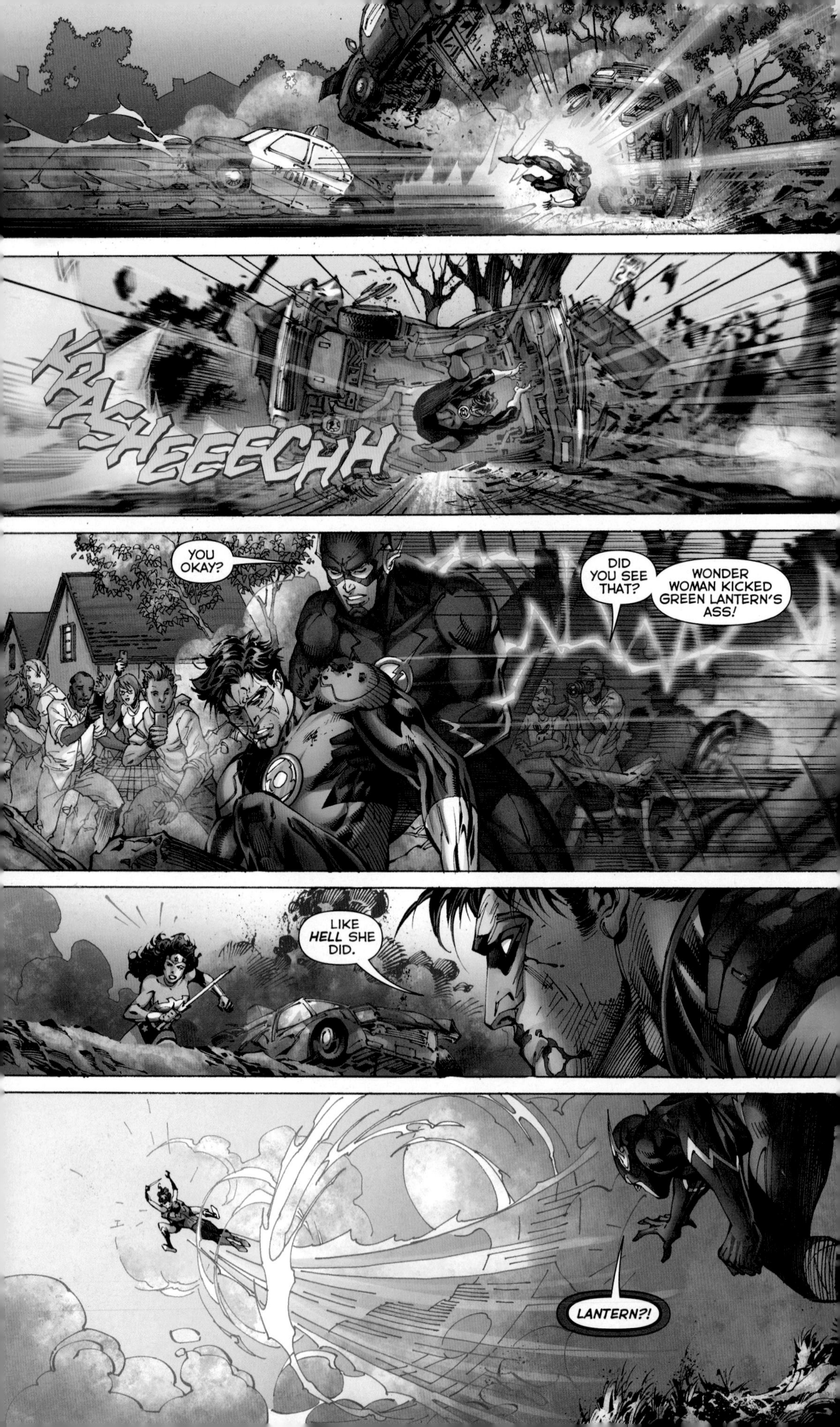
KRASHEEEECHH
YOU OKAY?
DID YOU SEE THAT?
WONDER WOMAN KICKED GREEN LANTERN'S ASS!
LIKE *HELL* SHE DID.
LANTERN?!

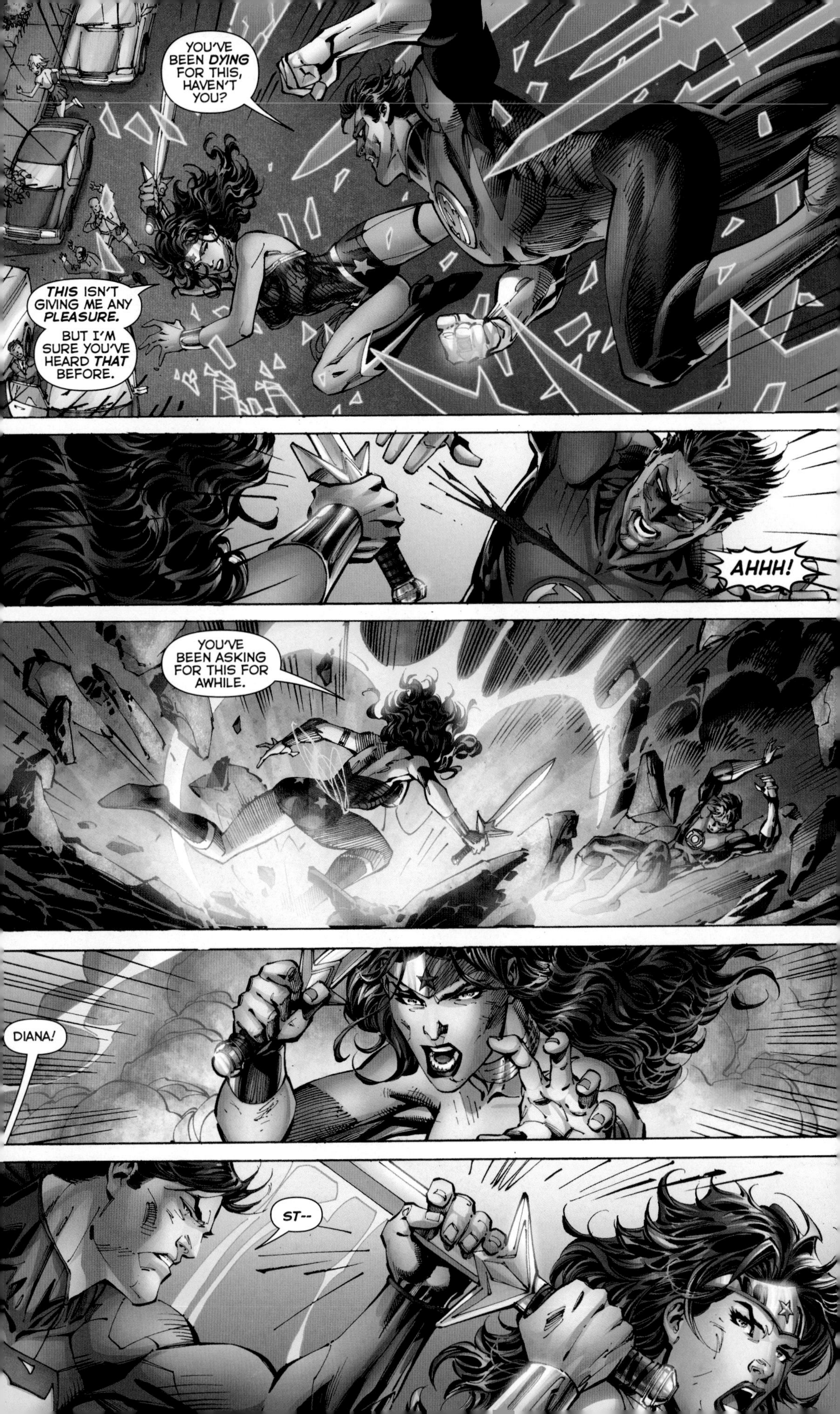
YOU'VE BEEN *DYING* FOR THIS, HAVEN'T YOU?
THIS ISN'T GIVING ME ANY *PLEASURE.*
BUT I'M SURE YOU'VE HEARD *THAT* BEFORE.
AHHH!
YOU'VE BEEN ASKING FOR THIS FOR AWHILE.
DIANA!
ST--

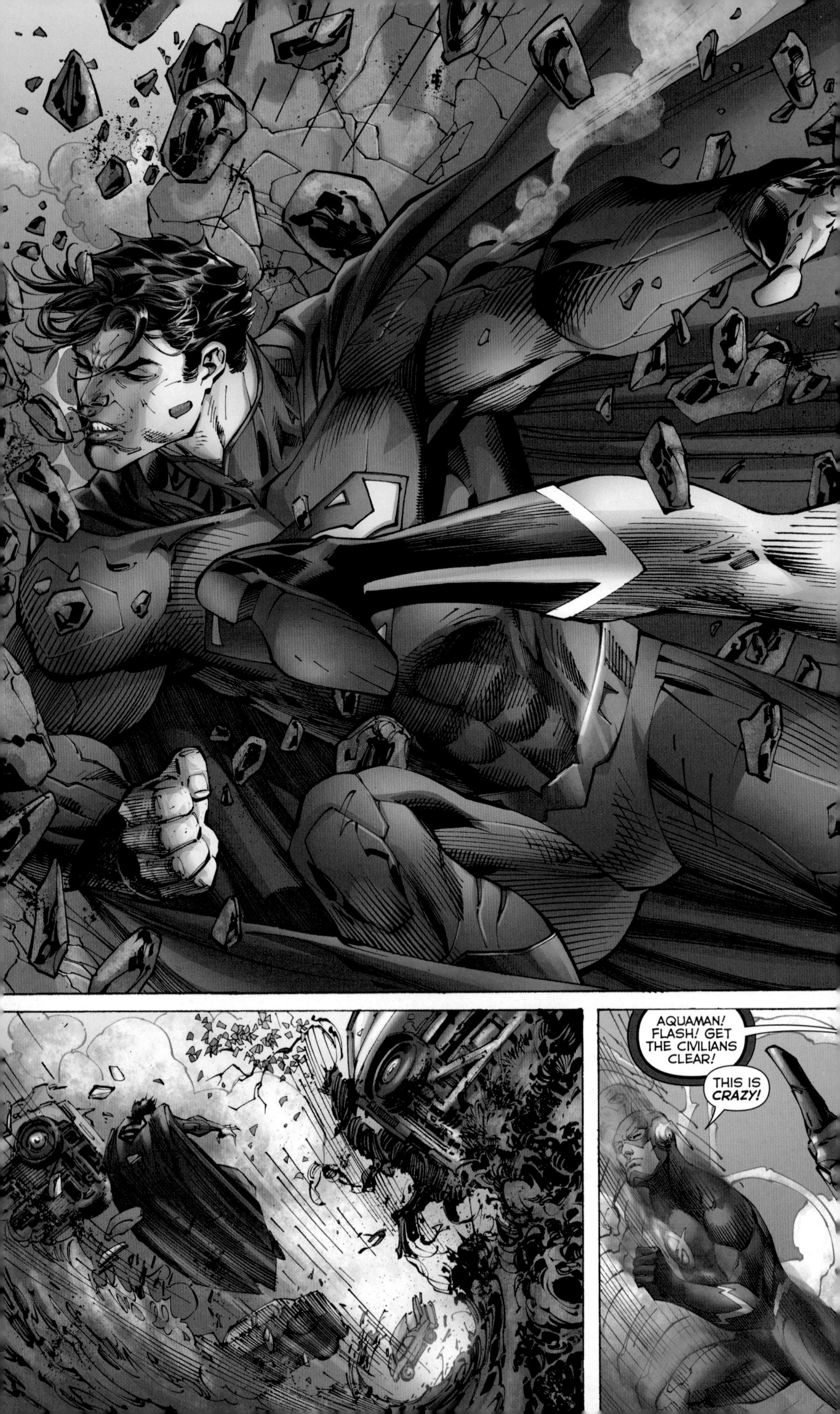
AQUAMAN! FLASH! GET THE CIVILIANS CLEAR!
THIS IS *CRAZY!*

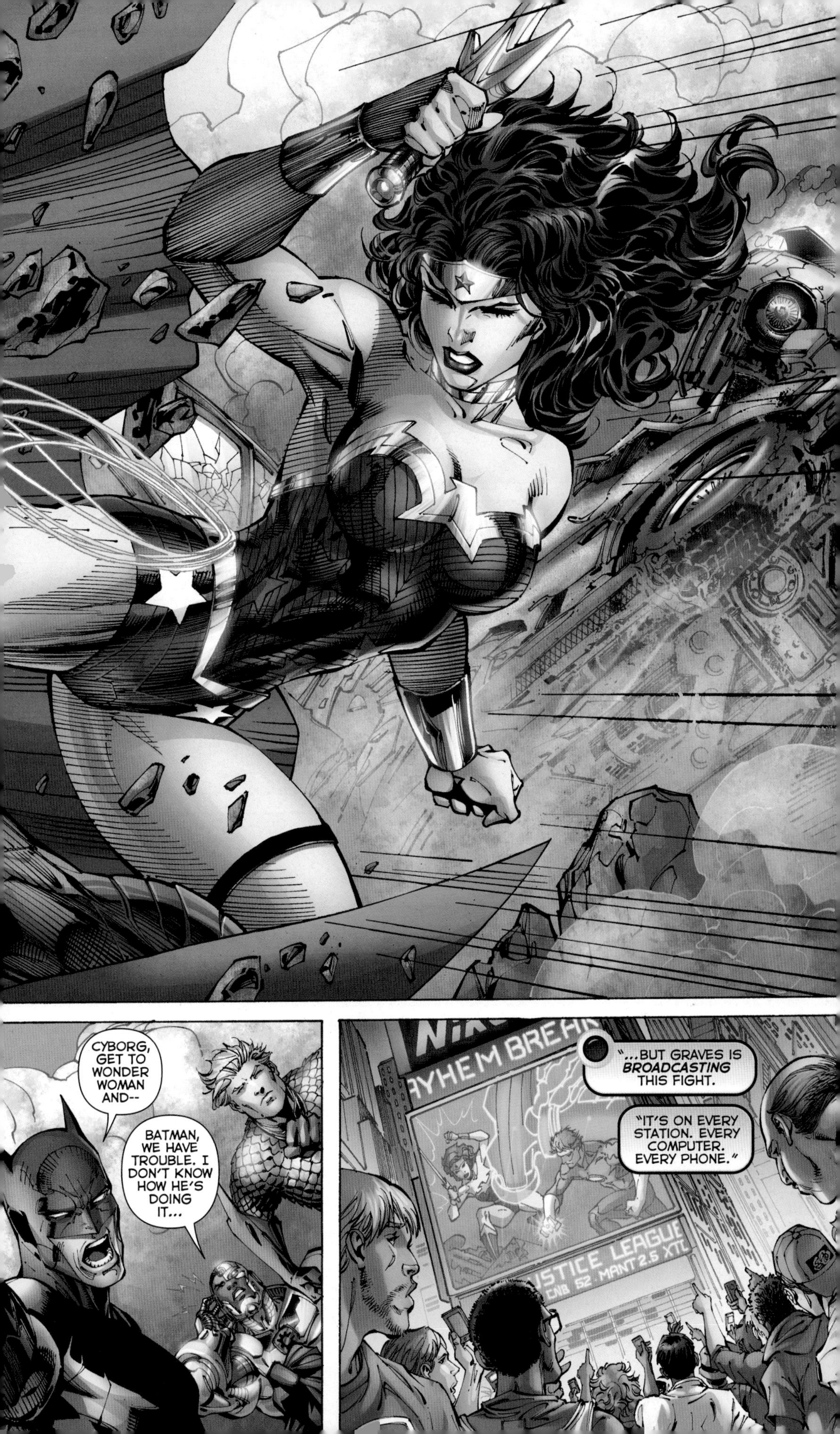
CYBORG, GET TO WONDER WOMAN AND--
BATMAN, WE HAVE TROUBLE. I DON'T KNOW HOW HE'S DOING IT...
"...BUT GRAVES IS BROADCASTING THIS FIGHT.
"IT'S ON EVERY STATION. EVERY COMPUTER. EVERY PHONE."
JUSTICE LEAGUE

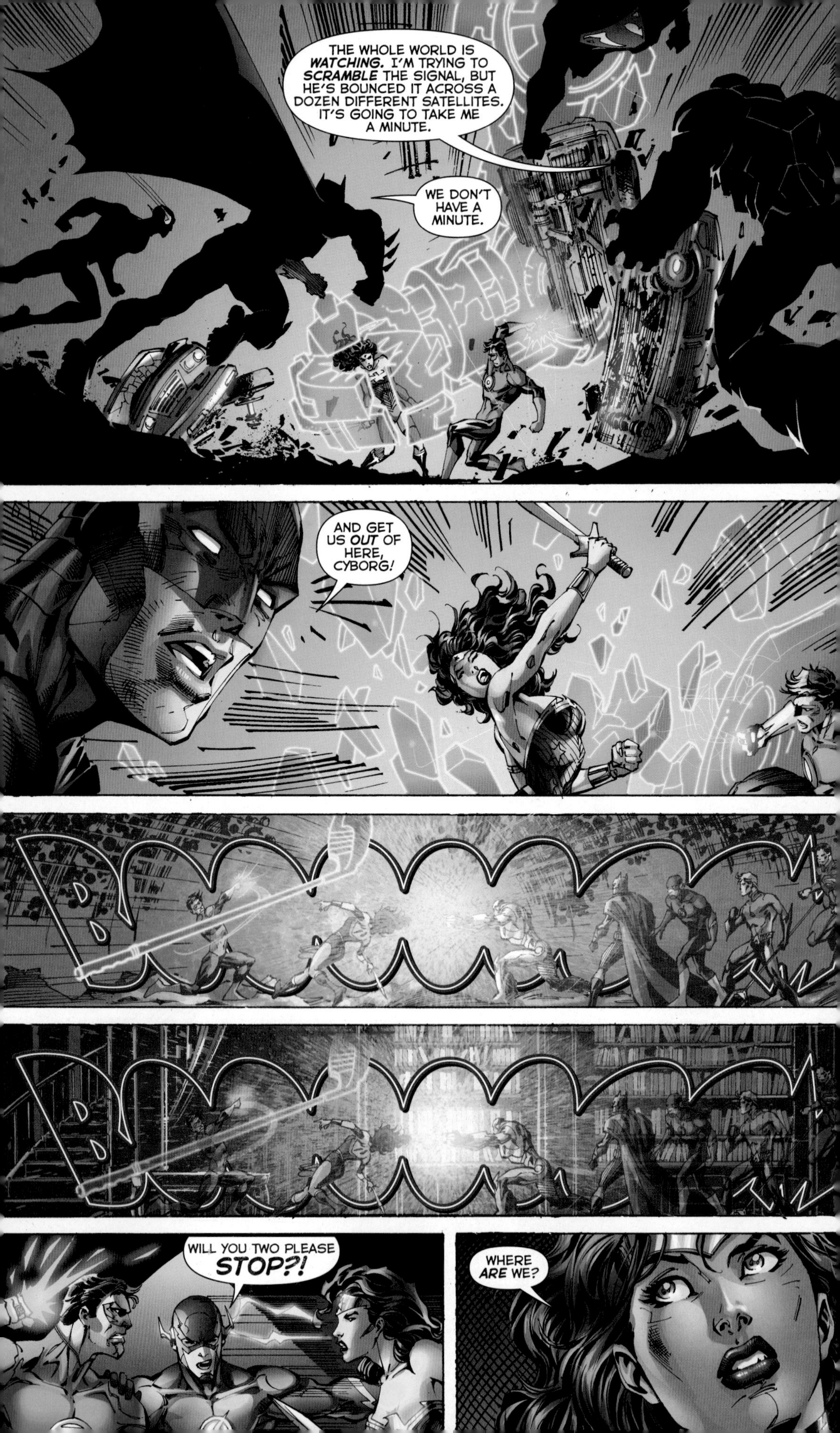
THE WHOLE WORLD IS WATCHING. I'M TRYING TO SCRAMBLE THE SIGNAL, BUT HE'S BOUNCED IT ACROSS A DOZEN DIFFERENT SATELLITES. IT'S GOING TO TAKE ME A MINUTE.
WE DON'T HAVE A MINUTE.
AND GET US OUT OF HERE, CYBORG!
WILL YOU TWO PLEASE STOP?!
WHERE ARE WE?

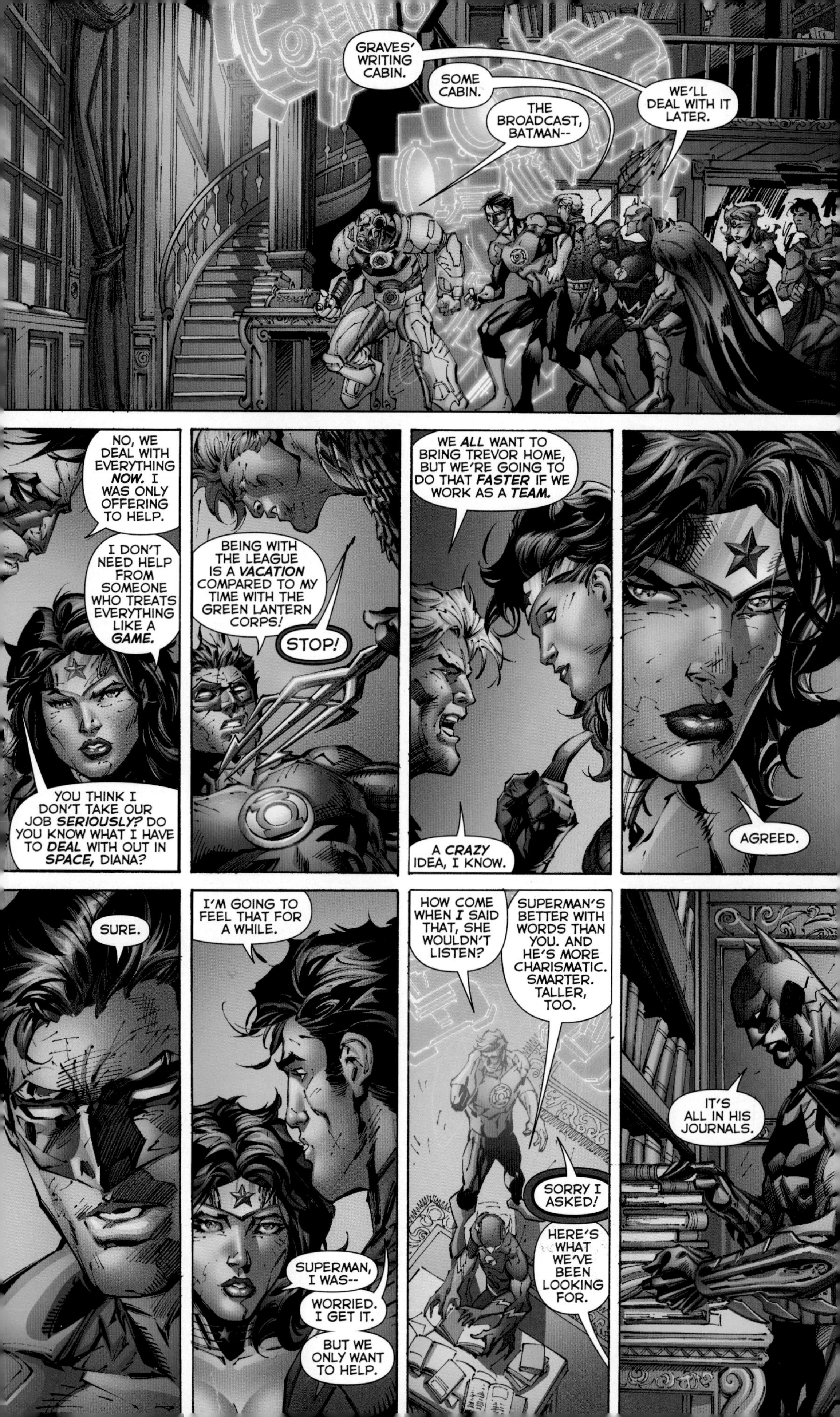
GRAVES' WRITING CABIN.
SOME CABIN.
THE BROADCAST, BATMAN--
WE'LL DEAL WITH IT LATER.
NO, WE DEAL WITH EVERYTHING NOW. I WAS ONLY OFFERING TO HELP.
I DON'T NEED HELP FROM SOMEONE WHO TREATS EVERYTHING LIKE A GAME.
YOU THINK I DON'T TAKE OUR JOB SERIOUSLY? DO YOU KNOW WHAT I HAVE TO DEAL WITH OUT IN SPACE, DIANA?
BEING WITH THE LEAGUE IS A VACATION COMPARED TO MY TIME WITH THE GREEN LANTERN CORPS!
STOP!
WE ALL WANT TO BRING TREVOR HOME, BUT WE'RE GOING TO DO THAT FASTER IF WE WORK AS A TEAM.
A CRAZY IDEA, I KNOW.
AGREED.
SURE.
I'M GOING TO FEEL THAT FOR A WHILE.
SUPERMAN, I WAS--
WORRIED. I GET IT.
BUT WE ONLY WANT TO HELP.
HOW COME WHEN I SAID THAT, SHE WOULDN'T LISTEN?
SUPERMAN'S BETTER WITH WORDS THAN YOU. AND HE'S MORE CHARISMATIC. SMARTER. TALLER, TOO.
SORRY I ASKED!
HERE'S WHAT WE'VE BEEN LOOKING FOR.
IT'S ALL IN HIS JOURNALS.

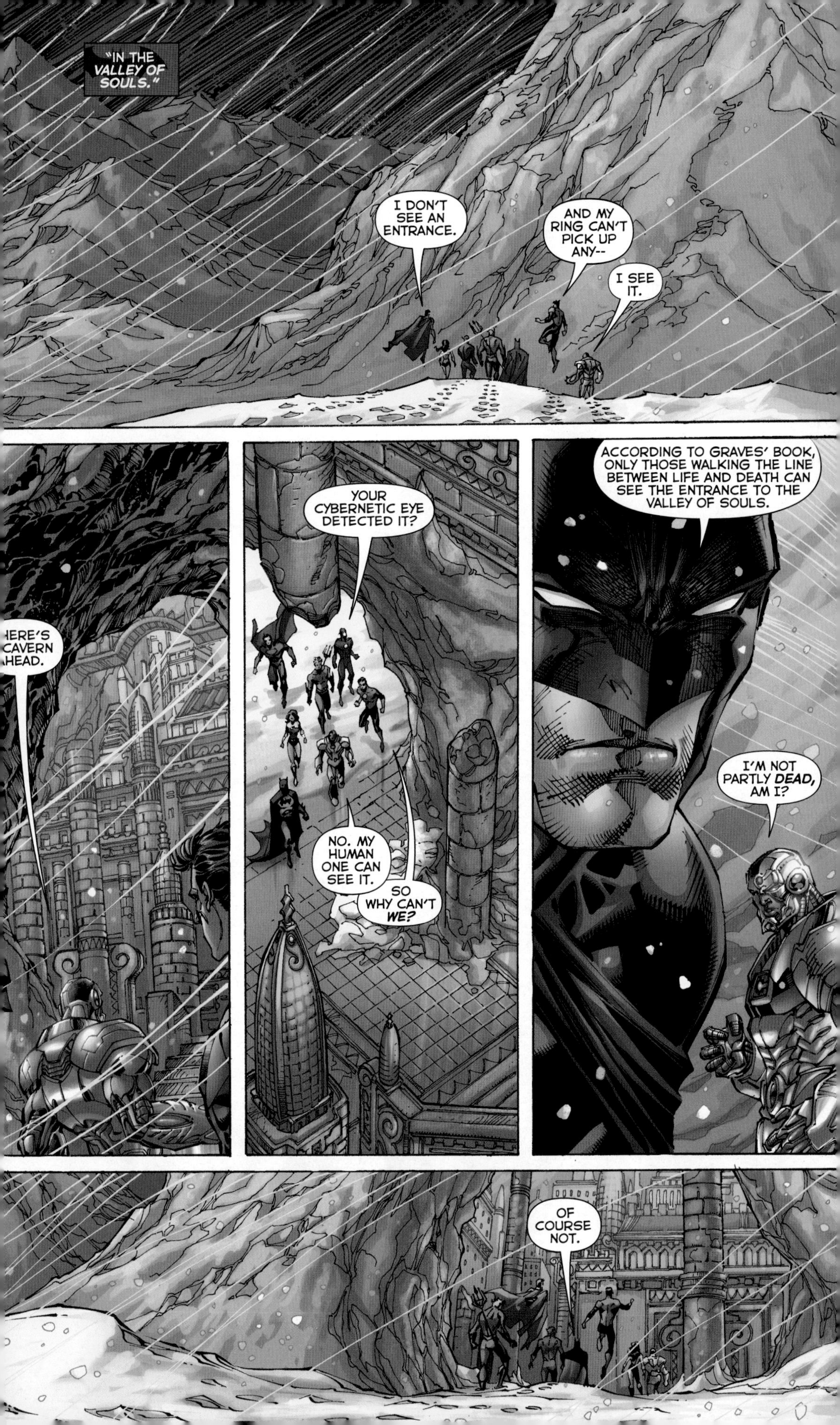
"IN THE VALLEY OF SOULS."
I DON'T SEE AN ENTRANCE.
AND MY RING CAN'T PICK UP ANY--
I SEE IT.
HERE'S CAVERN AHEAD.
YOUR CYBERNETIC EYE DETECTED IT?
NO. MY HUMAN ONE CAN SEE IT.
SO WHY CAN'T *WE?*
ACCORDING TO GRAVES' BOOK, ONLY THOSE WALKING THE LINE BETWEEN LIFE AND DEATH CAN SEE THE ENTRANCE TO THE VALLEY OF SOULS.
I'M NOT PARTLY *DEAD,* AM I?
OF COURSE NOT.

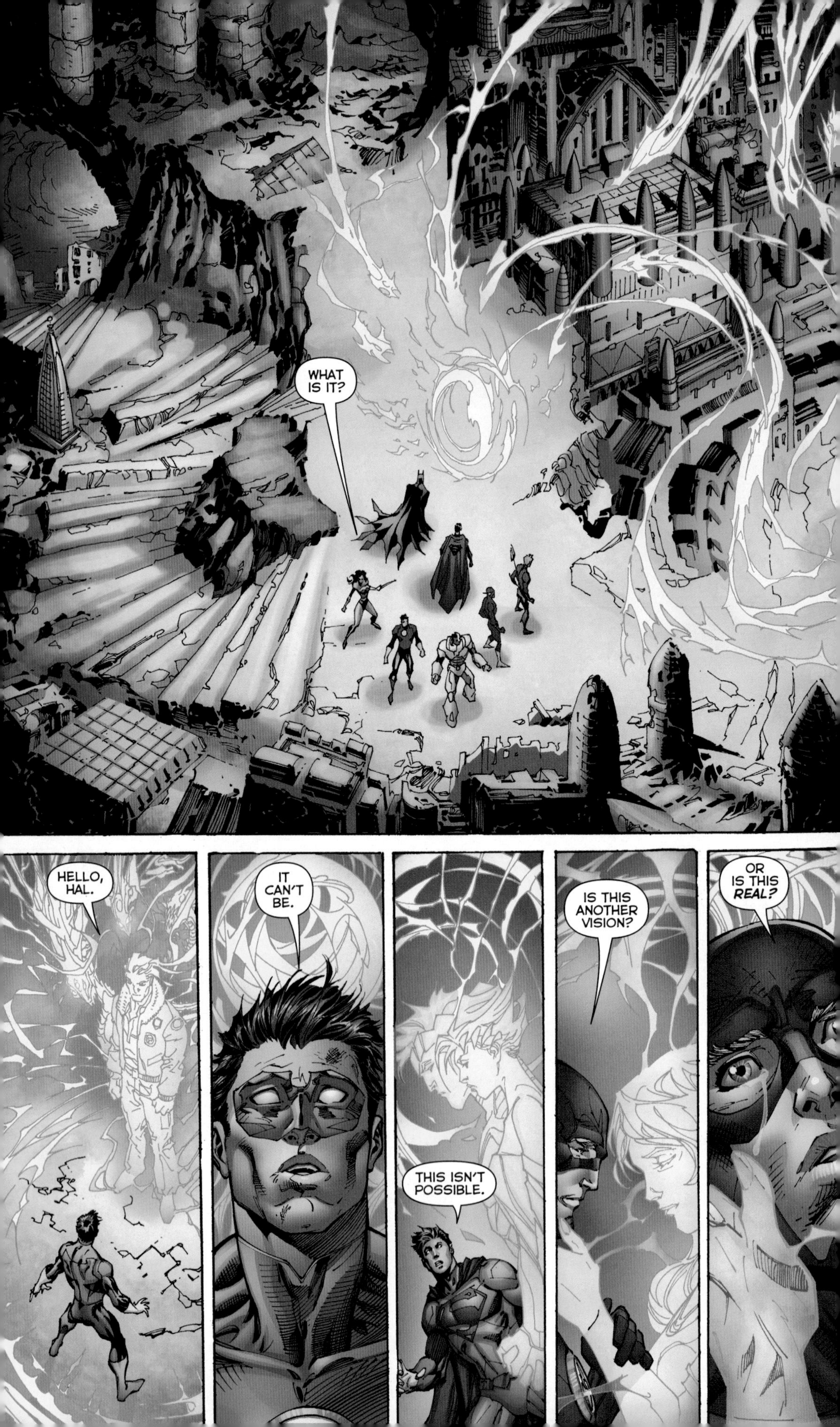
WHAT IS IT?
HELLO, HAL.
IT CAN'T BE.
THIS ISN'T POSSIBLE.
IS THIS ANOTHER VISION?
OR IS THIS *REAL?*

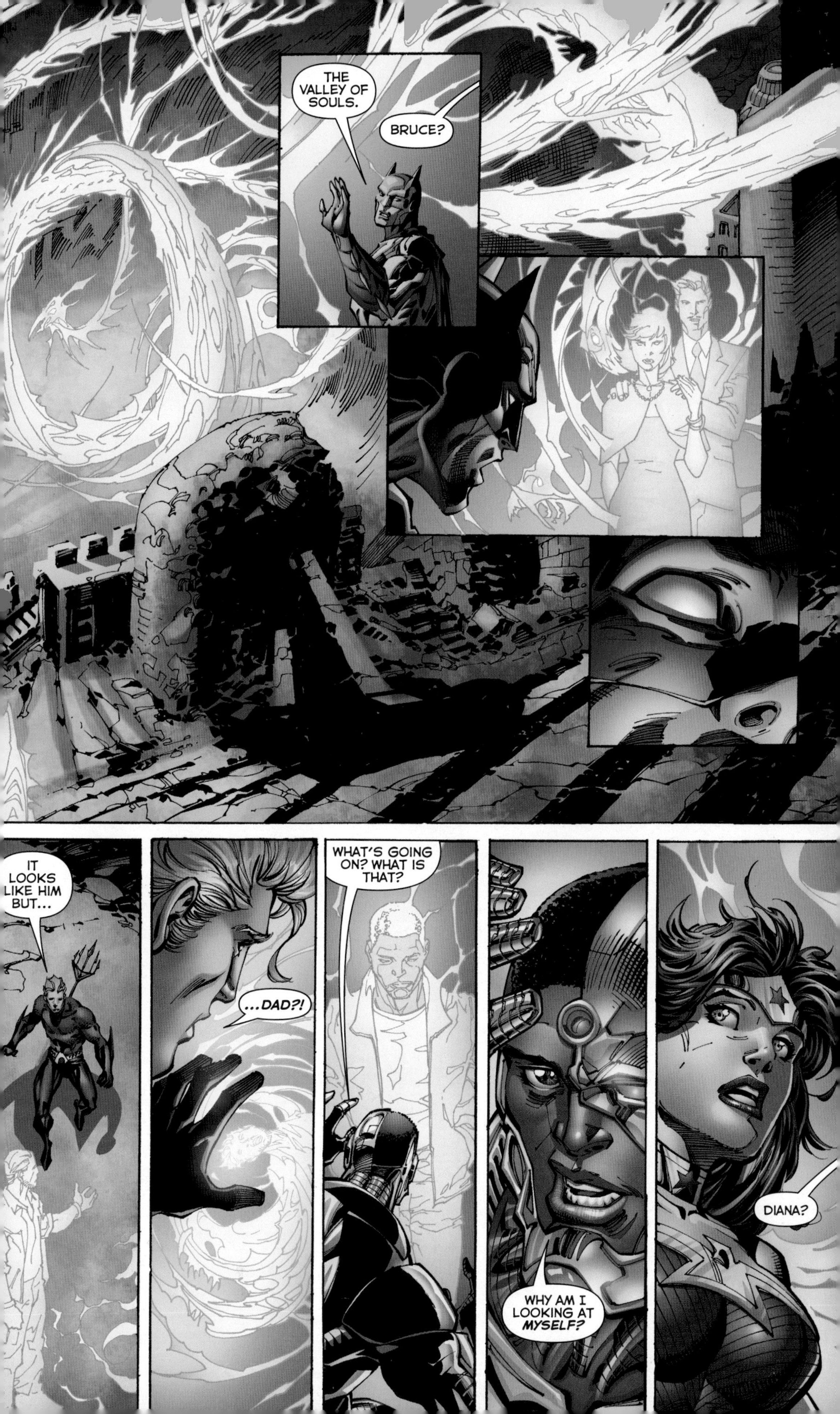
THE VALLEY OF SOULS.
BRUCE?
IT LOOKS LIKE HIM BUT...
...DAD?!
WHAT'S GOING ON? WHAT IS THAT?
WHY AM I LOOKING AT *MYSELF?*
DIANA?

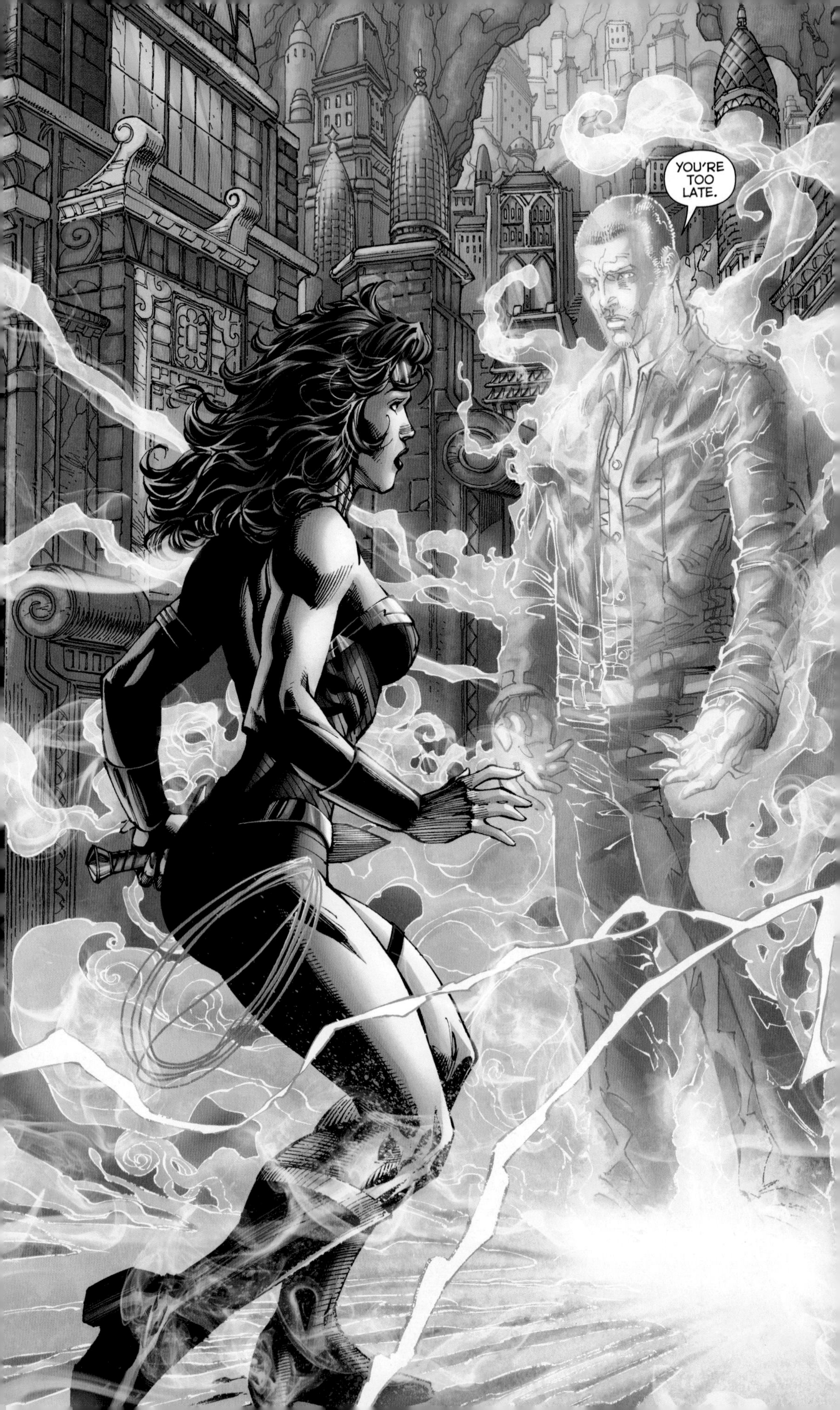
YOU'RE TOO LATE.

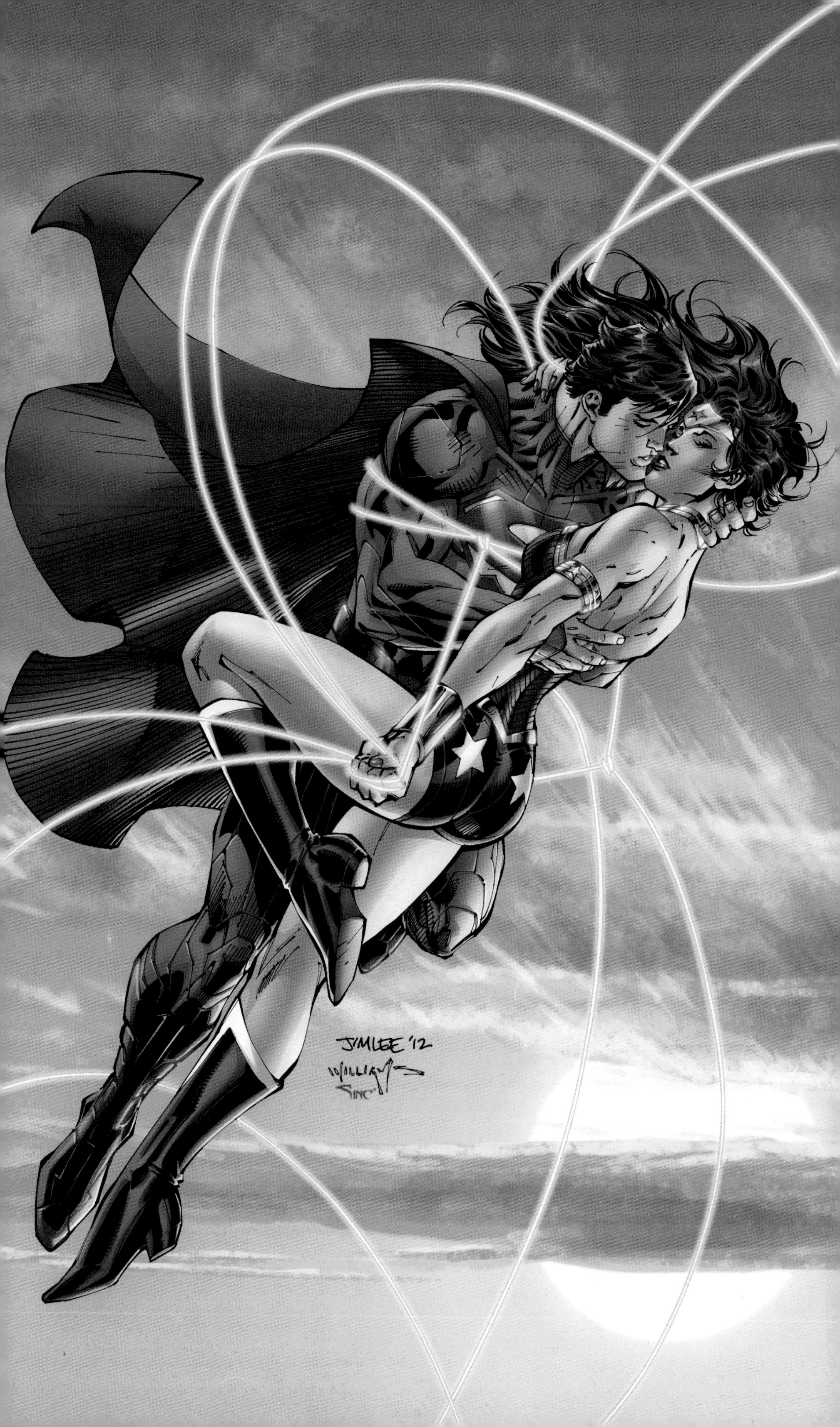
JIMLEE '12

THE VILLAIN'S JOURNEY CHAPTER FOUR: RESCUE FROM WITHIN

GEOFF JOHNS writer **JIM LEE with DAVID FINCH & IVAN REIS** pencillers **SCOTT WILLIAMS, SANDRA HOPE, JONATHAN GLAPION, MARK IRWIN, MATT BANNING, ROB HUNTER, JOE WEEMS, ALEX GARNER, TREVOR SCOTT, DAVID FINCH & JOE PRADO** inkers cover by **JIM LEE, SCOTT WILLIAMS & ALEX SINCLAIR**

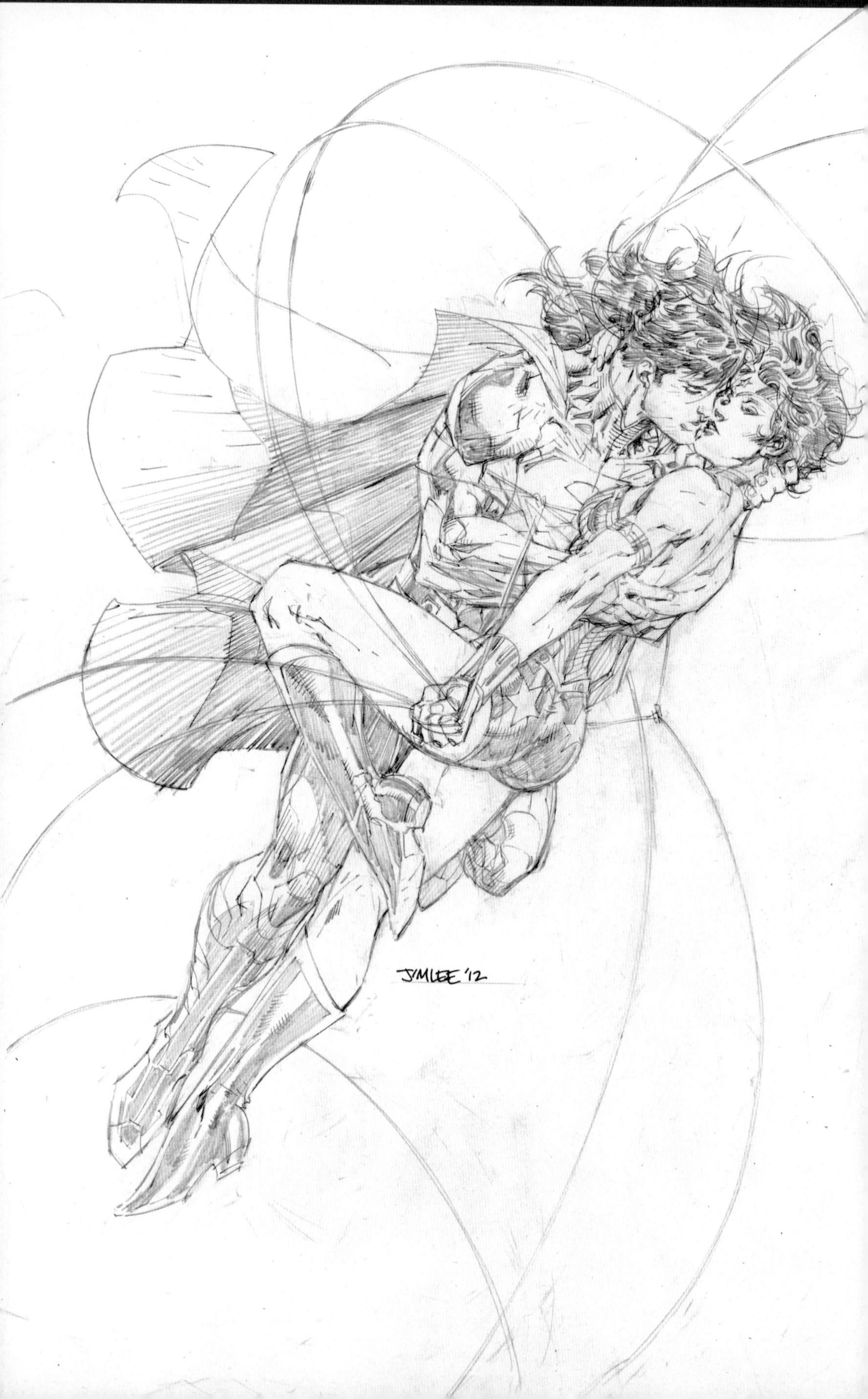

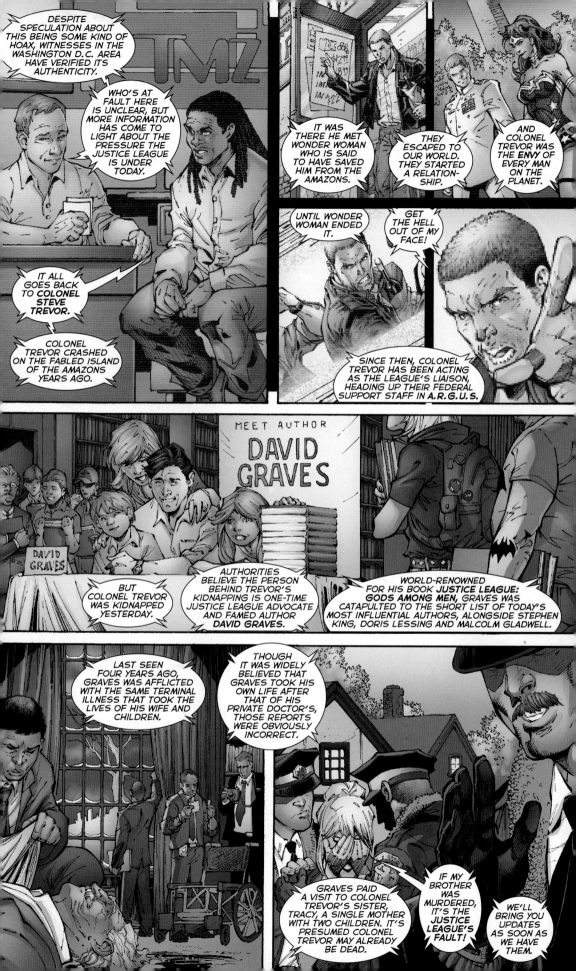

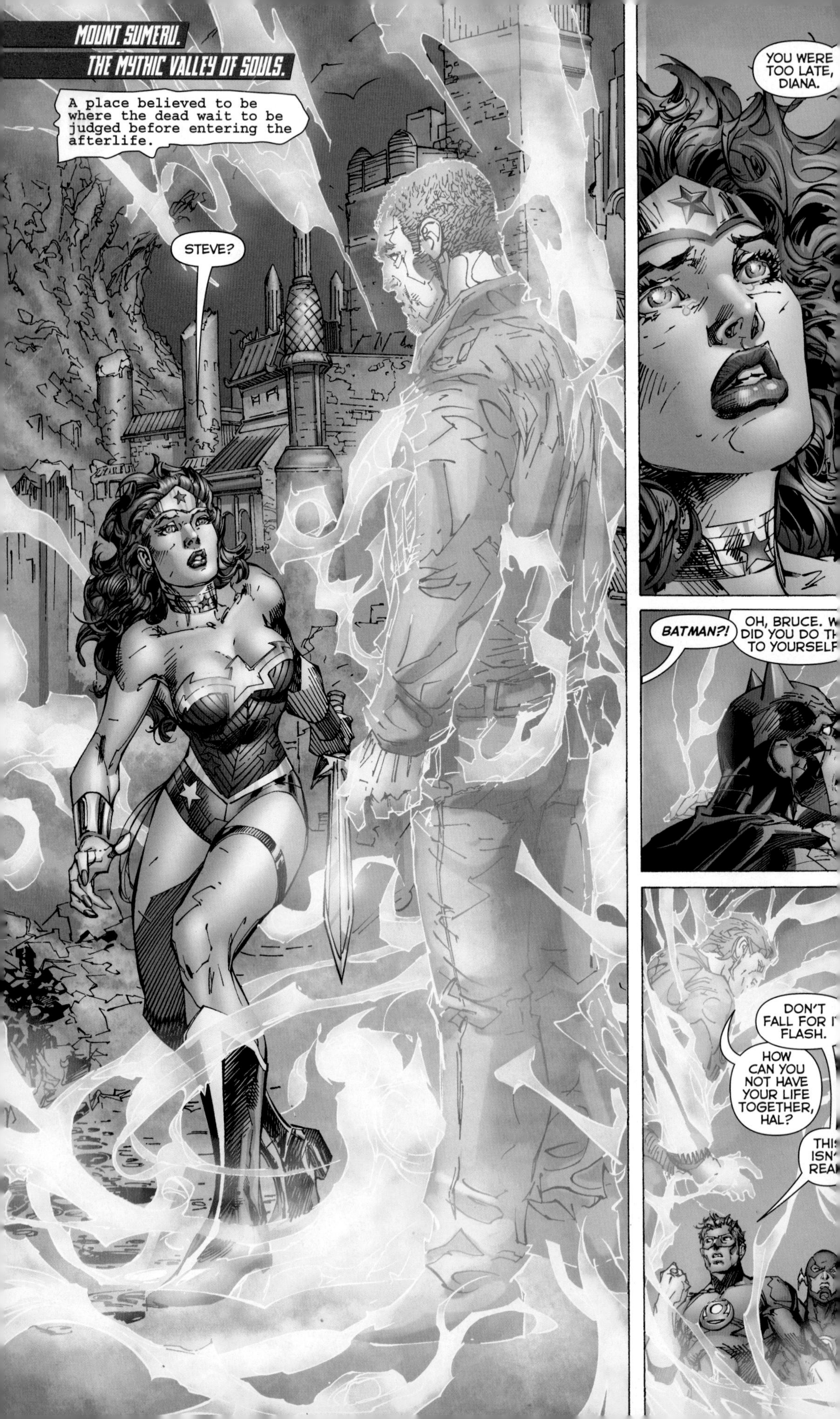
MOUNT SUMERU.
THE MYTHIC VALLEY OF SOULS.
A place believed to be where the dead wait to be judged before entering the afterlife.
STEVE?
YOU WERE TOO LATE, DIANA.
BATMAN?!
OH, BRUCE. W DID YOU DO TH TO YOURSELF
DON'T FALL FOR I FLASH.
HOW CAN YOU NOT HAVE YOUR LIFE TOGETHER, HAL?
THI ISN' REA

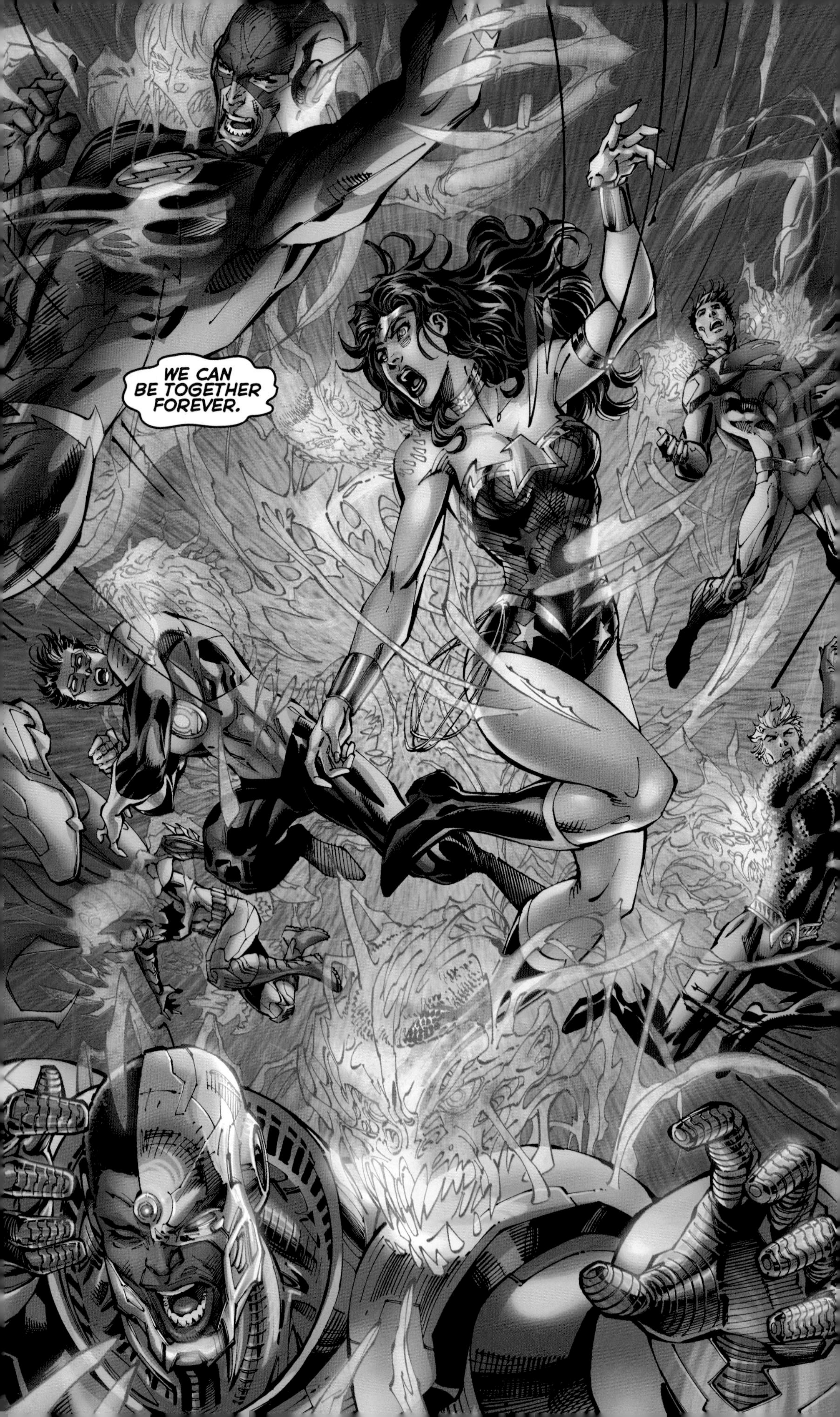
WE CAN BE TOGETHER FOREVER.

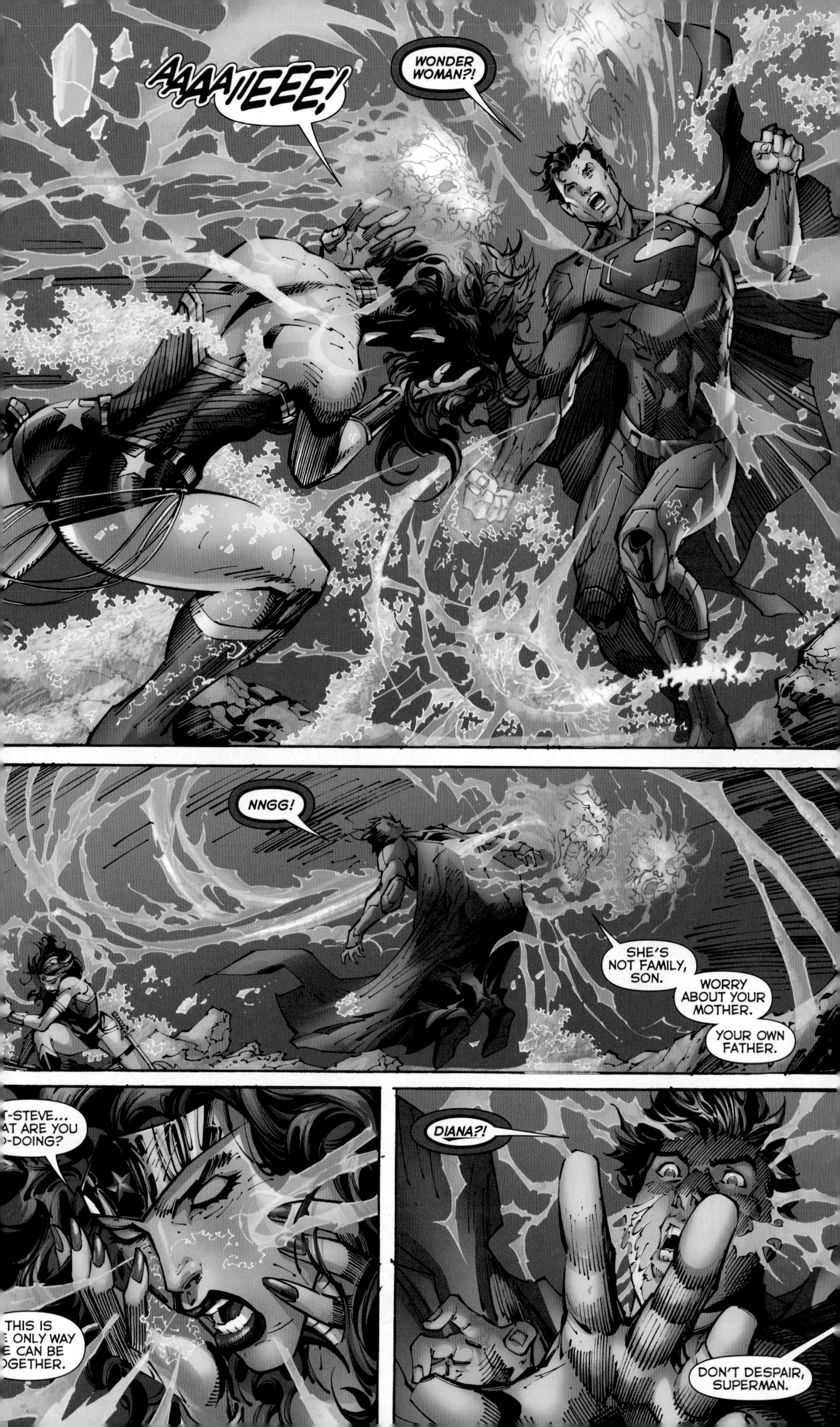
AAAAIIEEE!
WONDER WOMAN?!
NNGG!
SHE'S NOT FAMILY, SON.
WORRY ABOUT YOUR MOTHER.
YOUR OWN FATHER.
T-STEVE... AT ARE YOU D-DOING?
THIS IS E ONLY WAY E CAN BE OGETHER.
DIANA?!
DON'T DESPAIR, SUPERMAN.

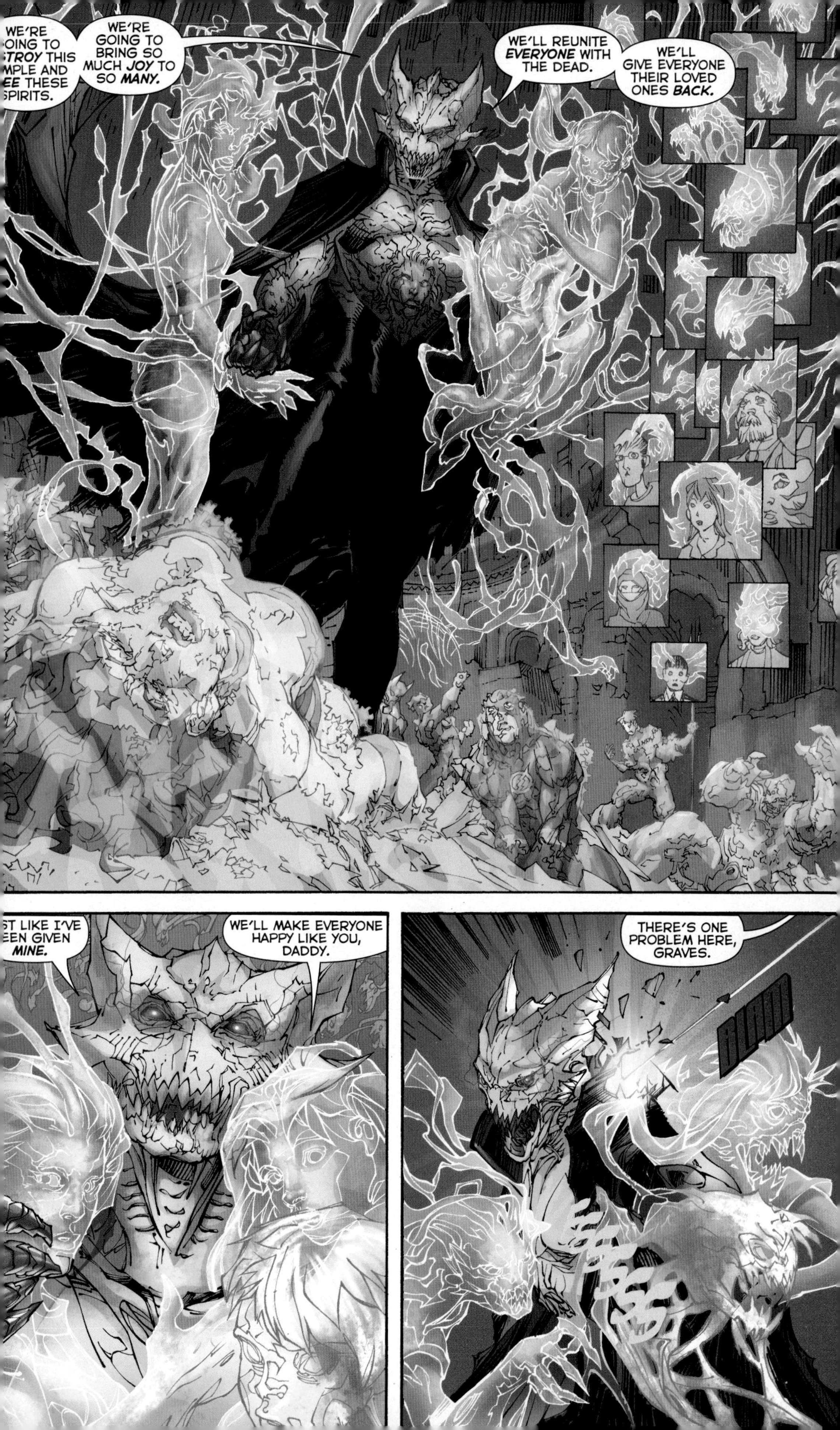
WE'RE OING TO STROY THIS MPLE AND EE THESE SPIRITS.
WE'RE GOING TO BRING SO MUCH JOY TO SO MANY.
WE'LL REUNITE EVERYONE WITH THE DEAD.
WE'LL GIVE EVERYONE THEIR LOVED ONES BACK.
ST LIKE I'VE EEN GIVEN MINE.
WE'LL MAKE EVERYONE HAPPY LIKE YOU, DADDY.
THERE'S ONE PROBLEM HERE, GRAVES.

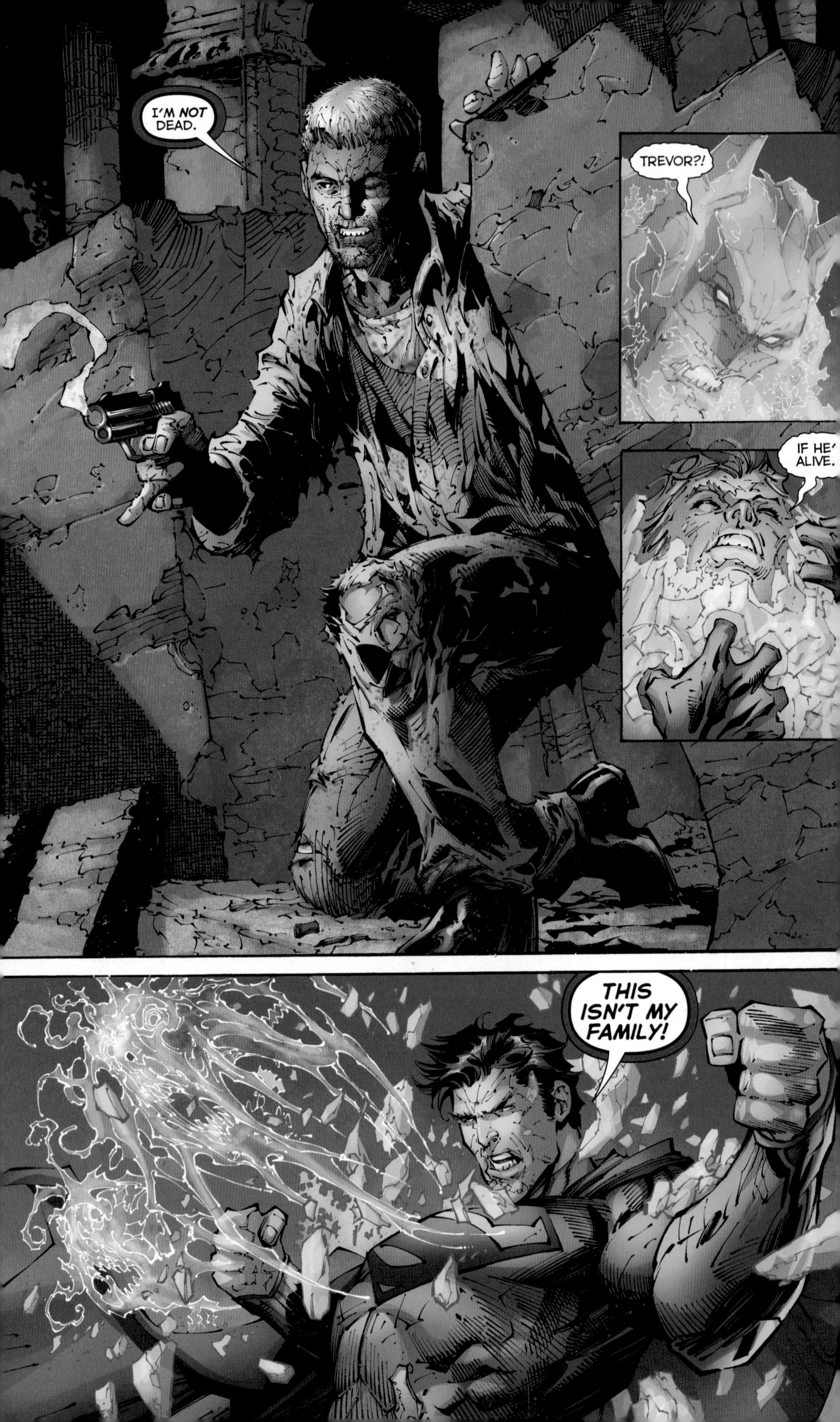
I'M NOT DEAD.
TREVOR?!
IF HE' ALIVE.
THIS ISN'T MY FAMILY!

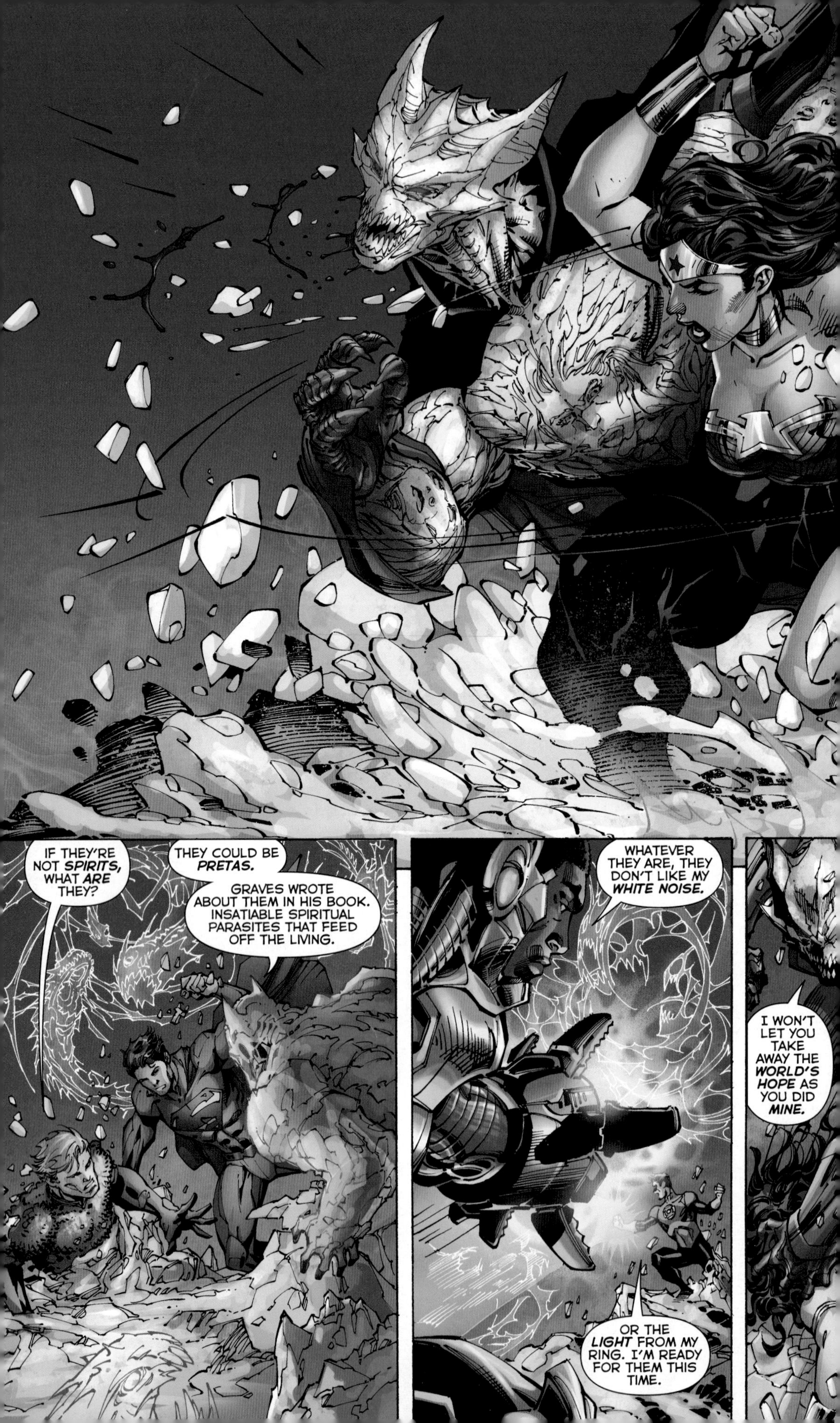
IF THEY'RE NOT SPIRITS, WHAT ARE THEY?
THEY COULD BE PRETAS.
GRAVES WROTE ABOUT THEM IN HIS BOOK. INSATIABLE SPIRITUAL PARASITES THAT FEED OFF THE LIVING.
WHATEVER THEY ARE, THEY DON'T LIKE MY WHITE NOISE.
OR THE LIGHT FROM MY RING. I'M READY FOR THEM THIS TIME.
I WON'T LET YOU TAKE AWAY THE WORLD'S HOPE AS YOU DID MINE.

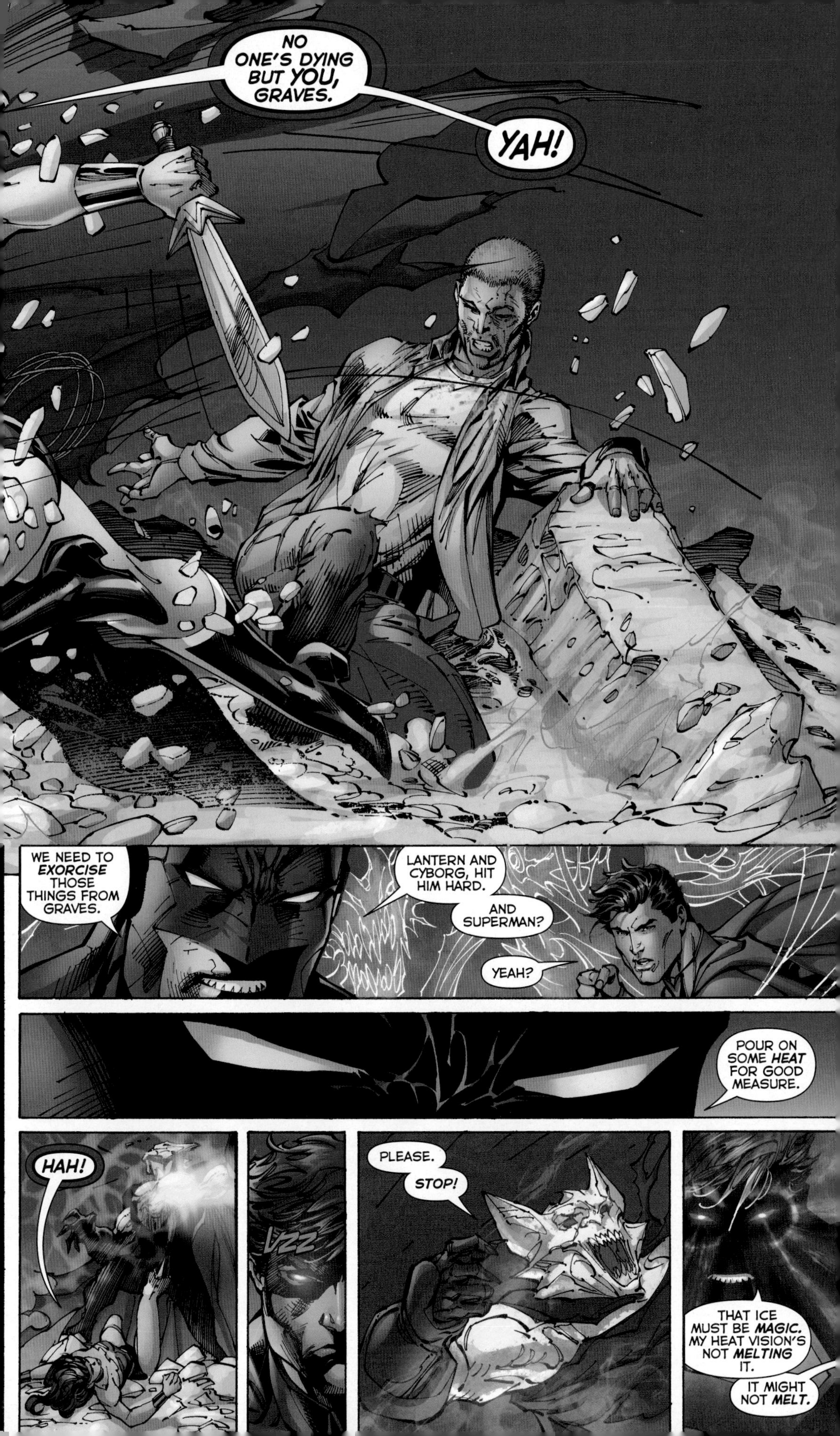
NO ONE'S DYING BUT YOU, GRAVES.
YAH!
WE NEED TO EXORCISE THOSE THINGS FROM GRAVES.
LANTERN AND CYBORG, HIT HIM HARD.
AND SUPERMAN?
YEAH?
POUR ON SOME HEAT FOR GOOD MEASURE.
HAH!
PLEASE.
STOP!
THAT ICE MUST BE MAGIC. MY HEAT VISION'S NOT MELTING IT.
IT MIGHT NOT MELT.

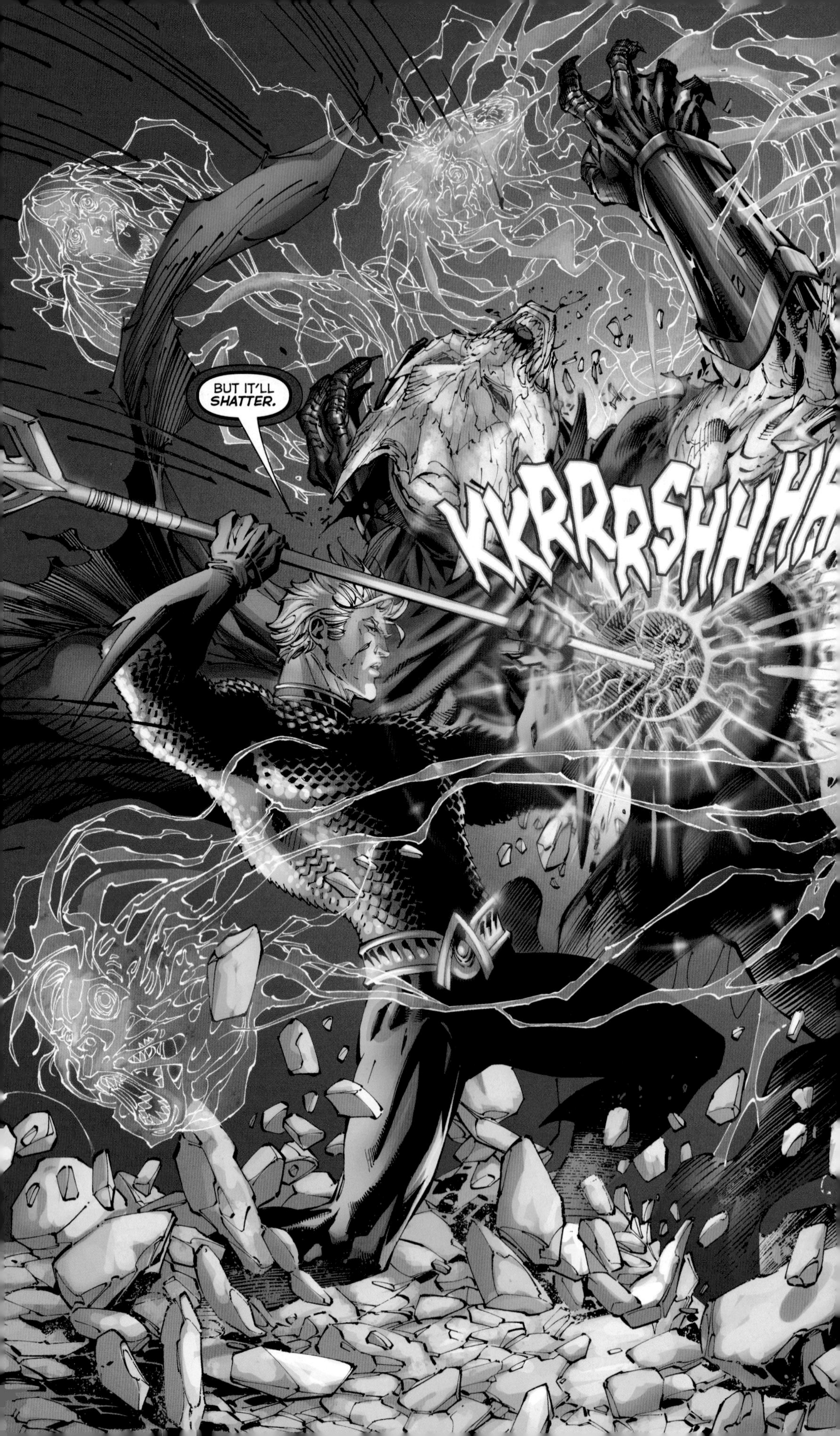
BUT IT'LL SHATTER.
KKRRRSHHH

THOSE SCREAMS. LIKE CHILDREN'S. WE SHOULD STOP.

REMEMBER, THEY AREN'T HIS CHILDREN.

KRK

WE CAN'T STOP, LANTERN.

KRAK

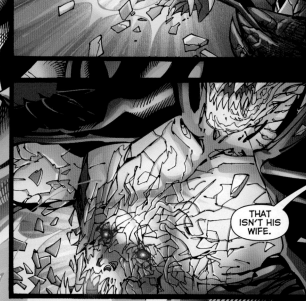

THAT ISN'T HIS WIFE.

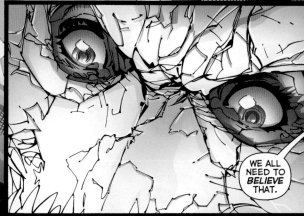

WE ALL NEED TO BELIEVE THAT.

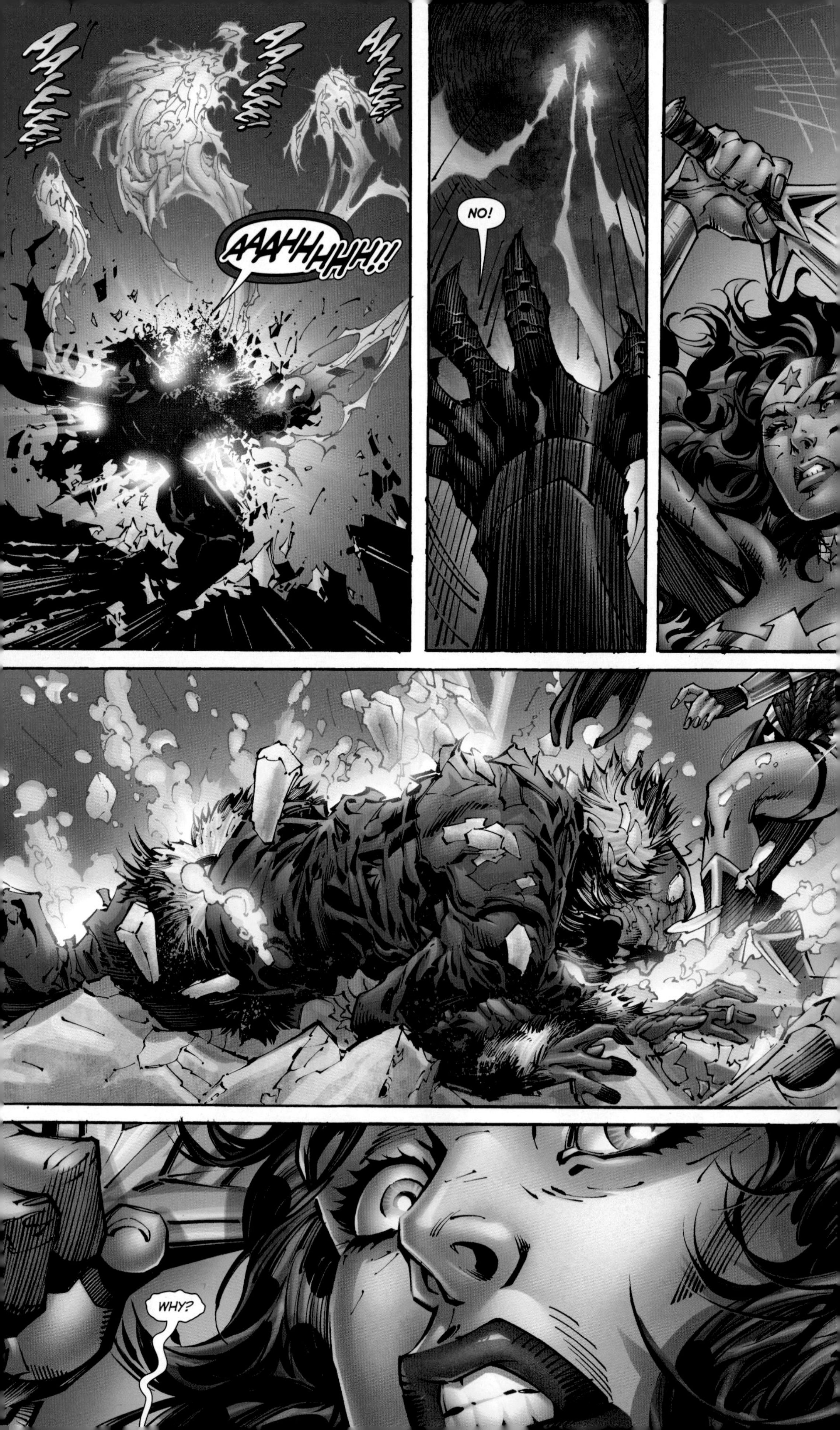
AAIEEE!
AAIEEE!
AAIEEE!
AAAHHHHH!!
NO!
WHY?

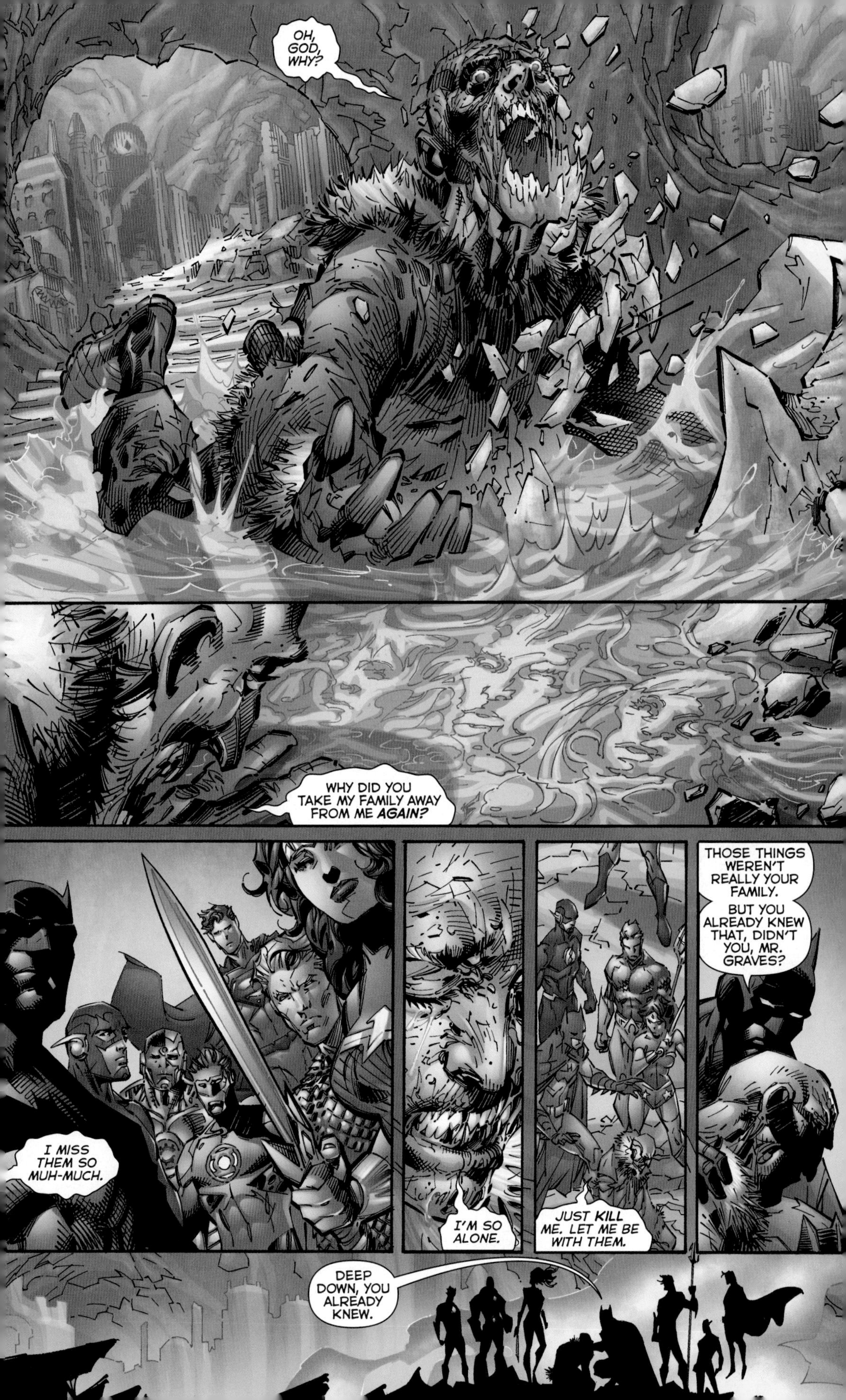
OH, GOD, WHY?
WHY DID YOU TAKE MY FAMILY AWAY FROM ME AGAIN?
I MISS THEM SO MUH-MUCH.
I'M SO ALONE.
JUST KILL ME. LET ME BE WITH THEM.
THOSE THINGS WEREN'T REALLY YOUR FAMILY.
BUT YOU ALREADY KNEW THAT, DIDN'T YOU, MR. GRAVES?
DEEP DOWN, YOU ALREADY KNEW.

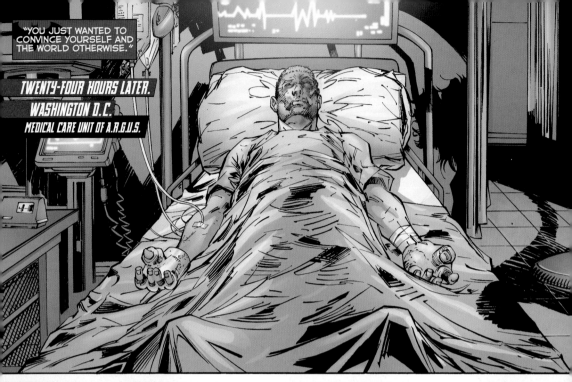

"YOU JUST WANTED TO CONVINCE YOURSELF AND THE WORLD OTHERWISE."

TWENTY-FOUR HOURS LATER.
WASHINGTON D.C.
MEDICAL CARE UNIT OF A.R.G.U.S.

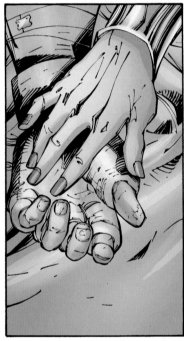

DIANA?

HI, STEVE.

THEY SAID YOU'VE GOT A FEW BROKEN RIBS ON TOP OF THOSE BROKEN FINGERS. AND SOME INTERNAL BLEEDING AND HEAD TRAUMA.

HOW BAD DO I LOOK?

YOU LOOK FINE.

THIS WAS MY FAULT.

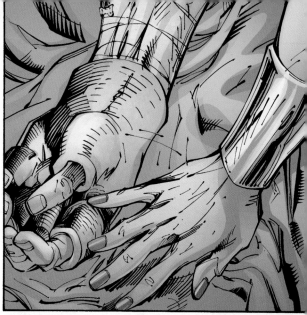

YOU'RE NOT DOING THIS *AGAIN,* ARE YOU?

I THOUGHT YOU WERE FAR ENOUGH AWAY, BUT I SHOULD'VE KNOWN BETTER. AFTER WHAT HAPPENED TO *BARBARA*--

WHAT HAPPENED TO *BARBARA MINERVA* WASN'T YOUR FAULT, EITHER. THE *CHEETAH*--

YOU NEARLY *DIED,* STEVE.

BUT *THIS* TIME YOU WERE TORTURED AND BEATEN AND ALMOST *KILLED* BECAUSE OF *OUR* RELATIONSHIP.

I'VE ARLY DIED A DRED TIMES, ANA. I'M A VERNMENT AGENT.

AND I WAS OUT IN THE FIELD PROTECTING THE WORLD *LONG* BEFORE I MET YOU.

OUR *RELATION-SHIP?* WHAT *RELATIONSHIP?!* YOU *ENDED* IT. YOU THREW IT *AWAY.*

TOO CLOSE? THE ONLY TIME I'VE SEEN YOU IN OVER A *YEAR* IS ON A *COMPUTER.*

YOU'RE STILL TOO CLOSE.

WHY ARE YOU STILL WORKING WITH THE LEAGUE?

BECAUSE THE LEAGUE *NEEDS ME!*

I PROTECT THE LEAGUE FROM ALL THE RED TAPE AND FEAR MONGERING THAT FESTERS IN WASHINGTON!

JUST LIKE I'VE PROTECTED *YOU* FROM IT SINCE THE DAY YOU CAME HERE!

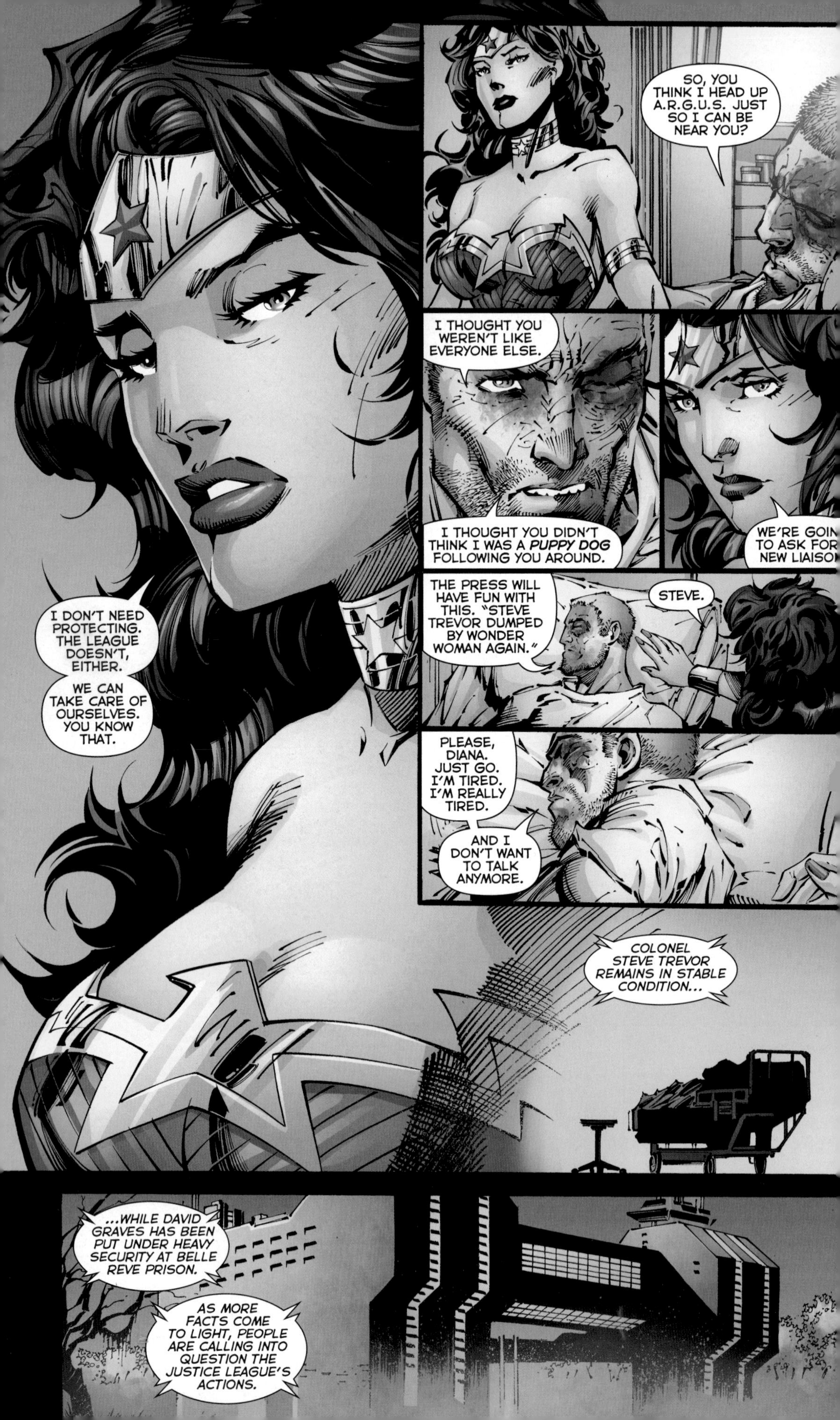
SO, YOU THINK I HEAD UP A.R.G.U.S. JUST SO I CAN BE NEAR YOU?
I THOUGHT YOU WEREN'T LIKE EVERYONE ELSE.
I THOUGHT YOU DIDN'T THINK I WAS A *PUPPY DOG* FOLLOWING YOU AROUND.
WE'RE GOIN TO ASK FOR NEW LIAISO
THE PRESS WILL HAVE FUN WITH THIS. "STEVE TREVOR DUMPED BY WONDER WOMAN AGAIN."
STEVE.
PLEASE, DIANA. JUST GO. I'M TIRED. I'M REALLY TIRED.
AND I DON'T WANT TO TALK ANYMORE.
I DON'T NEED PROTECTING. THE LEAGUE DOESN'T, EITHER.
WE CAN TAKE CARE OF OURSELVES. YOU KNOW THAT.
COLONEL STEVE TREVOR REMAINS IN STABLE CONDITION...
...WHILE DAVID GRAVES HAS BEEN PUT UNDER HEAVY SECURITY AT BELLE REVE PRISON.
AS MORE FACTS COME TO LIGHT, PEOPLE ARE CALLING INTO QUESTION THE JUSTICE LEAGUE'S ACTIONS.

YOU MIGHT BE A GREAT STRATEGIST, BATMAN, BUT YOU HAVE *NO IDEA* HOW TO BRING PEOPLE TOGETHER.

I KNOW ABOUT *THE OTHERS.* YOUR *SECOND* TEAM IS IN WORSE SHAPE THAN US.

I LEAD AN ENTIRE *CONTINENT.*

ATLANTIS? AND WHAT DO YOU DO FOR THEM *NOW?*

WE HAVE OTHER THINGS TO WORRY ABOUT *BEFORE* PICKING A NEW LEADER, *RIGHT?*

DO YOU KNOW HOW LONG IT TOOK ME TO EARN CENTRAL CITY'S TRUST?

YES. I WAS THERE. AND YOU WOULDN'T STOP COMPLAINING ABOUT IT.

GRAVES DIDN'T LIE, FLASH.

DAVID GRAVES AND HIS FA[...] WERE THE ONLY SURVIVOR[...] OF A GROUP OF PEOPLE DARKSEID HAD CORNERE[...] IN METROPOLIS.

THIS COULD *DESTROY* THAT. ALL BECAUSE OF GRAVES' LIES.

THEY ESCAPED HIS *OMEGA BEAMS*, BUT THEY BREATHED IN THE *ASH.*

GRAVE[S]

"WHO KNOWS WHAT THAT *COULD'VE* DONE TO THEM?"

WE...WE SHOULD'VE CONSIDERED *EVERY* POSSIBILITY.

EVEN IF WE *KNEW*, WAS THERE ANYTHING WE COULD'VE DONE?

WE COULD'VE *TRIED* TO HELP THEM.

WE...MADE A MISTAKE.

WE *CAN'T* AFFORD TO MAKE MISTAKES. WHEN WE MAKE MISTAKES, PEOPLE DIE!

WITH THE POWERS WE HAVE, IT'S UP TO US TO MAKE T[...] EARTH *SAFE.* MAKE SURE *EVERYONE'S* OKAY!

AS TWISTED AS IT WAS...THAT'S WHAT GRAVES WAS *TRYING* TO DO.

HE WAS TRYING TO HEL[P] EVERYONE, AN[...] THAT'S MORE THAN WE'VE BEEN DOING.

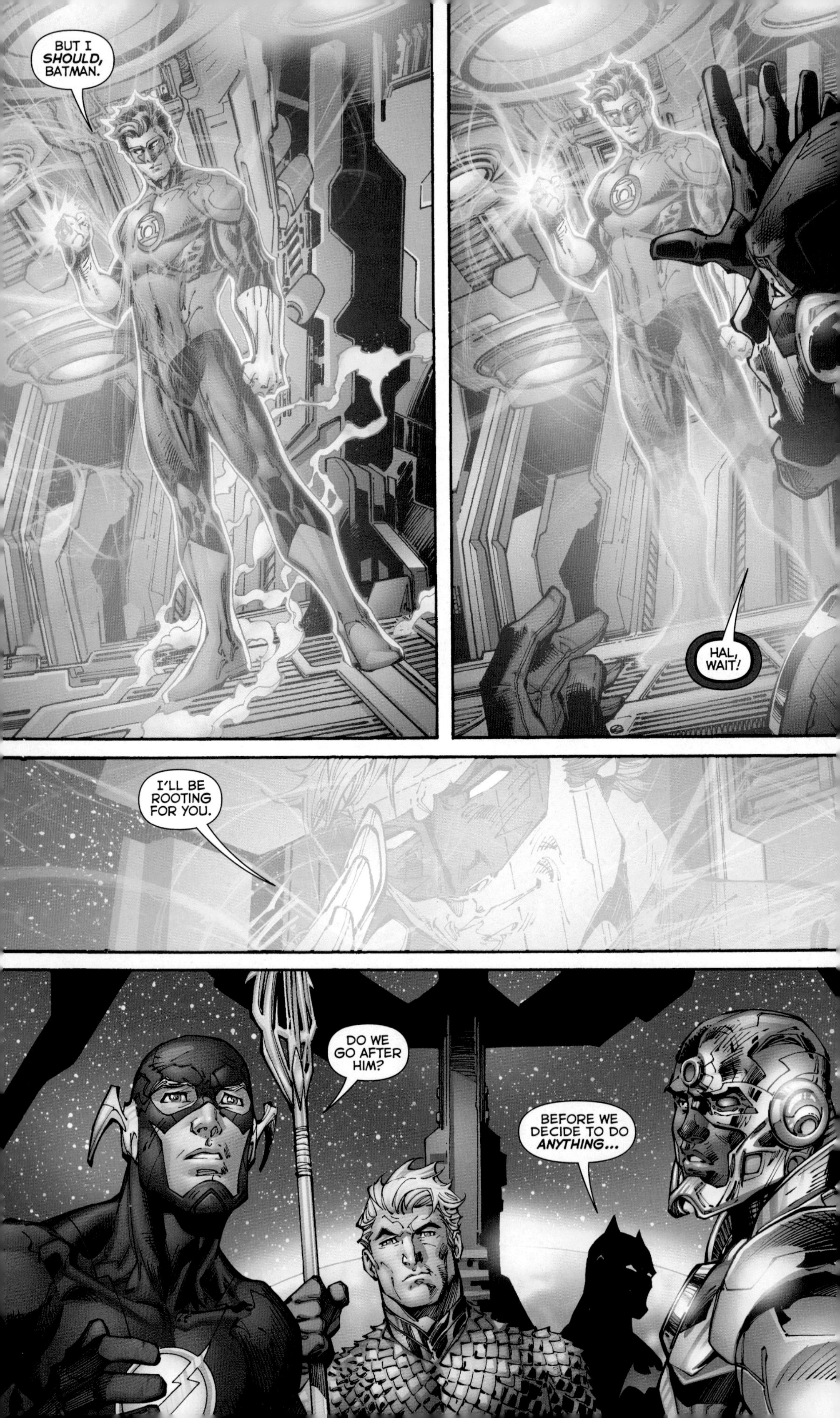

BUT I *SHOULD,* BATMAN.
HAL, WAIT!
I'LL BE ROOTING FOR YOU.
DO WE GO AFTER HIM?
BEFORE WE DECIDE TO DO *ANYTHING...*

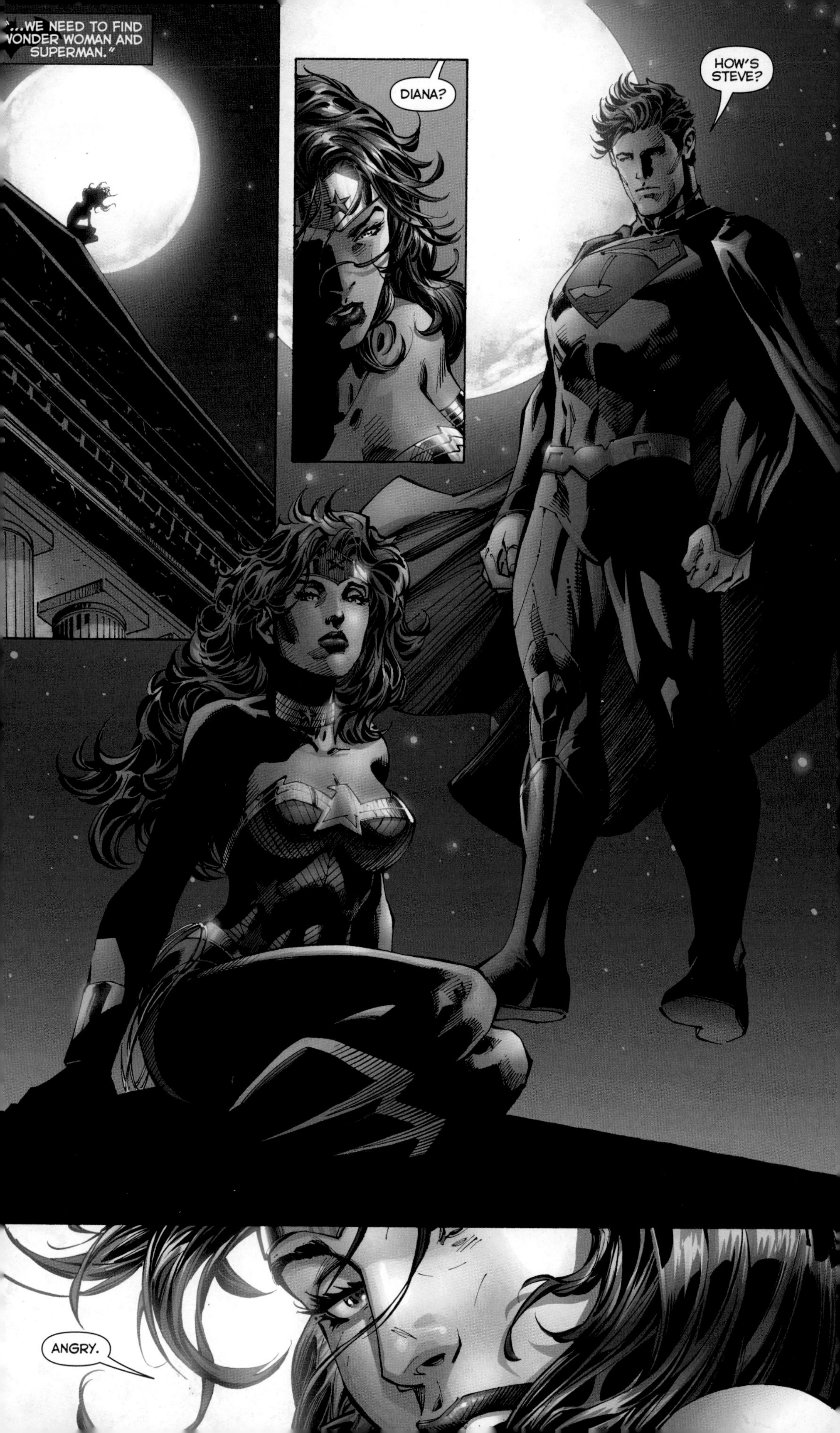
"...WE NEED TO FIND WONDER WOMAN AND SUPERMAN."
DIANA?
HOW'S STEVE?
ANGRY.

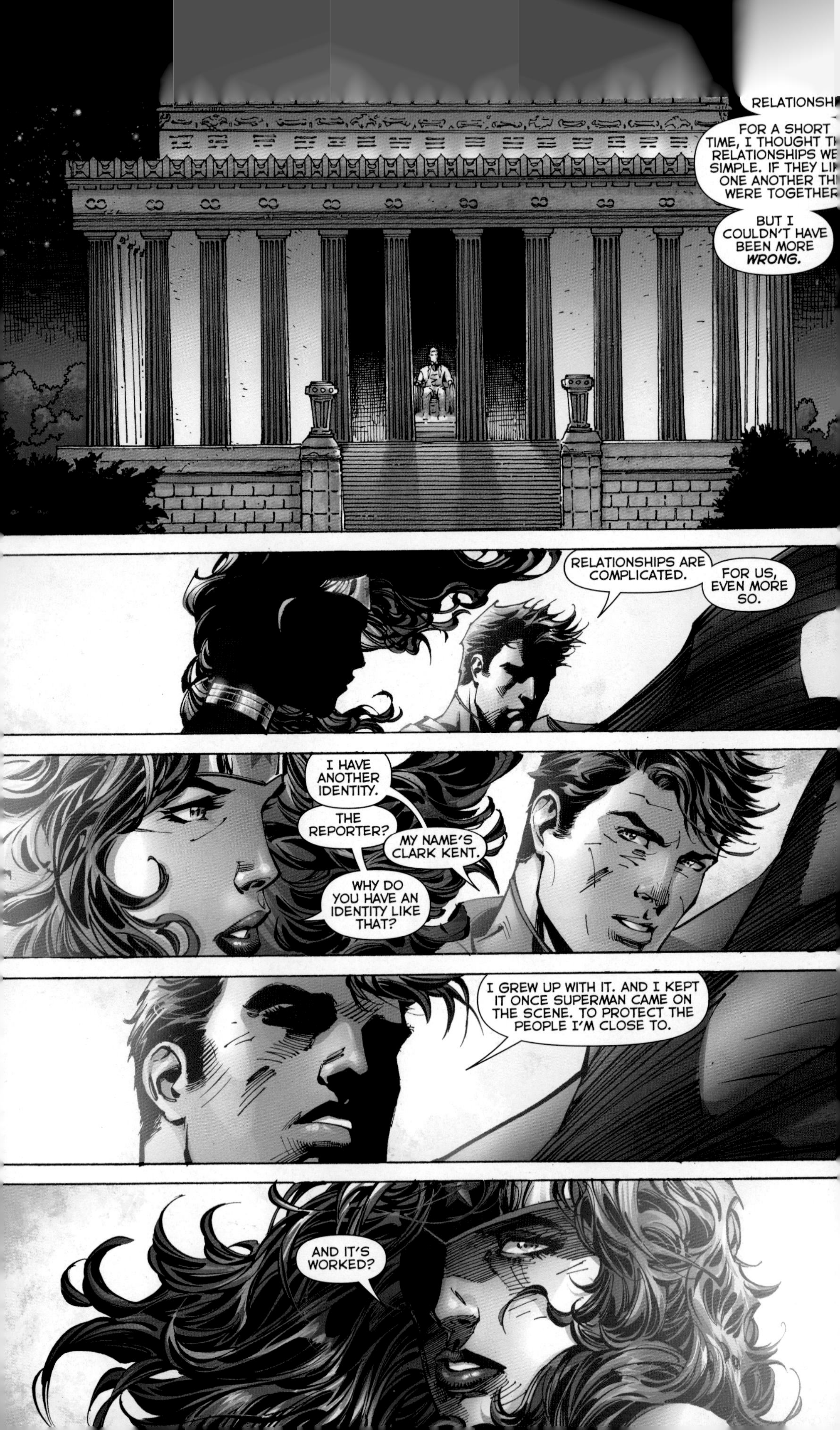

RELATIONSH
FOR A SHORT TIME, I THOUGHT T RELATIONSHIPS WE SIMPLE. IF THEY LI ONE ANOTHER TH WERE TOGETHER
BUT I COULDN'T HAVE BEEN MORE ***WRONG.***
RELATIONSHIPS ARE COMPLICATED.
FOR US, EVEN MORE SO.
I HAVE ANOTHER IDENTITY.
THE REPORTER?
MY NAME'S CLARK KENT.
WHY DO YOU HAVE AN IDENTITY LIKE THAT?
I GREW UP WITH IT. AND I KEPT IT ONCE SUPERMAN CAME ON THE SCENE. TO PROTECT THE PEOPLE I'M CLOSE TO.
AND IT'S WORKED?

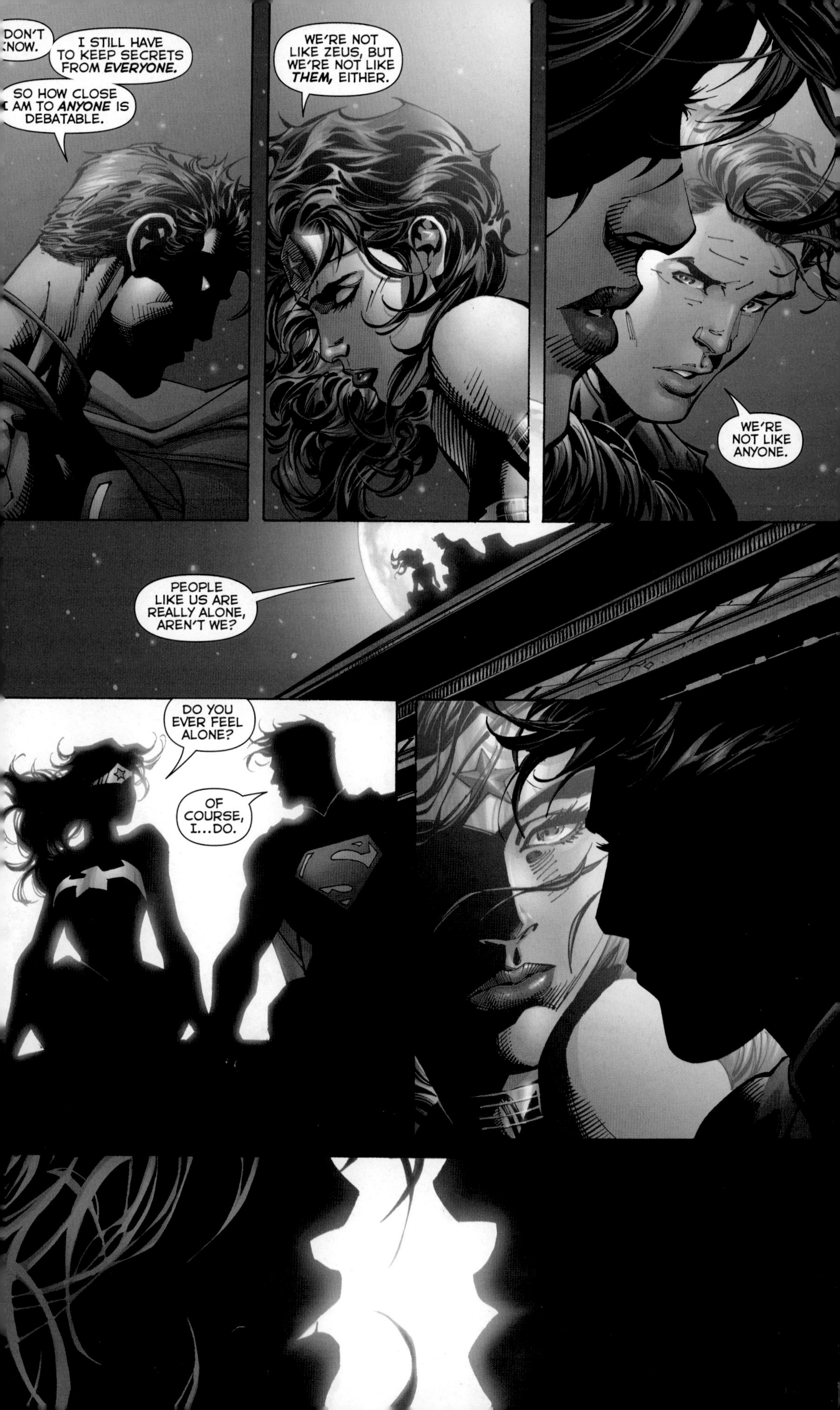

DON'T KNOW.
I STILL HAVE TO KEEP SECRETS FROM EVERYONE.
SO HOW CLOSE I AM TO ANYONE IS DEBATABLE.
WE'RE NOT LIKE ZEUS, BUT WE'RE NOT LIKE THEM, EITHER.
WE'RE NOT LIKE ANYONE.
PEOPLE LIKE US ARE REALLY ALONE, AREN'T WE?
DO YOU EVER FEEL ALONE?
OF COURSE, I...DO.

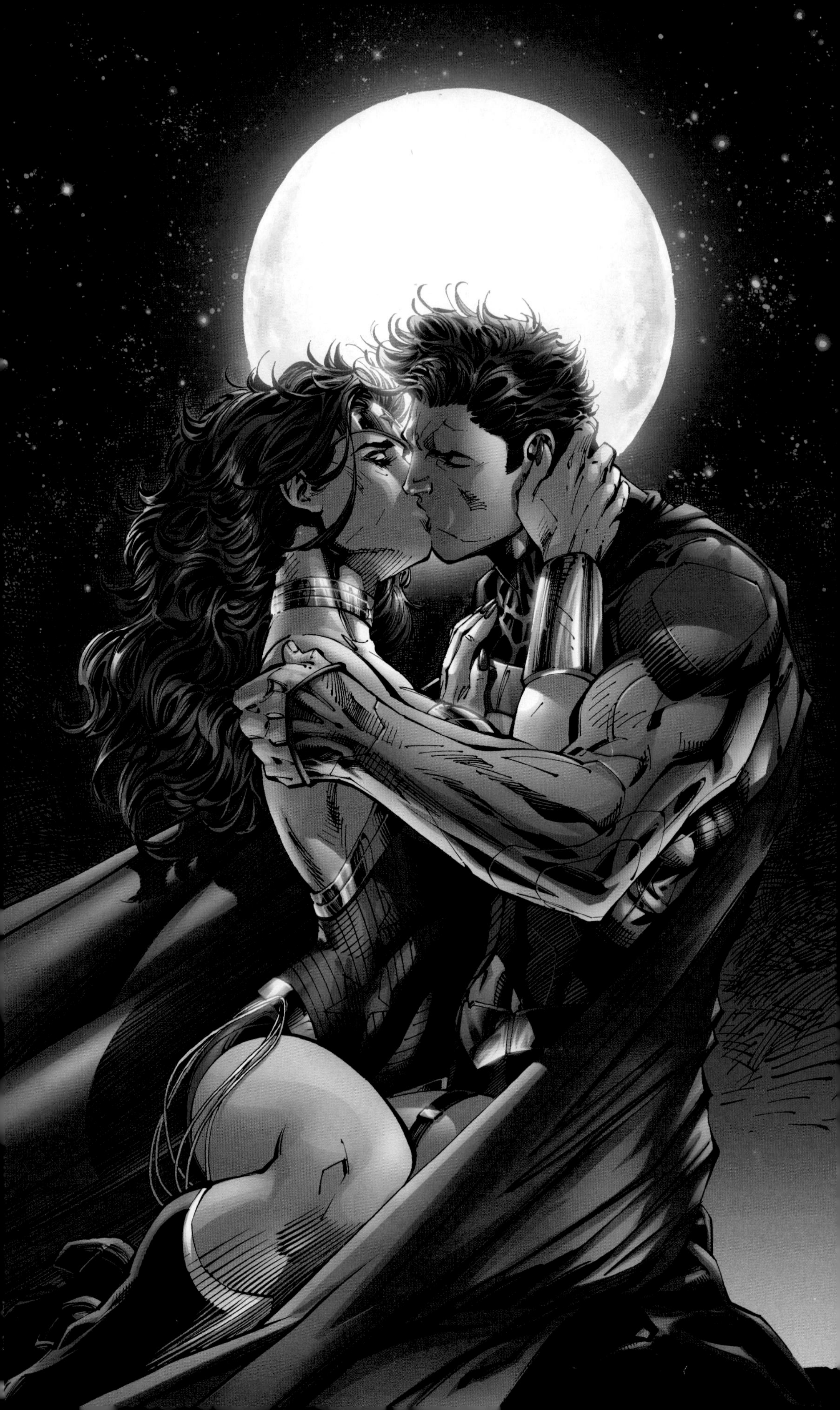

COMING IN THE SECOND YEAR OF JUSTICE LEAGU

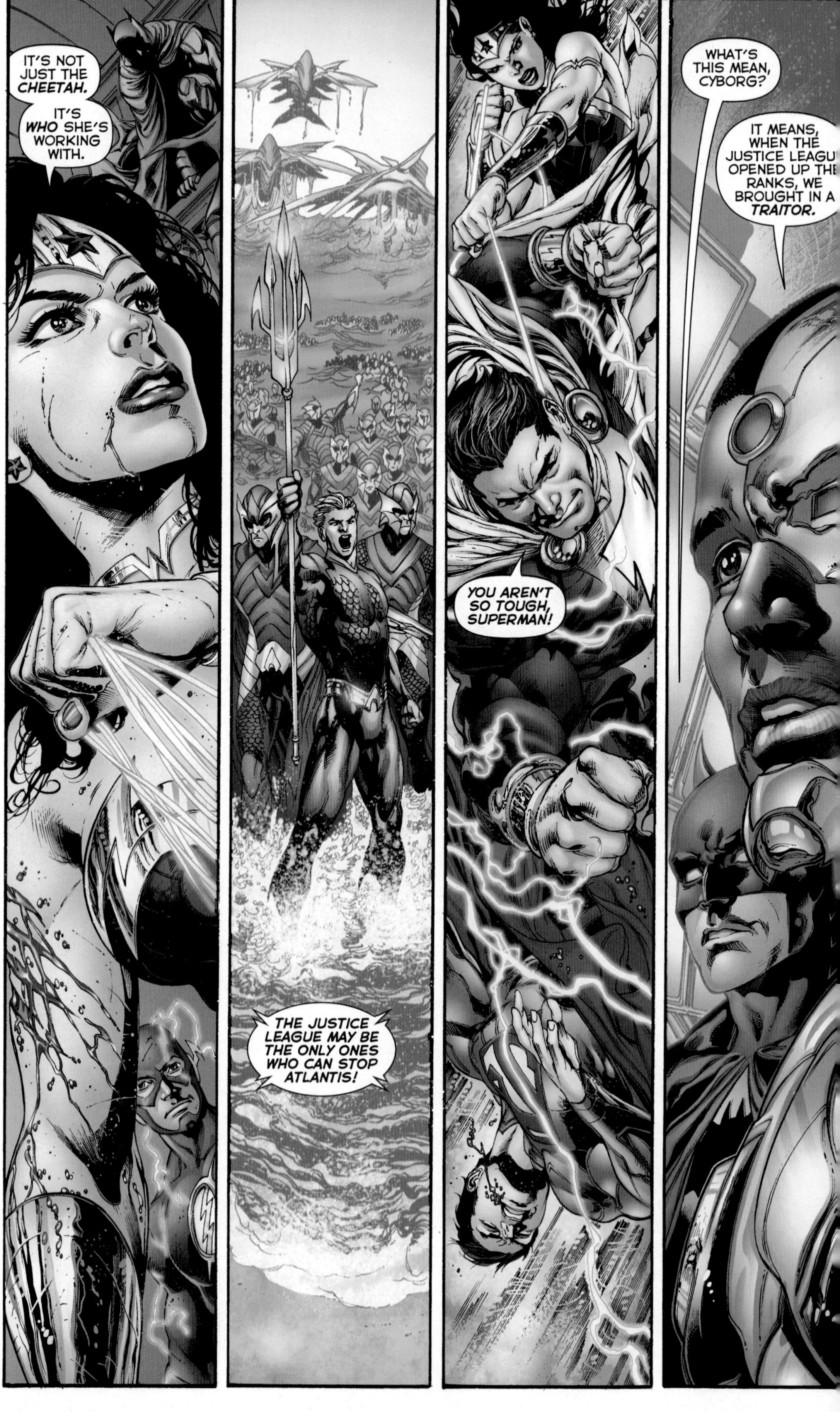
IT'S NOT JUST THE CHEETAH.
IT'S WHO SHE'S WORKING WITH.
THE JUSTICE LEAGUE MAY BE THE ONLY ONES WHO CAN STOP ATLANTIS!
YOU AREN'T SO TOUGH, SUPERMAN!
WHAT'S THIS MEAN, CYBORG?
IT MEANS, WHEN THE JUSTICE LEAGU OPENED UP THE RANKS, WE BROUGHT IN A TRAITOR.

AND COMING IN 2013

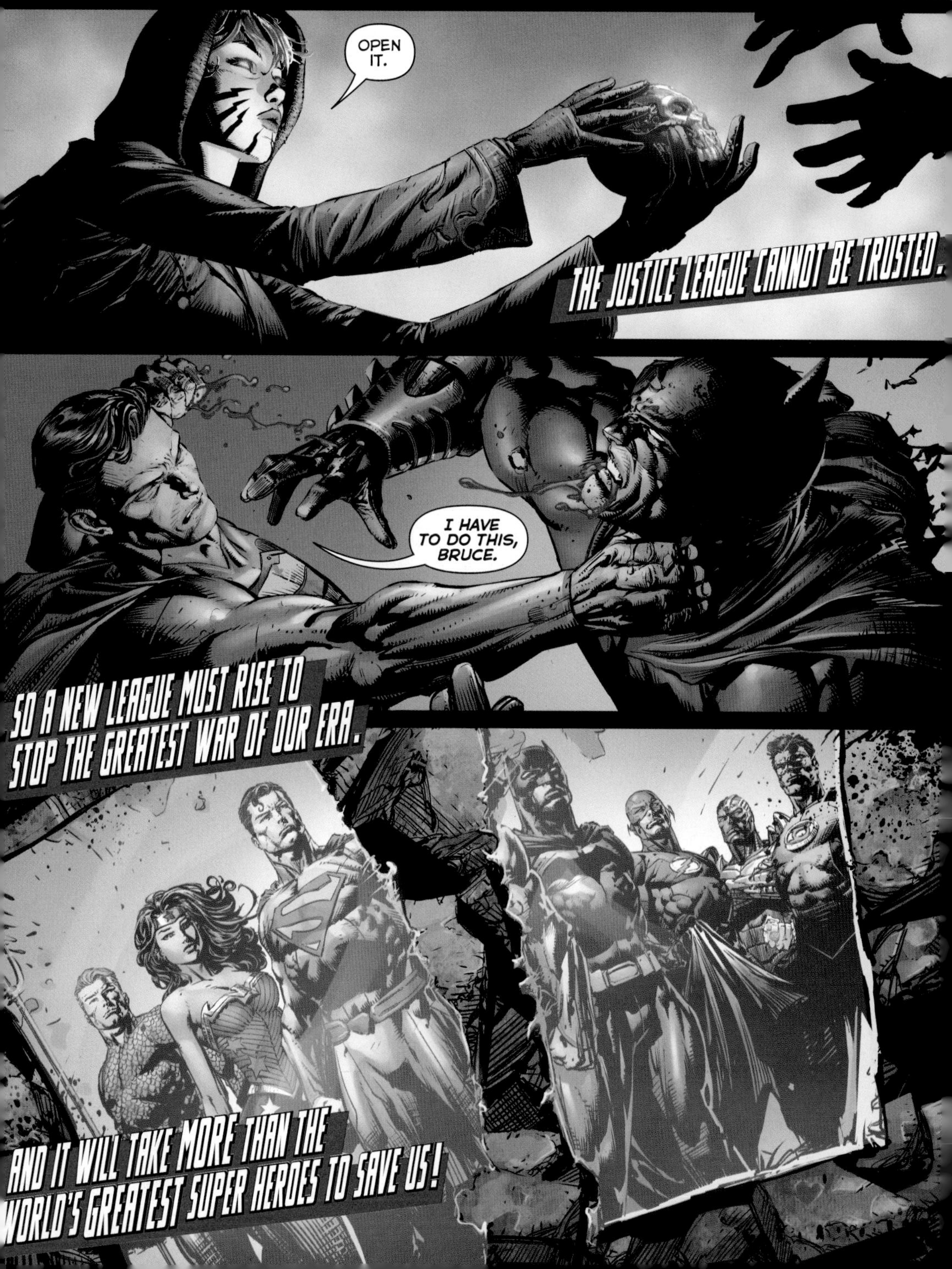
OPEN IT.
THE JUSTICE LEAGUE CANNOT BE TRUSTED.
I HAVE TO DO THIS, BRUCE.
SO A NEW LEAGUE MUST RISE TO STOP THE GREATEST WAR OF OUR ERA.
AND IT WILL TAKE MORE THAN THE WORLD'S GREATEST SUPER HEROES TO SAVE US!

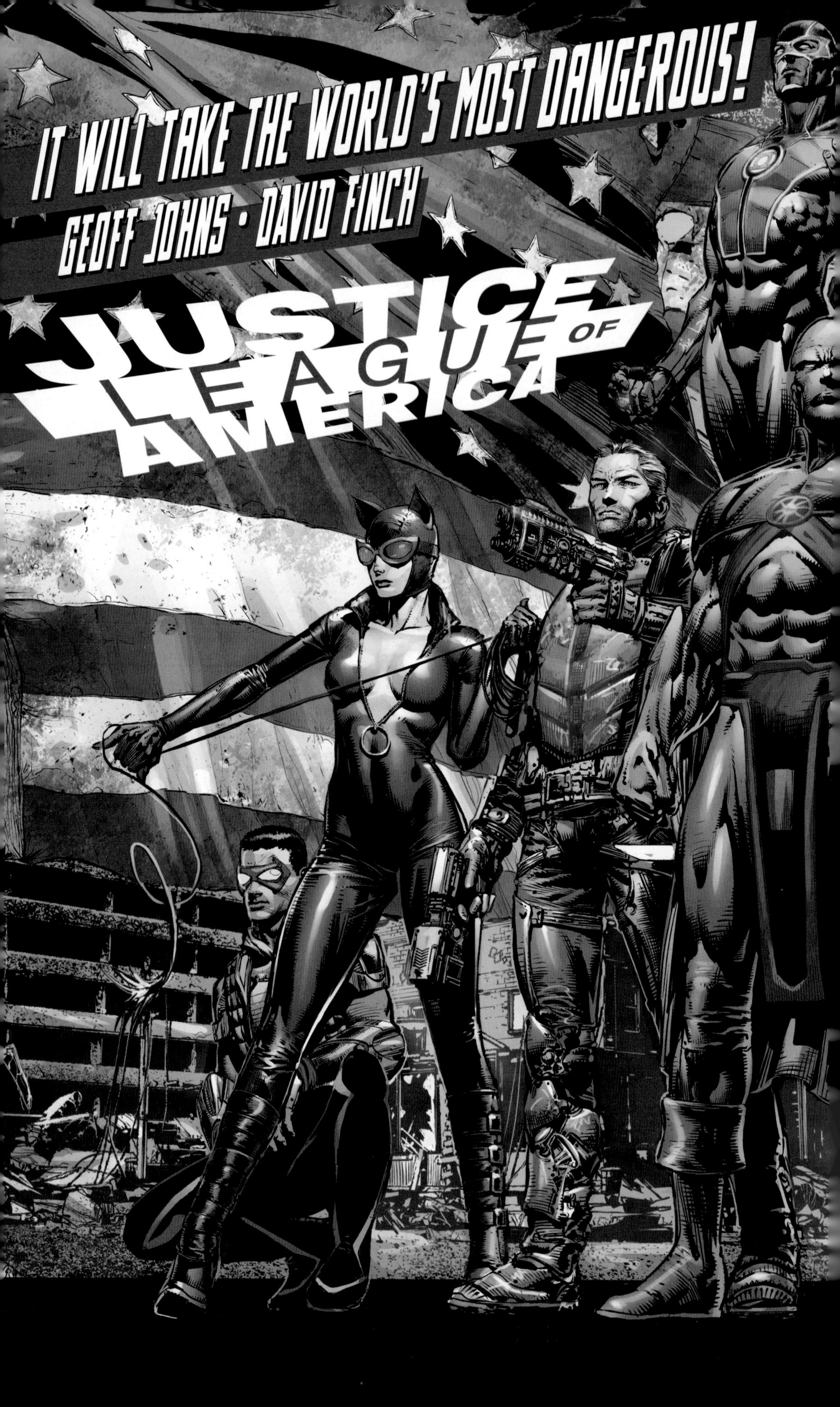
IT WILL TAKE THE WORLD'S MOST DANGEROUS!
GEOFF JOHNS · DAVID FINCH
JUSTICE LEAGUE OF AMERICA

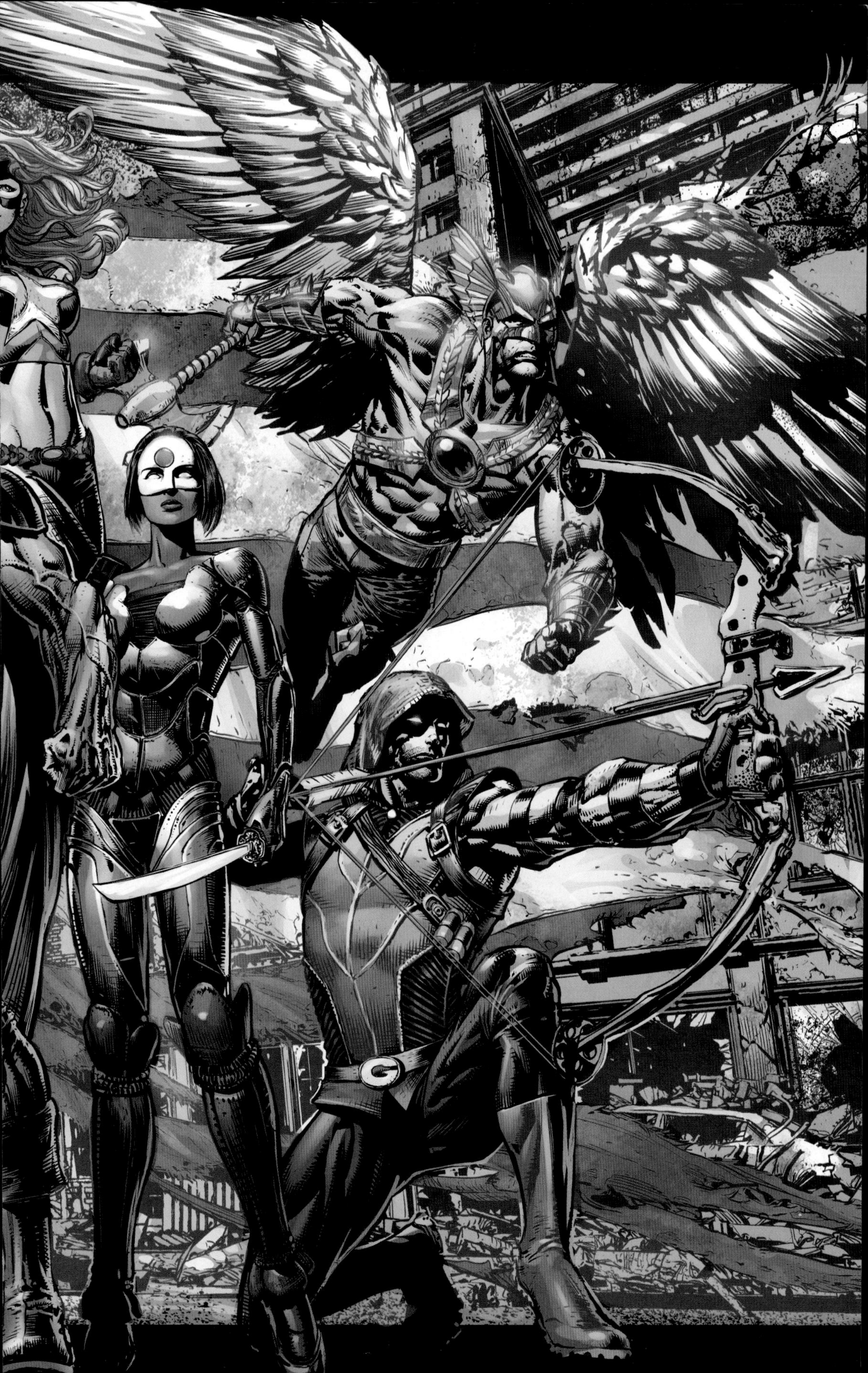

EPILOGUE: QUESTIONS

GEOFF JOHNS writer
ETHAN VAN SCIVER artist

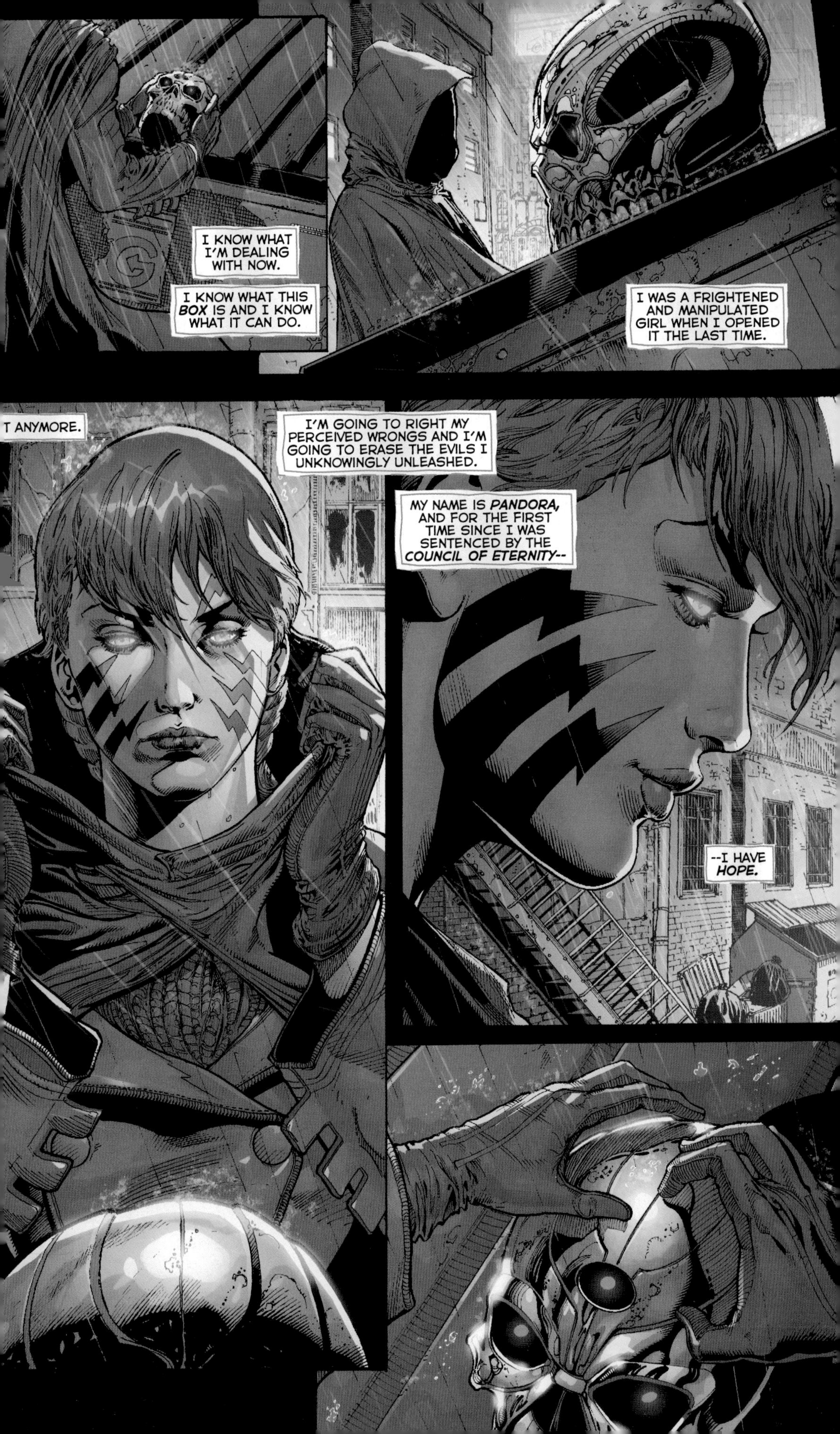

I KNOW WHAT I'M DEALING WITH NOW.
I KNOW WHAT THIS BOX IS AND I KNOW WHAT IT CAN DO.
I WAS A FRIGHTENED AND MANIPULATED GIRL WHEN I OPENED IT THE LAST TIME.
T ANYMORE.
I'M GOING TO RIGHT MY PERCEIVED WRONGS AND I'M GOING TO ERASE THE EVILS I UNKNOWINGLY UNLEASHED.
MY NAME IS PANDORA, AND FOR THE FIRST TIME SINCE I WAS SENTENCED BY THE COUNCIL OF ETERNITY--
--I HAVE HOPE.

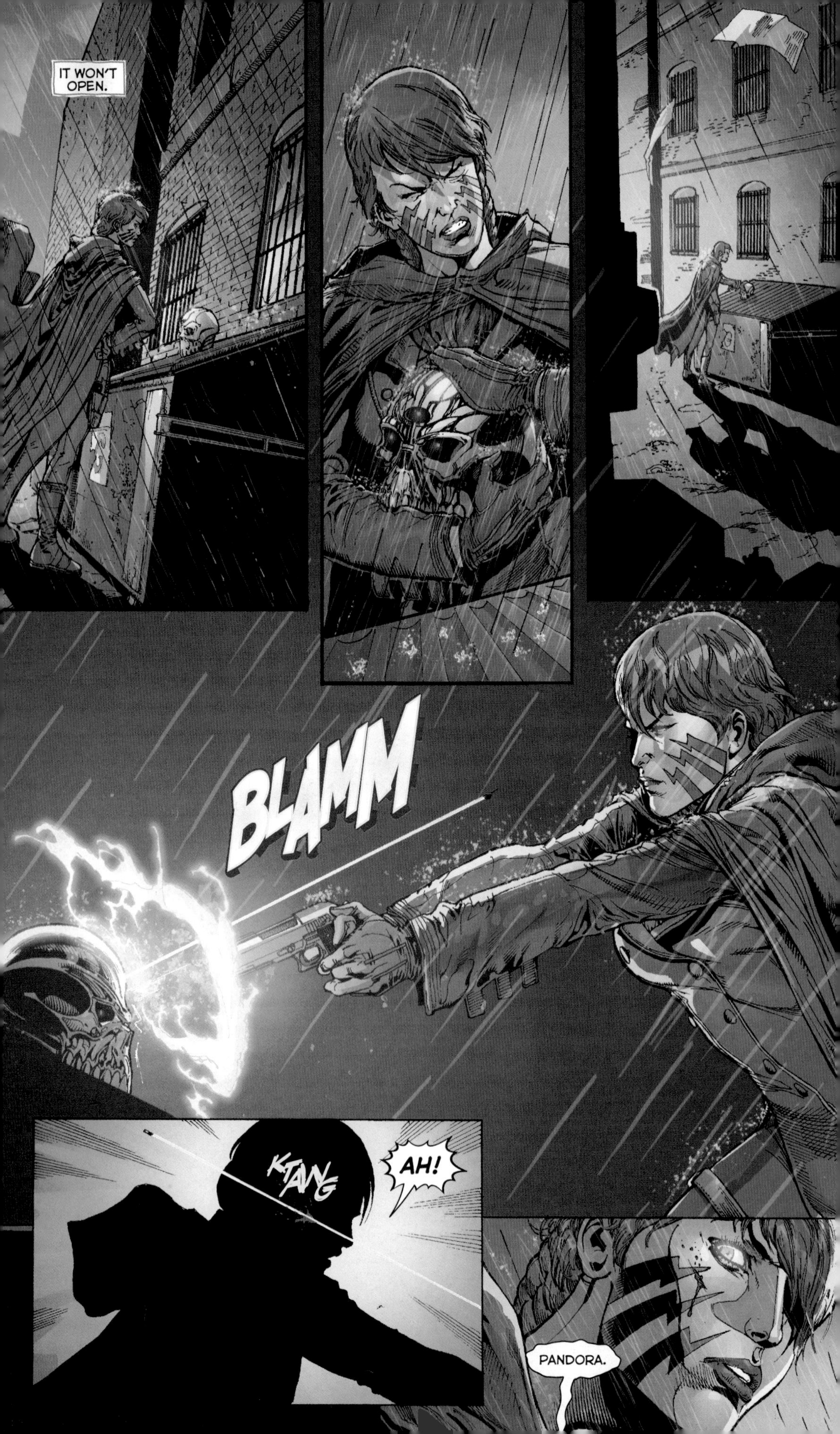
IT WON'T OPEN.
BLAMM
K-TANG
AH!
PANDORA.

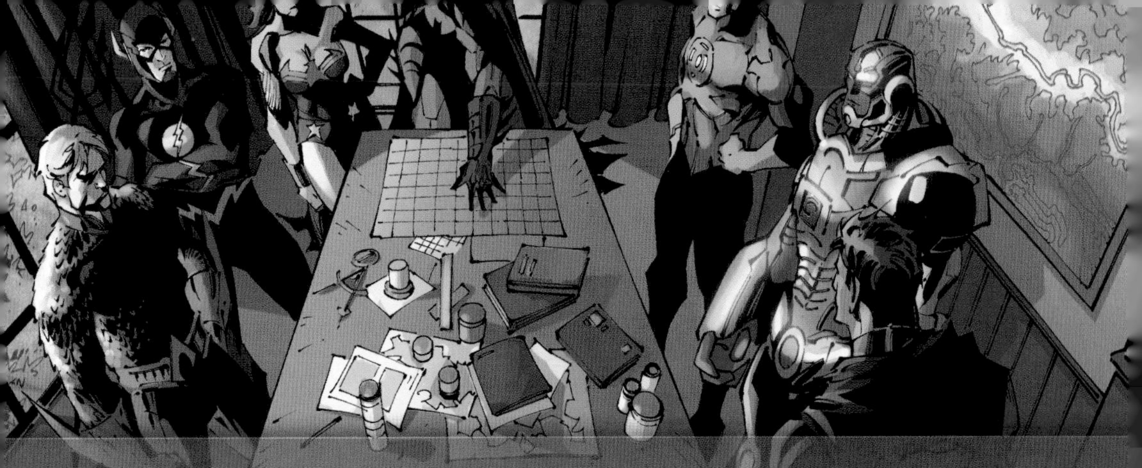

VARIANT COVER GALLERY

JUSTICE LEAGUE 7 combo pack
By Jim Lee, Scott Williams & Alex Sinclair

JUSTICE LEAGUE 7
by Gary Frank & Brad Anderson

JUSTICE LEAGUE 8 combo pack
By Jim Lee, Scott Williams & Alex Sinclair

JUSTICE LEAGUE 8
by Mike Choi & Marcelo Maiolo

JUSTICE LEAGUE 9 combo pack
By Jim Lee, Scott Williams & Alex Sinclair

JUSTICE LEAGUE 9
By Carlos D'Anda & Gabe Eltaeb

JUSTICE LEAGUE 10 combo pack
By Jim Lee, Scott Williams & Alex Sinclair

JUSTICE LEAGUE 10 combo pack
By Cully Hamner

JUSTICE LEAGUE 11 combo pack
By Jim Lee, Scott Williams & Alex Sinclair

JUSTICE LEAGUE 11
By Bryan Hitch & Paul Mounts

JUSTICE LEAGUE 11 Fan Expo Canada exclusive
By Jim Lee, Scott Williams & Alex Sinclair

JUSTICE LEAGUE 12
By Jim Lee, Scott Williams & Alex Sinclair

JUSTICE LEAGUE 12 combo pack
By Jim Lee, Scott Williams & Alex Sinclair

JUSTICE LEAGUE 12—second printing
By Jim Lee, Scott Williams & Alex Sinclair

JUSTICE LEAGUE 12 New York Comic Con exclusive
By Jim Lee, Scott Williams & Alex Sinclair

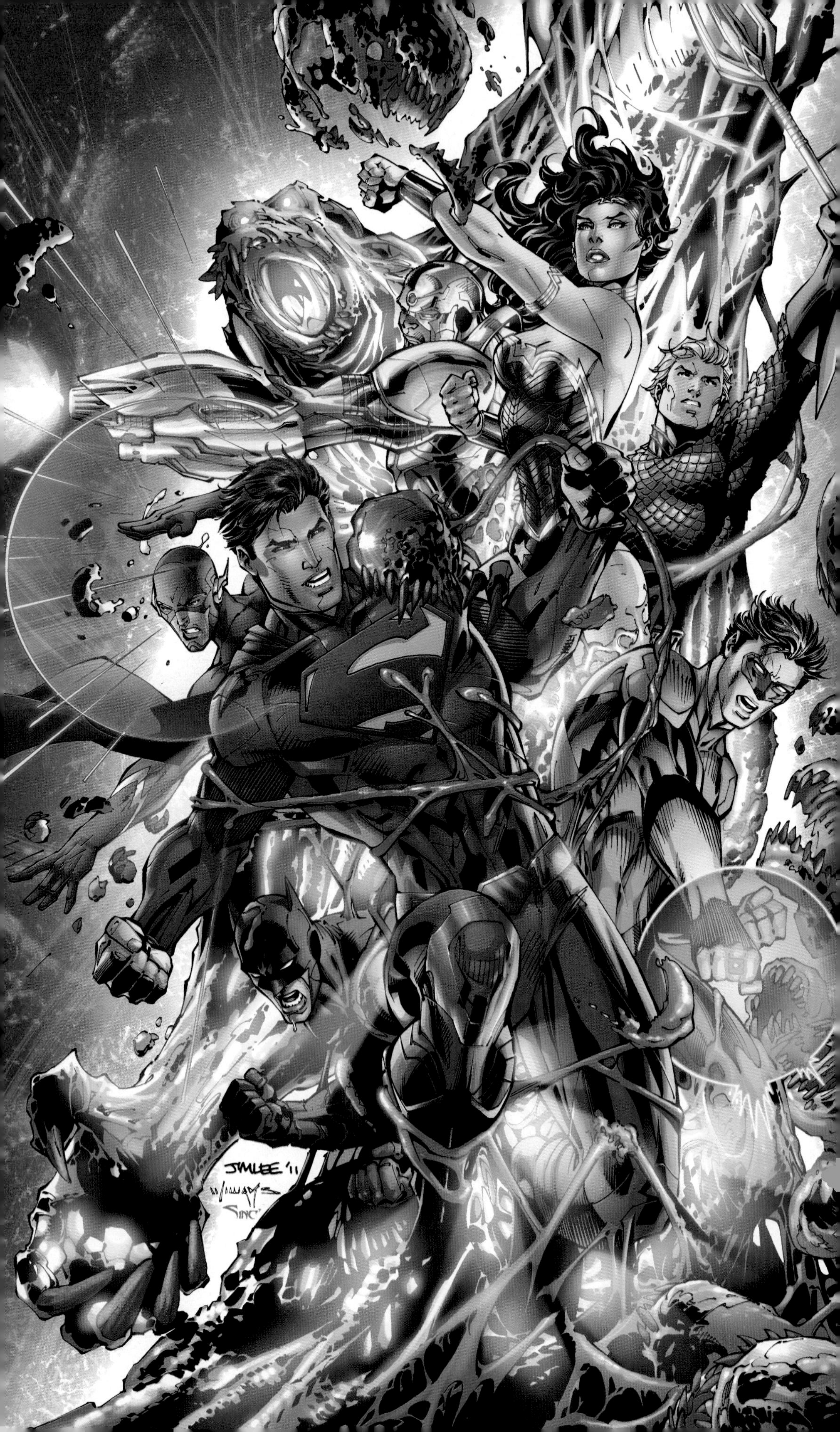

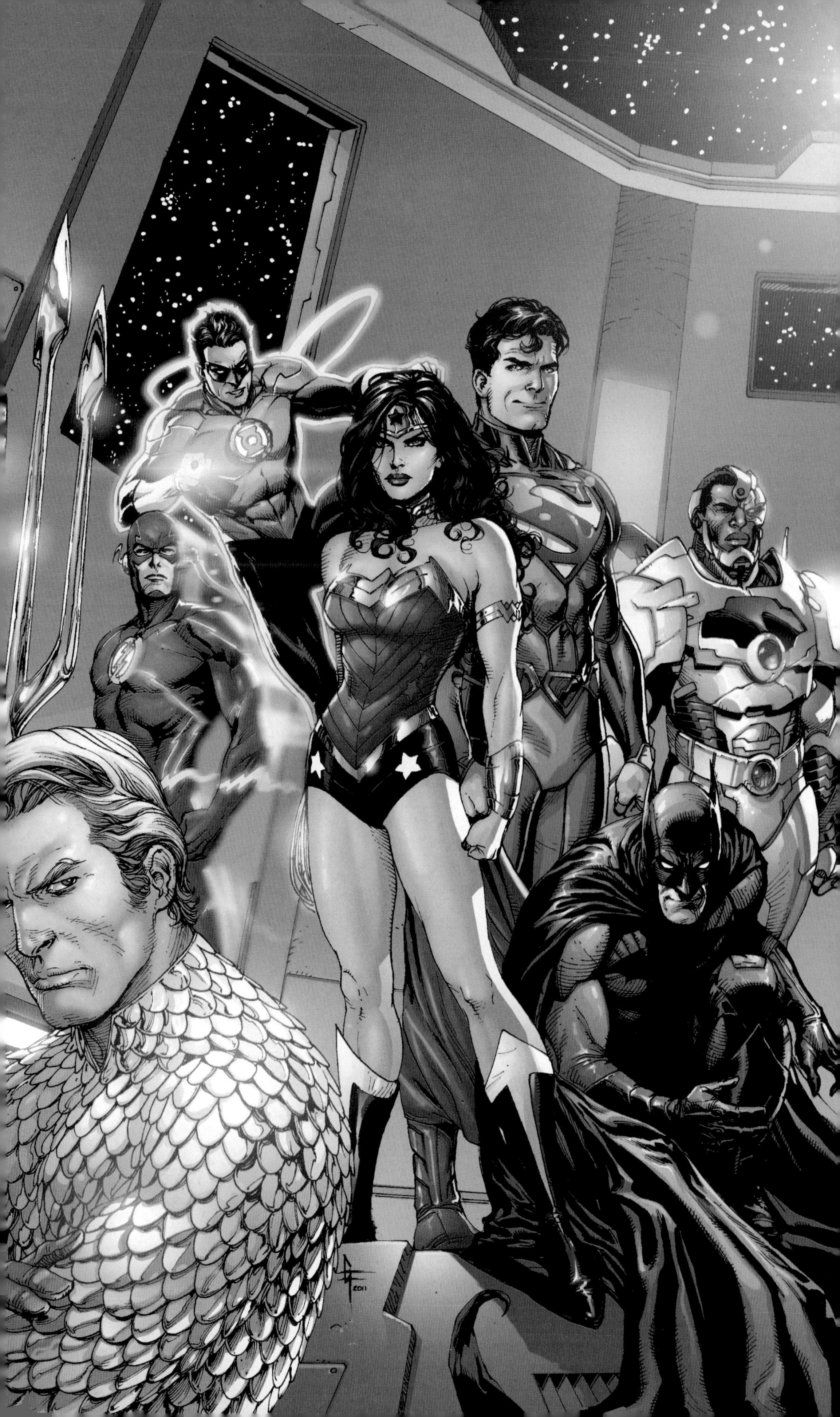

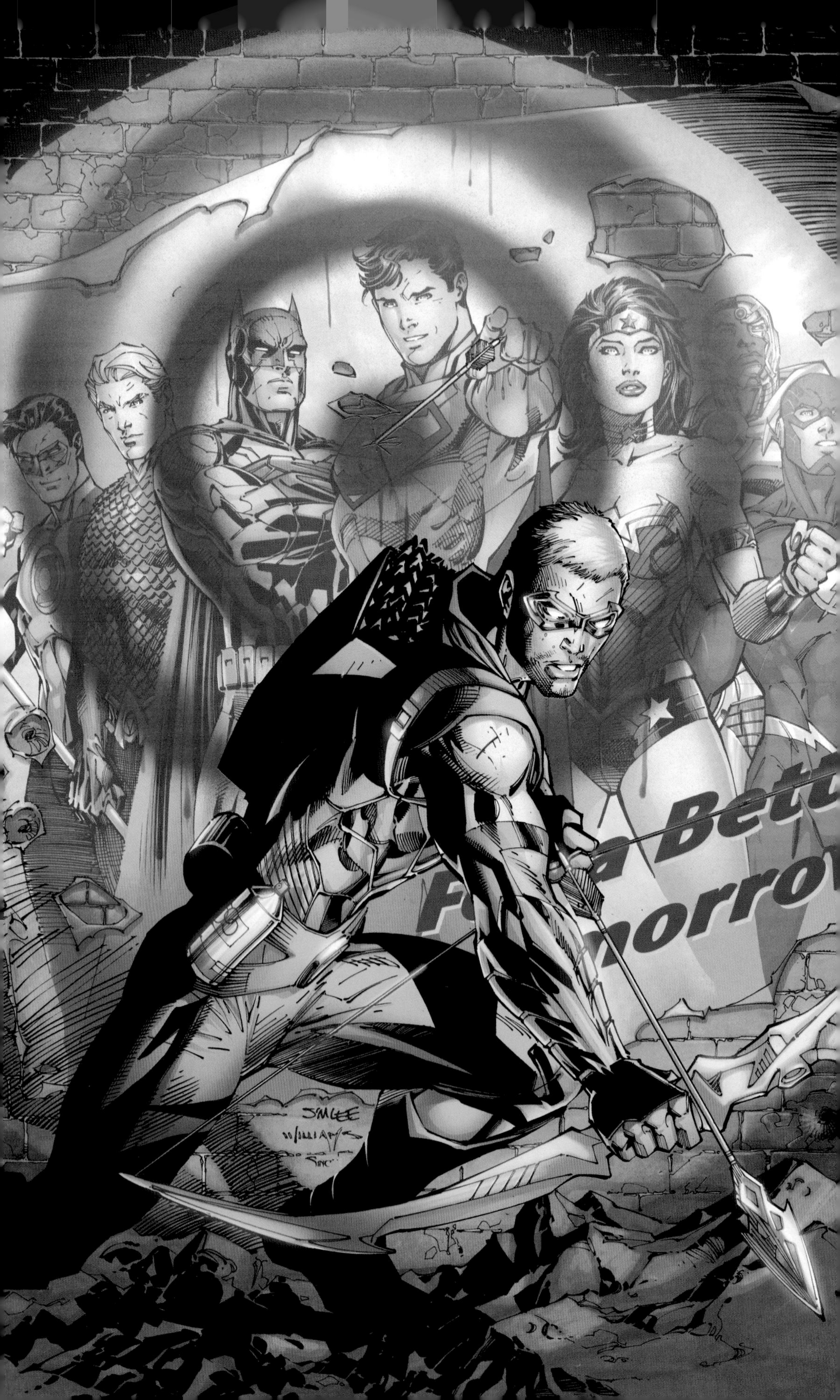

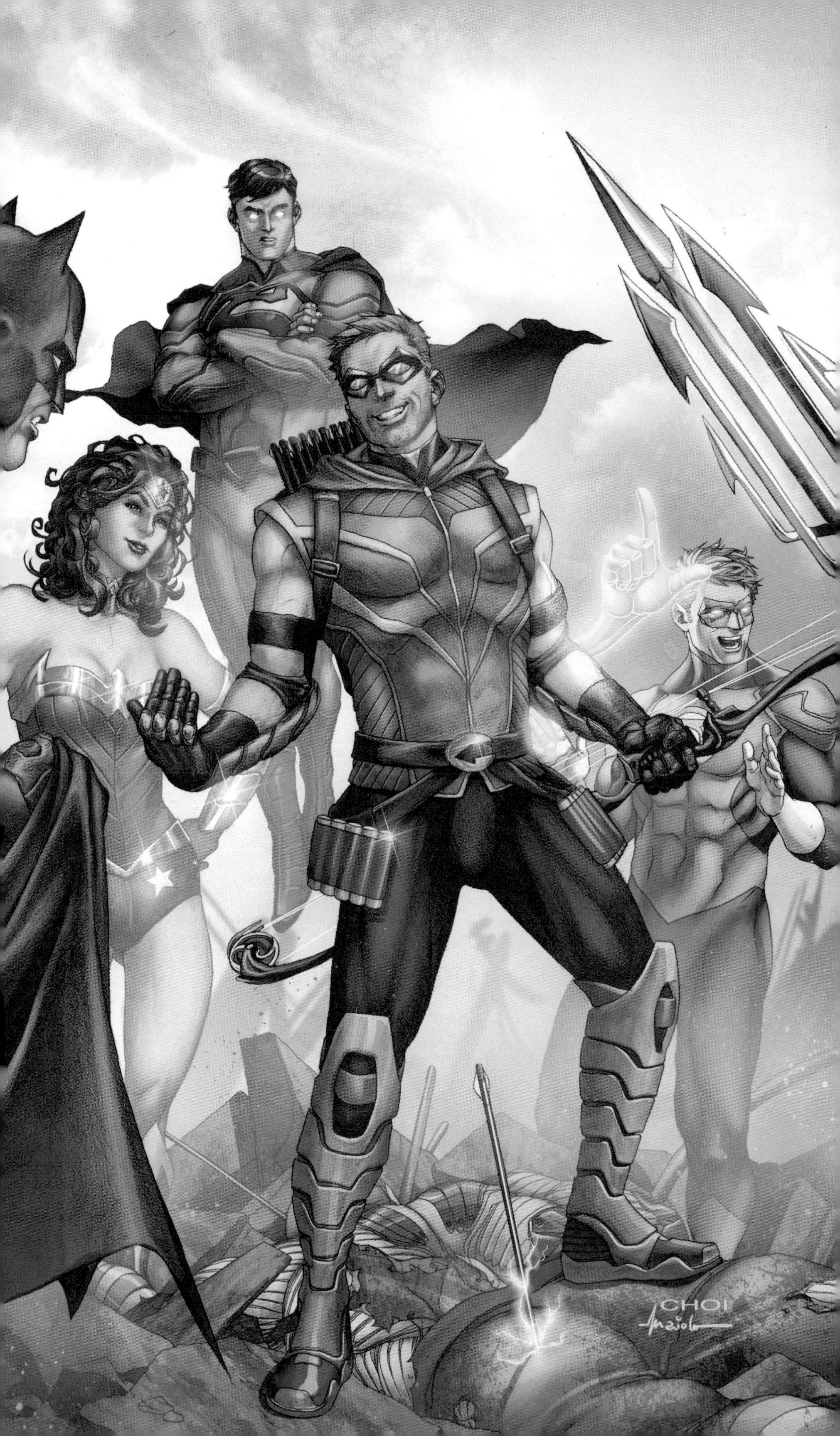
CHOI

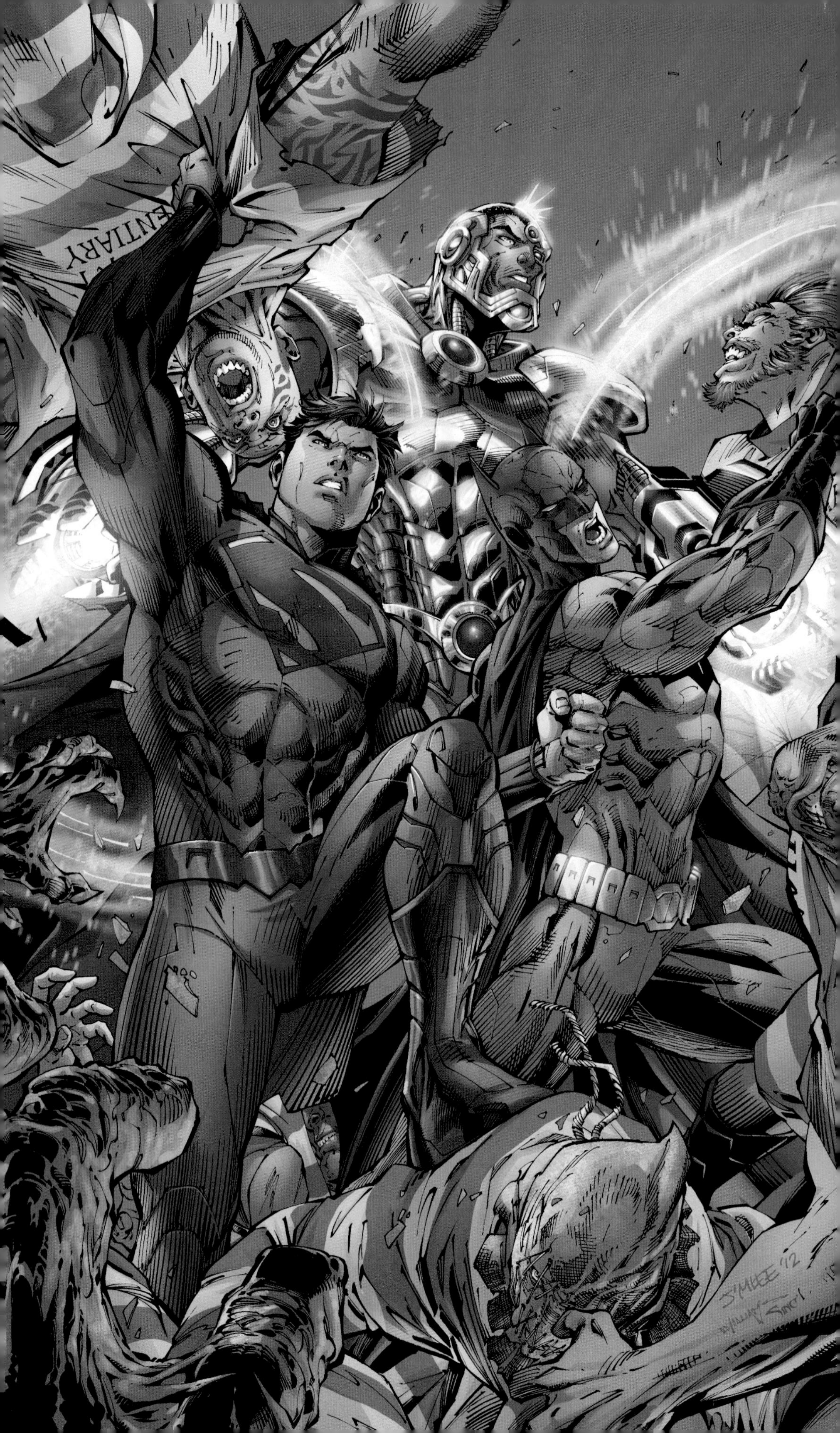

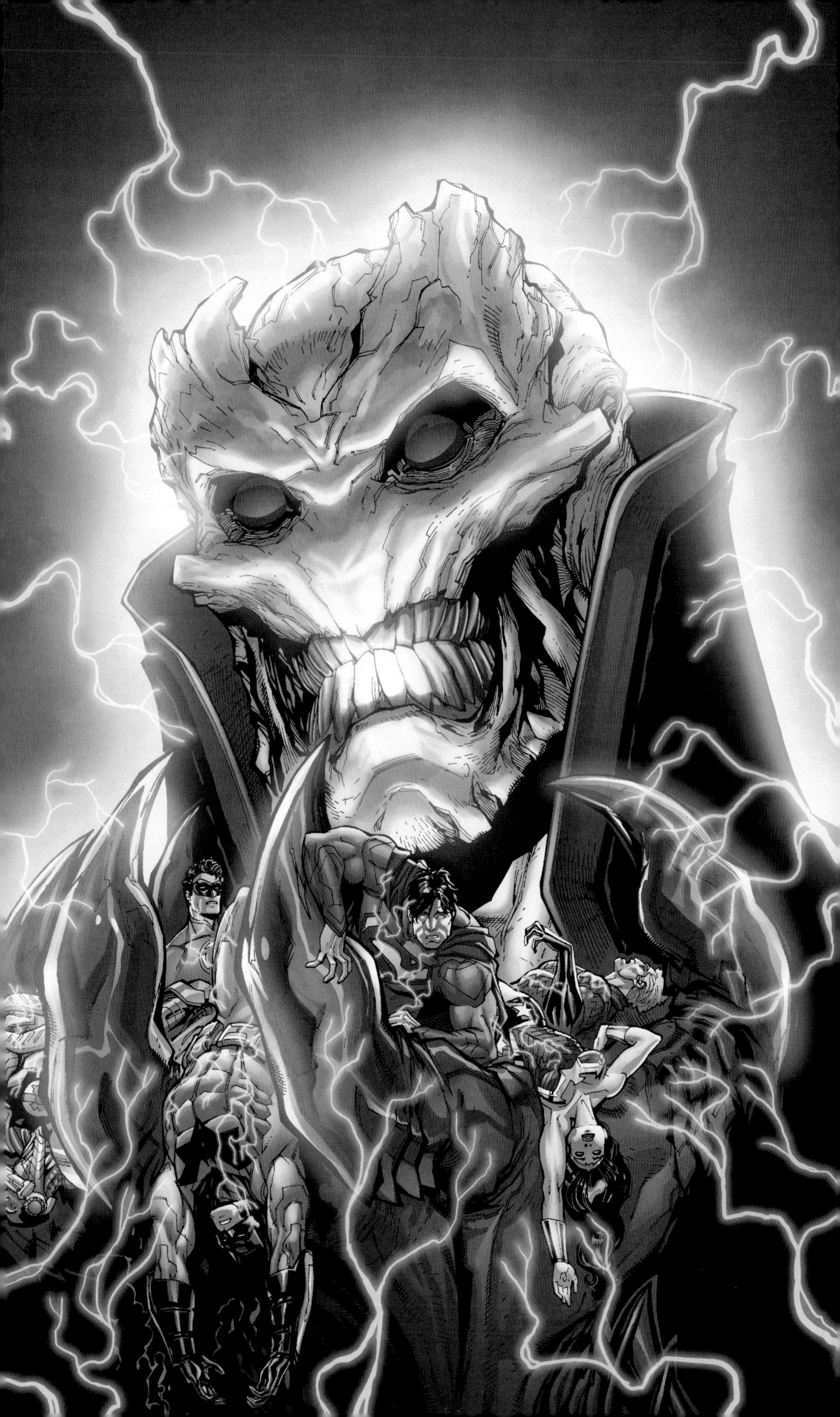

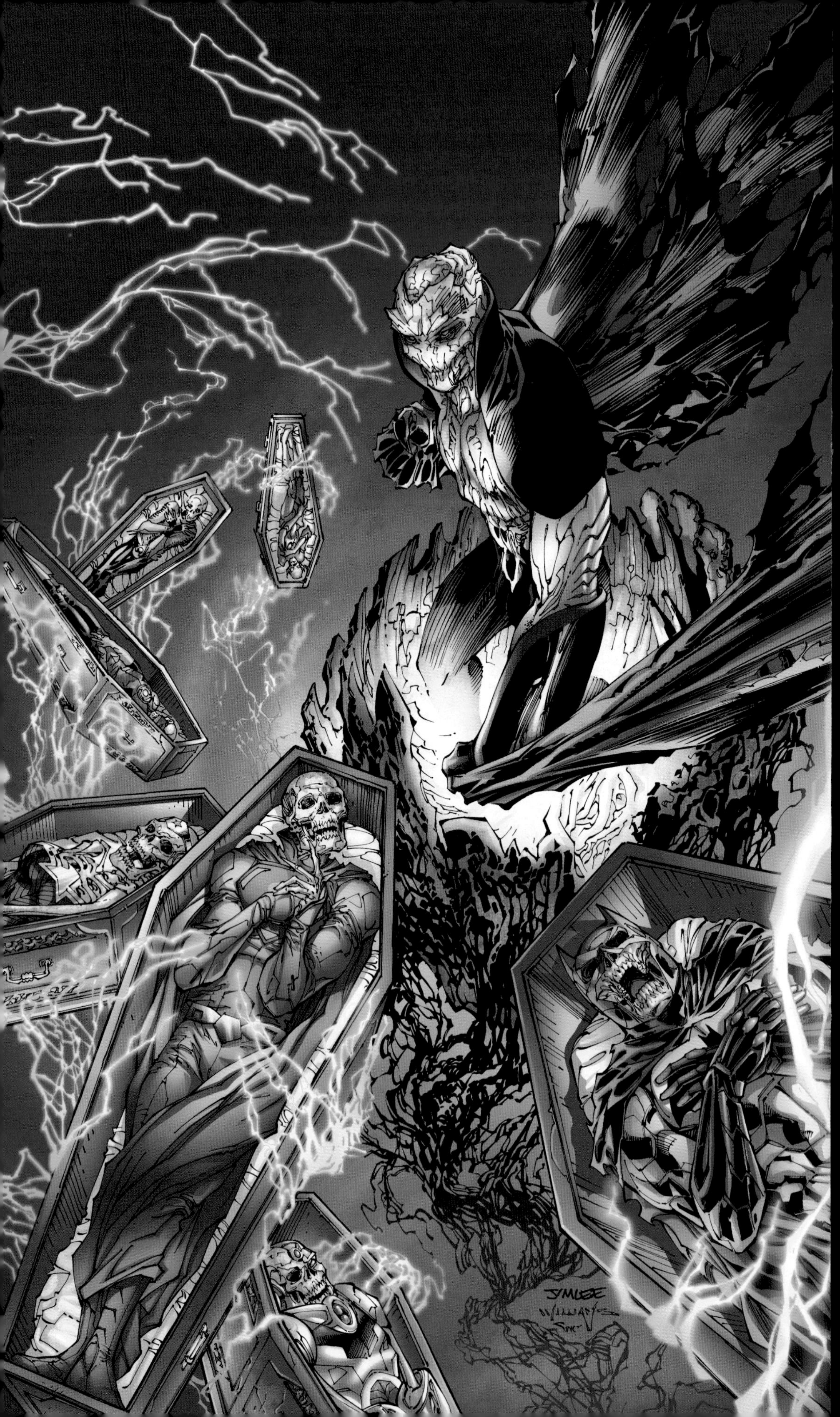

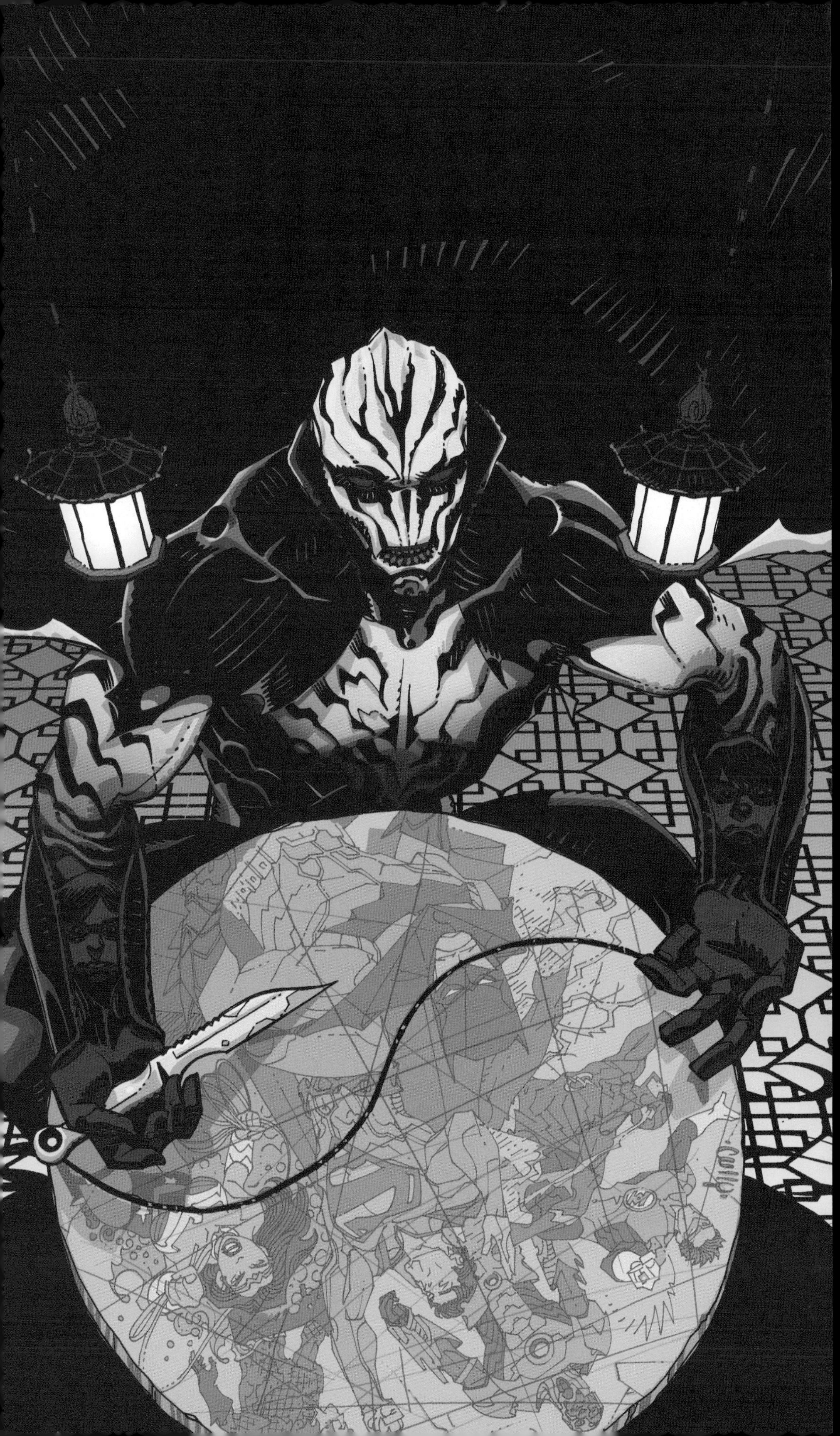

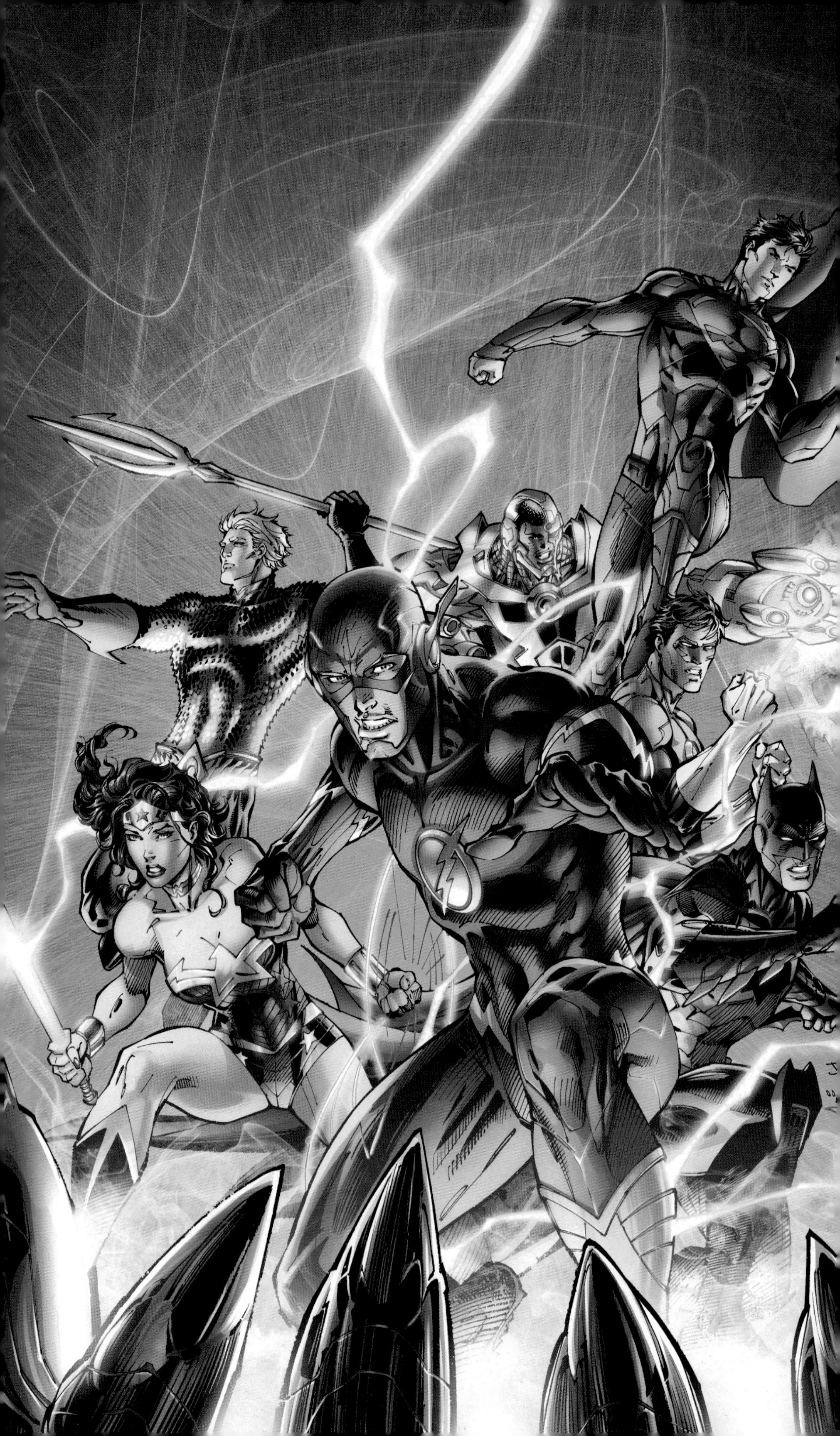

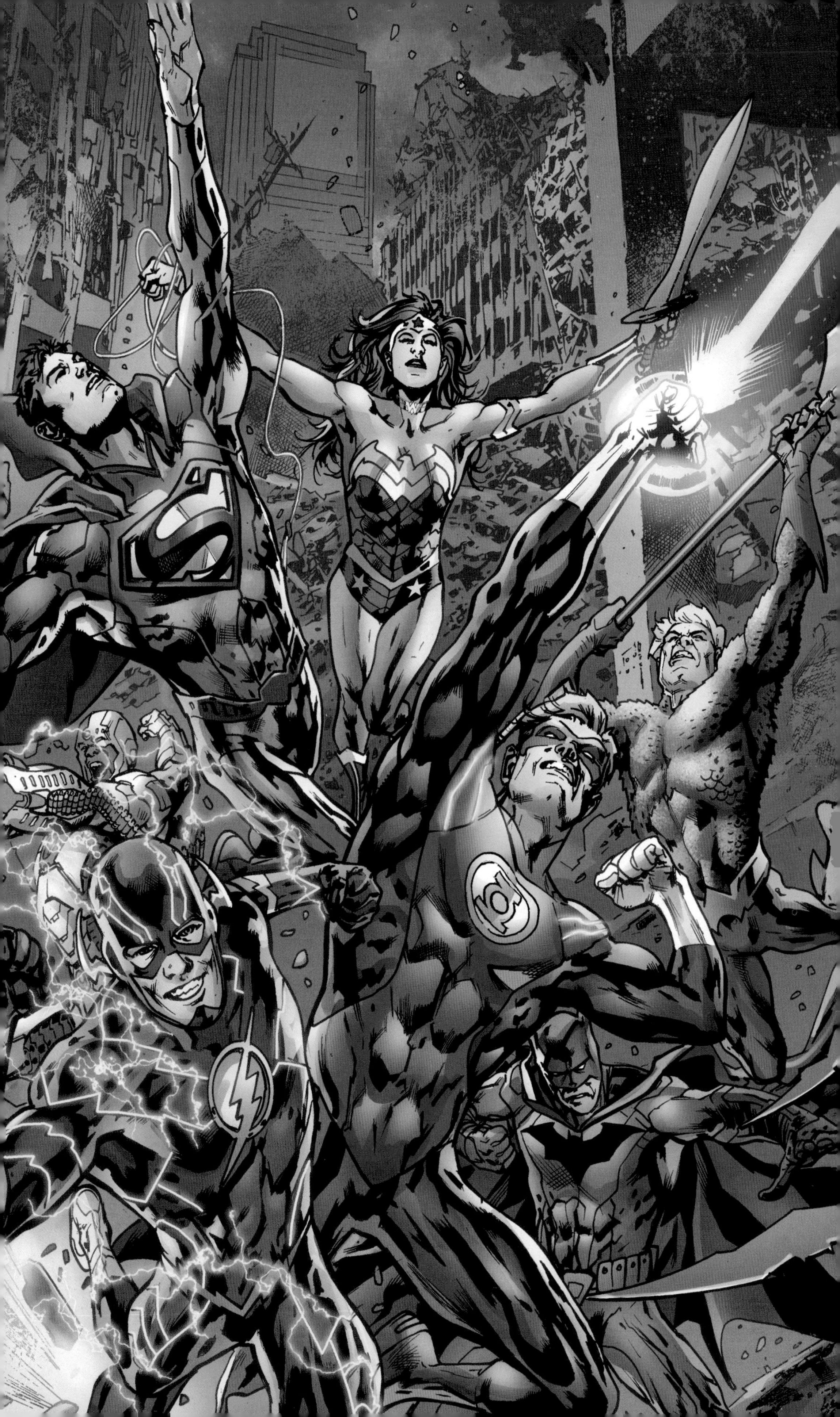

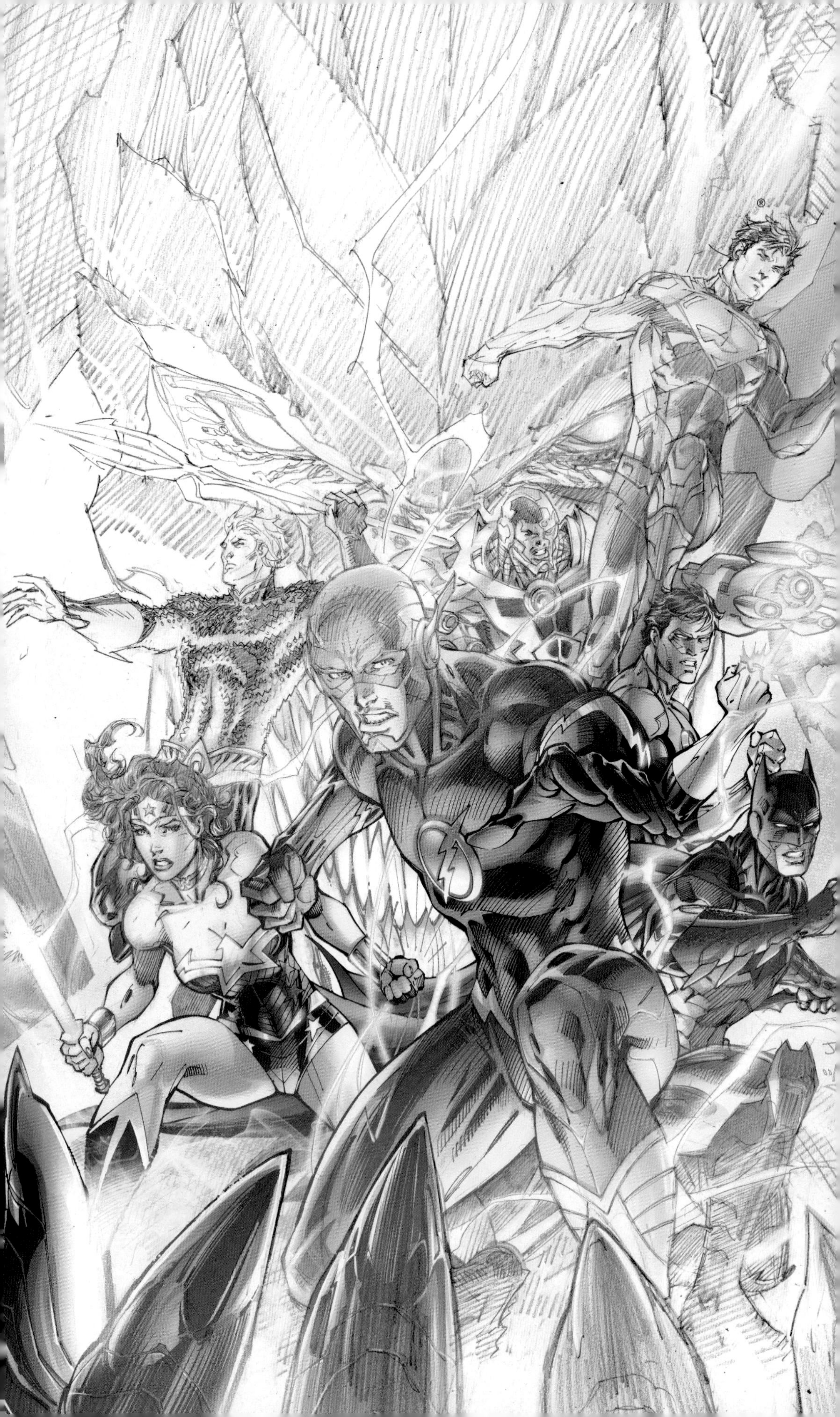

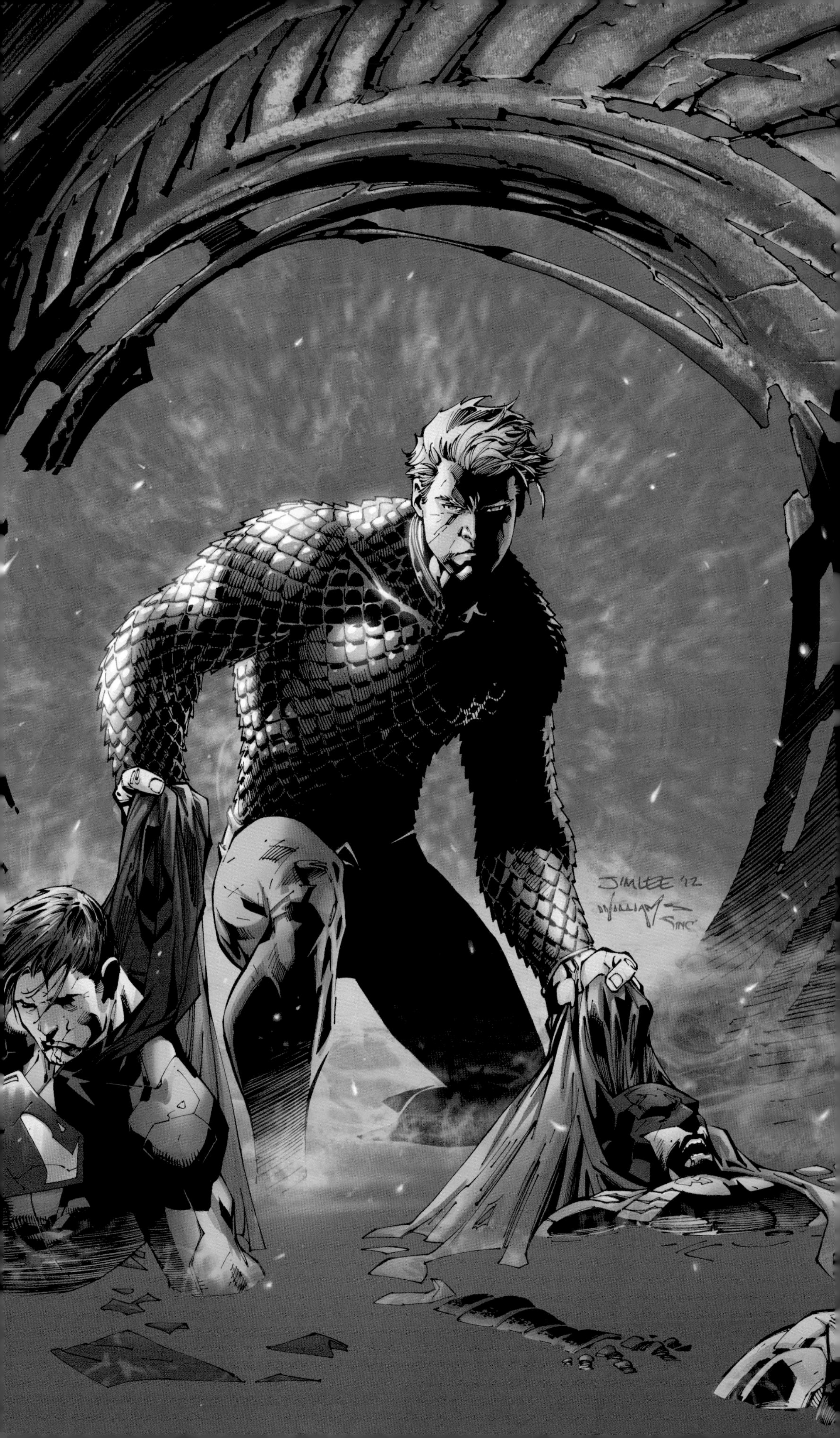
JIMLEE '12

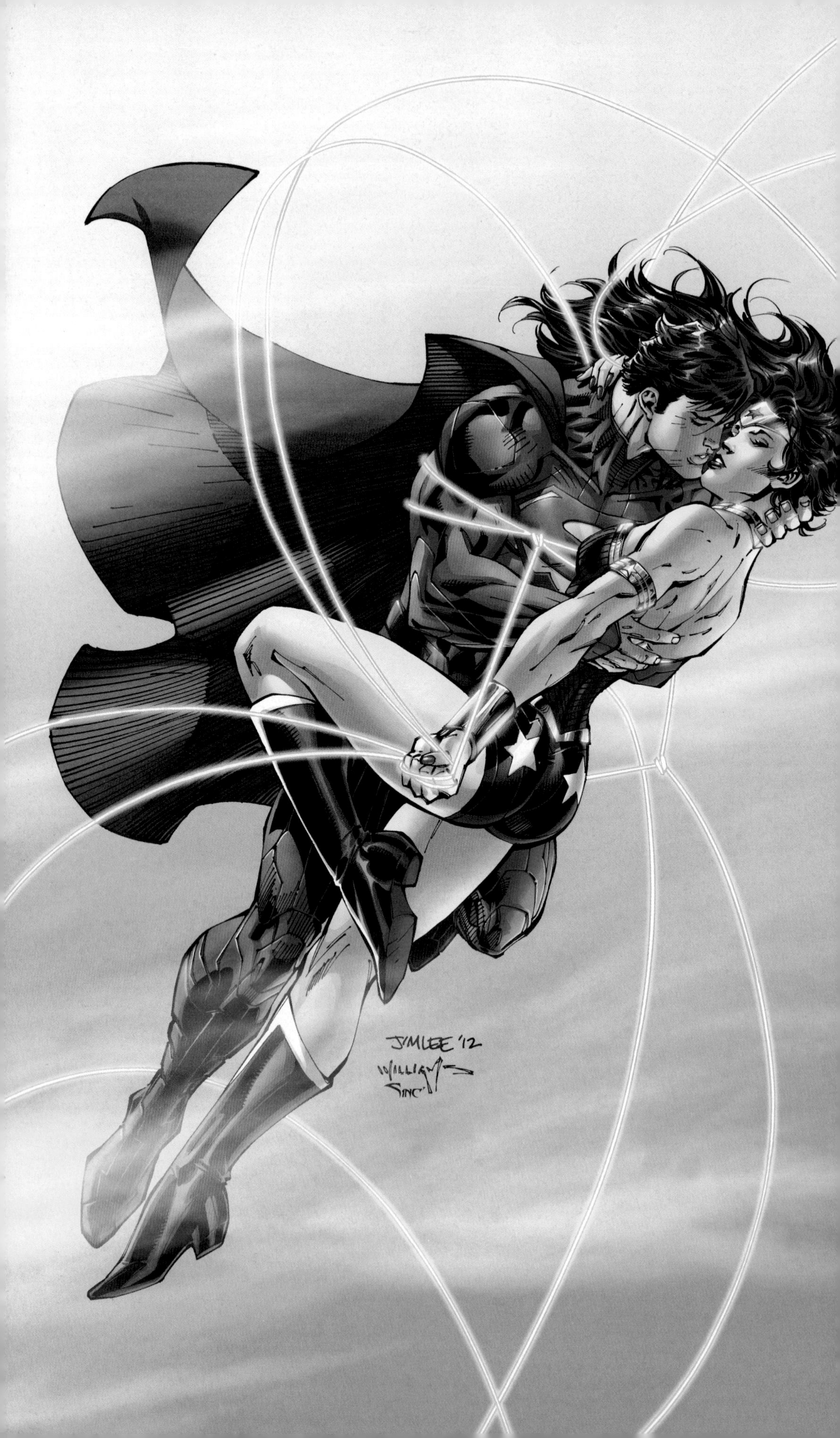
JIMLEE '12

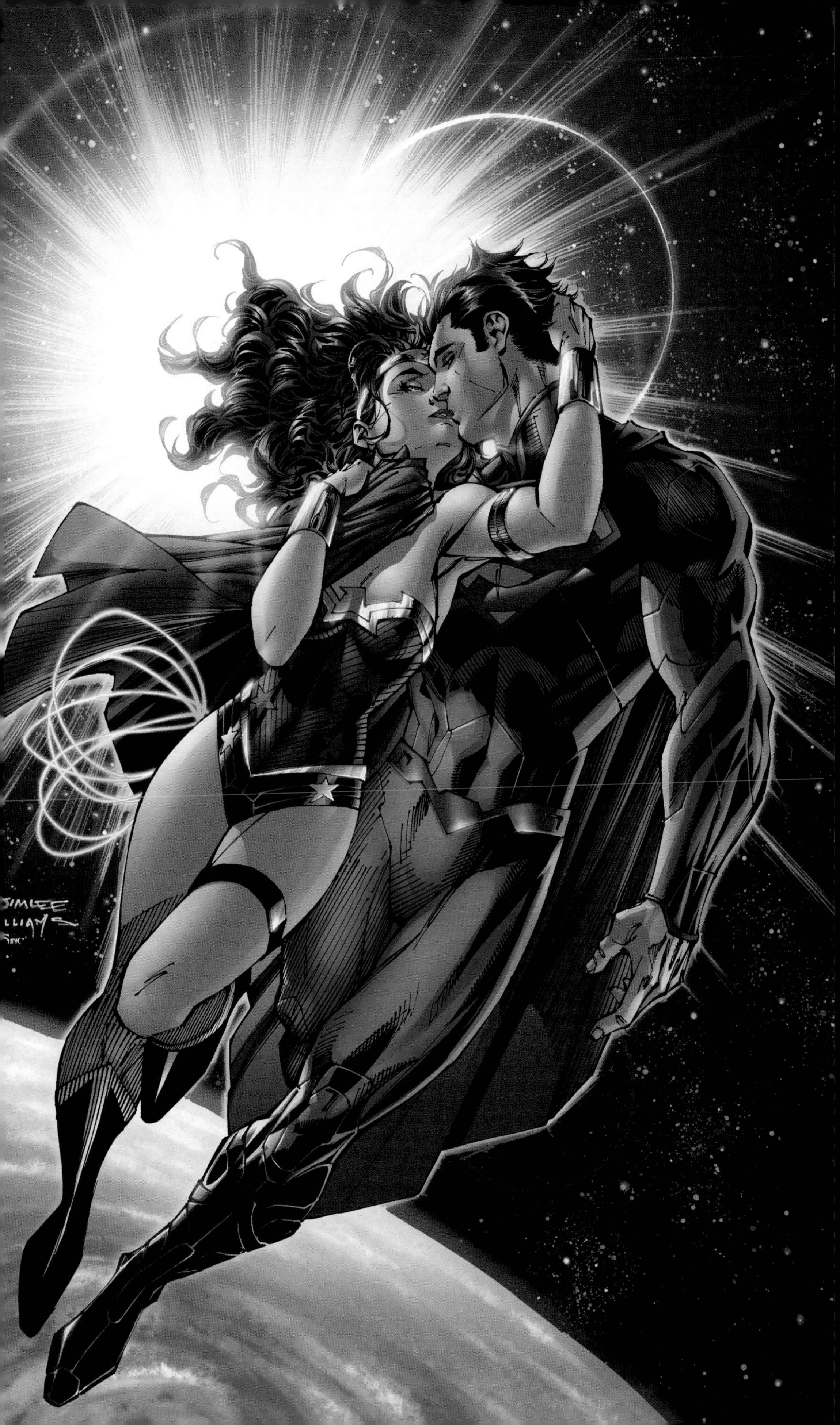
JIMLEE

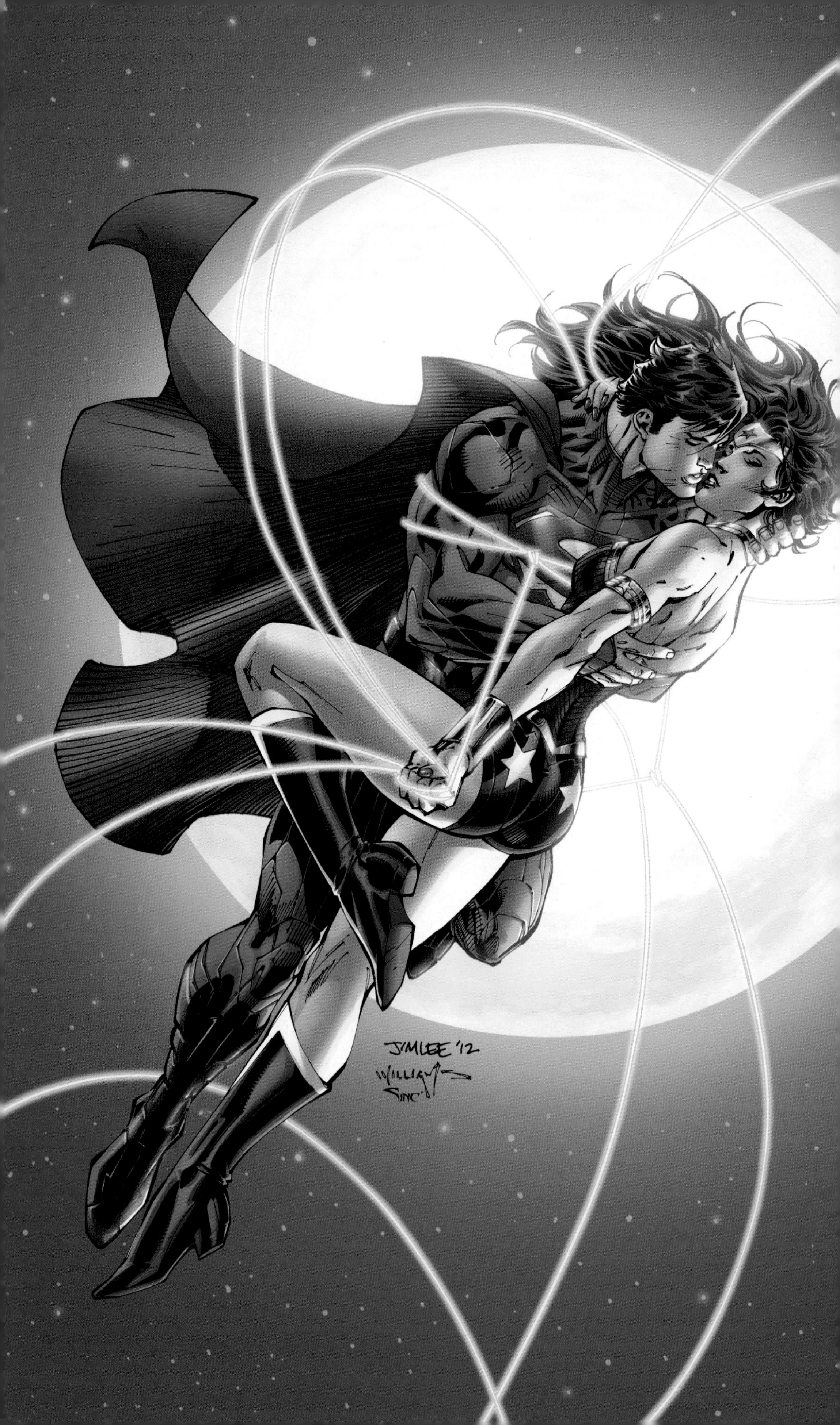
JIMLEE '12

START AT THE BEGINNING!

JUSTICE LEAGUE VOLUME 1: ORIGIN

AQUAMAN VOLUME 1: THE TRENCH

THE SAVAGE HAWKMAN VOLUME 1: DARKNESS RISING

GREEN ARROW VOLUME 1: THE MIDAS TOUCH

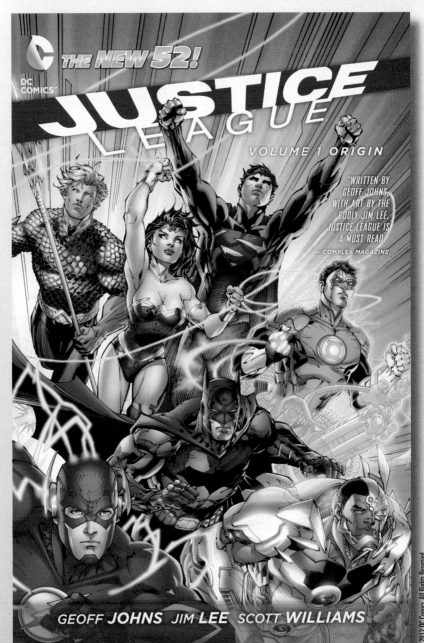

GEOFF **JOHNS** JIM **LEE** SCOTT **WILLIAMS**

DC COMICS™

START AT THE BEGINNING

GREEN LANTERN
VOLUME 1: SINESTRO

**GREEN LANTERN
CORPS VOLUME 1:
FEARSOME**

**RED LANTERNS
VOLUME 1:
BLOOD AND RAGE**

**GREEN LANTERN:
NEW GUARDIANS
VOLUME 1:
THE RING BEARER**

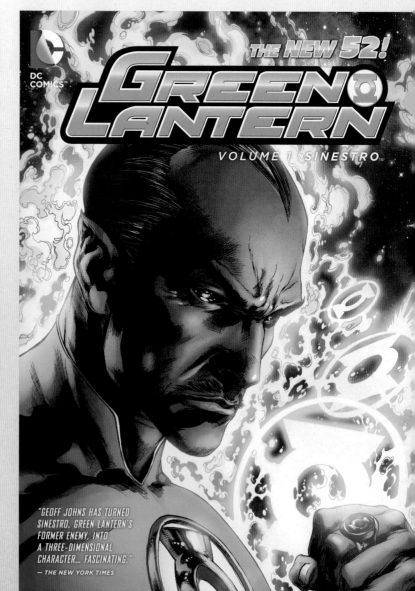

*"GEOFF JOHNS HAS TURNED
SINESTRO, GREEN LANTERN'S
FORMER ENEMY, INTO
A THREE-DIMENSIONAL
CHARACTER... FASCINATING."*
— THE NEW YORK TIMES

GEOFF JOHNS DOUG MAHNKE

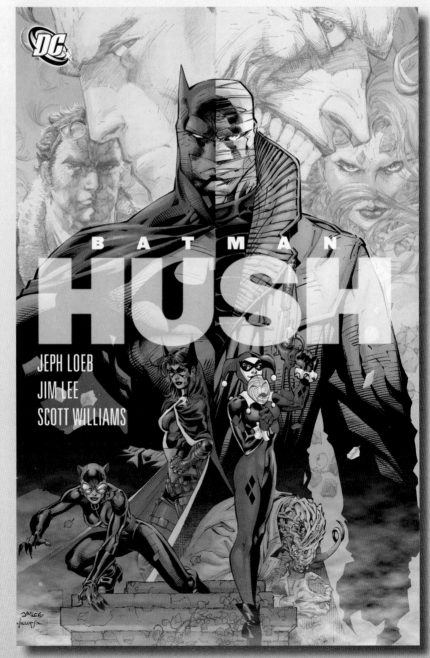

"Dynamit
—IG

"Intriguing
—AIN'T IT COOL NEW

"Comic-book art at its fines
—ENTERTAINMENT WEEKLY SHELF LIF

"Ambitiou
—USA TODA

FLASHPOINT
GEOFF JOHNS with ANDY KUBERT

"Heroic comic-book art at its finest" – ENTERTAINMENT WEEKLY / SHELF LIFE

GEOFF JOHNS · ANDY KUBERT · SANDRA HOPE

FLASHPOINT

"A soaring, if radical, tale that uses superheroes in ways that may surprise both first-time readers and long-time fans."
– THE ASSOCIATED PRESS

DC